PARALYMPIC LEGACIES

EDITORS:
DAVID LEGG AND KEITH GILBERT

PARALYMPIC LEGACIES

EDITORS:
DAVID LEGG AND KEITH GILBERT

Common Ground

First published in Champaign, Illinois in 2011
by Common Ground Publishing LLC
at the series imprint Sport and Society

Selections and editorial matter copyright © David Legg and Keith Gilbert 2011;
Individual chapters copyright © individual contributors 2011

All rights reserved. Apart from fair dealing for the purposes of study, research, criticism or review as permitted under the applicable copyright legislation, no part of this book may be reproduced by any process without written permission from the publisher.

Library of Congress Cataloging-in-Publication Data

The Paralympic legacies / editors, David Legg and Keith Gilbert.

   p. cm.

Includes bibliographical references and index.
ISBN 978-1-86335-896-5 (pbk : alk. paper) -- ISBN 978-1-86335-897-2 (pdf : alk. paper)
1. Paralympics. 2. Sports for people with disabilities. I. Legg, David, 1968- II. Gilbert, Keith, 1950- III. Title.

GV722.5.P37P37 2011
796.087--dc22

2011002624

Table of Contents

Part I : The Paralympic Legacy Debate

Chapter 1: Conceptualising Legacy 3
Keith Gilbert and David Legg

Chapter 2: The History of the Paralympic Games 13
David Legg and Robert Steadward

Chapter 3: An Overview of the Benefits of Hosting the Paralympic Games 21
David Legg and Keith Gilbert

Part II : Paralympic City Legacies

Chapter 4: The Toronto Olympiad for the Physically Disabled 35
'A.K.A.' the Fifth Summer Paralympic Games held in 1976
Ian Brittain

Chapter 5: Seoul 1988 47
The first Modern Paralympic Games
Justin Jeon and David Legg

Chapter 6: Barcelona 1992 53
The Coming of Age for the Paralympic Games
Patrick Jarvis

Chapter 7: Atlanta 1996 65
Trials and Triumphs of the Human Spirit
Travis Mushett and Ann Cody

Chapter 8: Sydney 2000 75
Moving from Post-Hoc Legacy to Strategic Vision and Operational Partnerships
Simon Darcy and Lois Appleby

Chapter 9: Athens 2004 99
Personal Reflections
Mary A. Hums

Chapter 10: Legacies and Tensions after the 2008 Beijing Paralympic Games 111
  Sun Shuhan and Jill M. Le Clair

Chapter 11: Vancouver 2010 131
  Dena Coward and David Legg

Chapter 12: London 2012 143
  The Right Choice for the Paralympic Games?
  Tony Sainsbury

Chapter 13: The Paralympic Games 155
  Legacy and Regeneration in Brazil
  Fernando Telles Ribeiro

Chapter 14: Winter Paralympic Games 165
  Founding Legacies 1976 - 1980
  Ted Fay

Chapter 15: Winter Paralympic Games 173
  Founding Legacies 1984 – 1988
  Ted Fay

Chapter 16: Winter Paralympic Games 181
  Summary of Legacies 1976 - 1988
  Ted Fay

Part III : Emerging Issues of Paralympic Legacy

Chapter 17: Legacy 191
  Generating Social Currency through Paralympic Excellence
  Phil Lane

Chapter 18: Paralympic Legacy in Physical 199
  Activity and Health
    A UK Perspective
  Paul Smith and Scott Fleming

Chapter 19: Physical Education and the 2012 Paralympic Legacy ... 213
  From Playground to Podium?
  Natalie Campbell

Chapter 20: Urban Regeneration and Paralympic Legacy for London 2012 217
Gavin Poynter

Part IV : Reconceptualising Paralympic Legacies

Chapter 21: A Metasynthesis of Paralympic Legacy 229
Keith Gilbert and David Legg

Chapter 22: Epilogue 239
The Plot Thins
Keith Gilbert and David Legg

The Paralympic Games: Legacy and Regeneration

Foreward

Dr. Robert D. Steadward, O.C., A.O.E., LLD

Many of us have been fortunate to have lived through and witnessed the most significant changes in the Paralympic movement's recent history and the impacts that they have made on the world as we know it today. In this manner it is so very difficult to talk about the Movement and sport for athletes with disability in this brief forward since I have been involved with the movement for nearly five (5) decades. I have been privileged to work closely with athletes, managers, coaches and parents within disability, sport settings and the association with sport has therefore taken up a great part of my life.

It has been fifty (50) years (September 25th 1960) since the humble beginnings with our first Paralympic Games in Rome in 1960. At that time, the Paralympic Movement worldwide was a mere fledgling competition caught within the superstructure of international sport. Over the years we struggled for our rights, recognition, respect and equality in order to equate ourselves with the so-called "normal" realm of sport. In the past, our focus was on rehabilitation through the implementation of remedial exercise and not through sport. This was known, as the 'medical model'.

In time, our struggle was alleviated through our commitment to sport excellence, athleticism and high level sport competitions and in order to survive we had to adapt and master change. We did more than survive; we experienced unprecedented growth and development. We have been ambassadors and role models extending far beyond sport. Our athletes have been an inspiration for society as a whole. As a result, the status, visibility, profile, and credibility of our movement, continues to grow to this very day. Indeed, there were significant historical changes that took place through the 70's, 80's, 90's and on into the 21st Century.

1976 saw athletes with visual impairments and amputation compete for the first time in the Summer Paralympic Games. It was also the beginning of our Winter Paralympic Games. In 1980, athletes with cerebral palsy were added to the program. As a result of these changes, it became necessary to create a new umbrella international body that would govern the future of Paralympic sport. But this structure did not last very long as it was necessary to create a democratic organization made up of member nations and athletes with the assurance that it become a sport structure and not a medical one. This led to the foundation of a wonderful relationship with the IOC, the creation of the IPC and the first modern Summer Paralympic Games in Seoul, Korea in 1988.

The 1990's allowed us to grow and market our brand and product in the number of countries participating in IPC activities. It also allowed us to enhance the quality of our athletes and to further our relationship with the IOC and other international federations.

In the year 2000, in Sydney, Australia, one of the most significant pieces of Paralympic history was signed between the former President of the IOC, the late Juan Antonio Samaranch and I as the President of the IPC. This document, a result of nearly 20 years of negotiating and relationship building, formally linked our two movements together and since that date the relationship has continued to grow and prosper to the benefit of both movements. Eventually the IPC has become a great international sporting organization.

But, what constitutes greatness. If we look over the past 20 years of our history, we might reflect that they were indeed the years of growth, progress and improvement. However, I suggest that they were the *result*, not the *cause* of our greatness as we had to excel in our organizational developments as well as in our sports. I believe greatness has shown itself in the works of our volunteer committees, in our Headquarter's staff, in the success of our athletes at Paralympic Games and in our historical Agreement/MOU with the IOC. All of these were the *acorns*, but they were not the *oak*.

Is democracy the determining factor towards greatness? We have, unmistakably, demonstrated time and again our need and our desire for openness, transparency, and the absolute liberty to make our views known. We have not hesitated in expressing our opinions and engaging in open discussion on issues that are felt deeply by each of our members. But, even in such virtues as liberty and freedom, we sometimes find that personal and political agendas cloud the way to clear and rational process.

So, today we may be large, powerful, free and bold, but my personal belief is that these qualities alone will not make us great. No, our greatness is in our passion, our honesty and our spirit.

It is in that spirit which prizes the glory of our athletes above all. And, it is in that spirit of generosity and fairness that raises us above the lowest human level. It is with us when we review our history. It swells at the recollection of how far we have come in such a brief period of time. This spirit of ours is fierce to protect and support the Paralympic ideals. It is noble, holding in the highest esteem that role and responsibility with which we have been tasked.

And, when this spirit prevails, our organization will be wise and energetic because such an organization will be led by those who are themselves guided by the same spirit. Such an organization, in the true interest of those over whom it is responsible, will find the same spirit establishing itself throughout the entire movement. Such are the blessings of greatness, borne on the pillars of hope and dreams for our future. It is this spirit which I have found everywhere there was an IPC flag waving; it is this spirit which has done so much during our brief history, to draw us and hold us together.

In order that we do hold together in the future, I believe there are three (3) pillars upon which the IPC should be based: Unity, Tolerance and Respect. During my tenure as President of the IPC from 1989-2001, I consistently promoted the unity of the Paralympic Movement, between the IPC, the sports, the IOSDs, the NPCs and most importantly the athletes. This unity was essential to our growth and development, for without constant contact we would have no athletes. It is the Sports that feed athletes to the NPCs and IOSDs and it is the NPCs and IOSDs who ensure representation in the Paralympic movement.

But, relationships do not just happen overnight. It takes time to nurture them and to build trust, confidence, credibility and acceptance among them. There must also be accountability and responsibility for our member nations, with full participation in our General Assemblies and Games. Only then can we have balanced representation in our Paralympic Movement.

I ask you; have we achieved greatness and success in the Paralympic Movement over our short history? If you read carefully and study this book you will be able to draw your own conclusions.

Dr. Robert D. Steadward, O.C., A.O.E., LLD
Founding President International Paralympic Committee (1989-2001)
Honorary President International Paralympic Committee (2001 to current)

Acknowledgements

Many different individuals have contributed to the writing of this book. Indeed, when we first started to put together the proposal draft and first documents for the publisher Common Ground we were speaking to friends and work colleagues to try to better understand the conceptual basis and theoretical framework for this text. At that time several important people came together at different times to discuss the proposal and comment on its use in the higher education and practical contexts. Therefore thanks go to Professor Otto J. Schantz, Associate Professor Alan Edwards, Professor Karin Volkwein – Caplan, friends and contributors to this book and fellow staff members, and postgraduate students at the University of East London and Mount Royal University, who provided valuable advice and direction. It goes without saying perhaps that we need to thank the individual authors who have spent their own time to make this text the first of its kind in the world. We would like to thank Kathryn Otte from Common Ground Publishing for her continued support and her editing skills throughout the past year. Also thanks go to our families and in particular our children Jackson, Isaac, Cade and Tamsyn, Caja, Phillip and partners Julie and Yuen Ching for their support throughout. Both of us understand the basic premise of the difficult concepts in this book and we understand that this book represents the beginning of an unknown journey which will not be completed until we have further enriched Paralympic research and perhaps more importantly cultivated and stimulated debate and perhaps some controversy.

David Legg and Keith Gilbert   December 2010

Contributors

Lois Appleby

Lois Appleby is the former Chief Executive of Tourism Victoria (Australia), a senior position in the Victorian Government which she held from 2001-2006. Lois then retired from full time work in 2006. During her five years as CEO of Tourism Victoria, international visitor numbers to Victoria continued to increase and the marketing of regional Victoria became a priority. Under her management Tourism Victoria became the number one tourism agency in Australia. Lois took an active interest in the positioning and marketing of Melbourne and Victoria through all the major events, but especially for the 2006 Commonwealth Games. Prior to her move to Melbourne in 2001, Lois was the Chief Executive of the Sydney 2000 Paralympic Games, a position she held for six years. She was responsible for the overall day to day management and marketing of the Games. Through her leadership and collaborative relationship with the organizing committee for the Olympic Games, the delivery of the Paralympic Games was a joint effort of both organizing committees leading to the outstanding success of the Games. The Games were declared "the best ever" by the President of the International Paralympic Committee raising the standards for all Games to follow.

Ian Brittain

Ian Brittain, PhD, is currently Project Manager for 'Peace, Olympics, Paralympics' in the Centre for Peace and Reconciliation Studies at Coventry University, UK. He has written extensively in the field of disability and Paralympic sport including The Paralympic Games Explained published by Routledge in 2009. He has also been researching the history of the Paralympic Games for over ten years, collecting material and data from around the world. In addition to his academic work Ian has also been an Executive Board member of the International Stoke Mandeville Wheelchair Sports Federation, Sports Co-ordinator for the International Wheelchair and Amputee Sports Federation World Games in Rio de Janiero in 2005 and has attended the last three summer Paralympic Games in Sydney, Athens and Beijing.

Natalie Campbell

Natalie gained her undergraduate degree from Plymouth University, her teaching qualification from Thames Valley University and has a Masters in Human Performance from Brunel University. She is currently completing her PhD in Paralympic studies at the University of East London. Natalie's academic interests are grounded in the sociology of sport and include the student-athlete, disability studies, performance lifestyle and education. Before starting her PhD Natalie was the Lead Athlete Support Manager for the U.K. Talented Athlete Scholarship Scheme (TASS). As well as being a strength and conditioning coach, Natalie is also a competitive rower and basketball player.

Ann Cody

Ann Cody is Director of Policy and Global Outreach for BlazeSports America and leads the organization's efforts domestically and internationally with government and non-profit sectors. BlazeSports is the direct legacy organization of the 1996 Atlanta Paralympic Games. As a three-time Paralympian and gold medalist in Athletics, Ann retired from competition to work for the Atlanta Paralympic Organizing Committee in sports planning and venue management. In 2005 Ann was elected to the Governing Board of the International Paralympic Committee and serves as the IPC's liaison to the United Nations.

Dena Coward

Dena Coward is passionate about sport and the opportunities and legacies sport provides. So when the opportunity came around to work on an event that would host the world's best athletes in her home town she jumped at it. Dena was the Director of Paralympics with the Vancouver Organizing Committee for the 2010 Olympic and Paralympic Winter Games from 2005 to 2010 and oversaw the planning of the 2010 Paralympic Winter Games.

Simon Darcy

Simon Darcy PhD is an Associate Professor and Research Director of the School of Leisure, Sport and Tourism at the University of Technology, Sydney. He teaches subjects including environmental planning, public policy, venue management, diversity management and research methods across the School's undergraduate and postgraduate programs. He has held research grants with the Australian Research Council, Australian Sports Commission, Australian Paralympic Committee, Australian Rugby Union and the Football Federation Australia. His sport related research has included sport participation patterns, inclusive planning processes, volunteer management, planning issues for major sport developments, and Olympic and Paralympic planning and legacy processes. Since incurring a spinal injury in 1983 Simon is a power wheelchair user and has been active in the advocacy and research of issues facing people with disabilities. He has held and holds a variety of board positions with sport and disability organizations and represents the perspective of people with disabilities on a range of government committees.

Ted Fay

Ted Fay, PhD, is a professor of Sport Management at the State University of New York (SUNY) at Cortland. He holds a doctorate from the University of Massachusetts in Amherst, a MPA in Public Affairs from the University of Oregon, and a B.A. in government from St. Lawrence University. Dr. Fay served as a senior research fellow at the Center for the Study of Sport in Society at Northeastern University. Fay has an extensive background in international sport including the Olympic and Paralympic movements. He has had a varied career as an educator, advocate and activist involved in a number of human rights initiatives, environmental policy and protection campaigns, and community organizing efforts. Fay is recognized as an international expert on issues related to the integration and inclusion of athletes with a disability in mainstream sport. He was involved in the drafting of Article 30.5 of the United Nations Convention on the Human Rights for Persons with a Disability that addresses issues involving culture, leisure, and sport. He has worked with or for a number of national and international sport federations including U.S. Ski & Snowboard Association, the US Biathlon Association, USA Hockey, US Team Handball Federation and the International Paralympic Committee over a span of 30 years as a national team coach, program director, marketing and strategic consultant, international games and event official and executive director of national and world championship events in cross country skiing, biathlon and ice hockey. Fay has been actively involved in nine Winter Paralympic Games (1980 – 2010) and was a member of the 1988 U.S. Winter Olympic Team in Calgary Alberta.

Scott Fleming

Scott Fleming PhD, is Professor of Sport and Leisure Studies at the Cardiff School of Sport, UWIC. He is also an Honorary Research Fellow at the Asia-Pacific Centre for the Study and Training of Leisure, Zhejiang University, China, and was Chair of the Leisure Studies Association between 2004 and 2009. He serves on the Editorial Boards of Leisure Studies and Sociological Research Online, and on the Editorial Advisory Board of the Journal of Hospitality, Leisure, Sport and Tourism Education. He has published extensively on aspects of the sociology of sport and leisure and on research ethics for over twenty years, and has co-edited (amongst others) Leisure and Tourism: International Perspectives on Cultural Practice (2009), Events Management - Education, Impacts and Experiences (2006), and New Leisure Environments: Media, Technology and Sport (2003).

Keith Gilbert

Keith Gilbert, PhD, is a Professor in the School of Health & Bioscience at the University of East London and Director of the Centre for Disability, Sport & Health. He researches in the area of sport sociology and disability sport and has a strong interest in qualitative, interpretive and narrative research methodologies. He has numerous publications and has edited several books in the broad areas of sport, sociology, cultural studies, and disability which include the following: *'The Paralympics: Empowerment or Sideshow'; 'Sexuality, Sport and the Culture of Risk'; 'Extending the Boundaries: Theoretical Frameworks for Research in Sports Management'; 'Some like It Hot: The Beach as Cultural Dimension'; 'Life on the Margins: Implications for Health Research'; 'Reconstructing Lives: The Problem of Retirement from Elite Sport'; 'Striving for Balance: Modernity and Elite Sport from an Islamic Perspective*. Along with the above, Dr. Gilbert has written over 55 published research articles. He has been an Executive Board Member of the International Council of Sports Science and Physical Education (ICSSPE) and is currently on the publications Board of (ICSSPE). Professor Gilbert is chief editor of the International Journal of Sport in Society and he has two book series, one in the area of Disability and Sport and the other in the broad area of Sport in Society. He was the Assistant Chef de Mission [Administration] of the Australian Paralympic Team in Sydney 2000 and maintains a healthy relationship with Australian and British sport. Dr. Gilbert was an IOC research scholarship winner. He was awarded an Australian Prime Ministers medal for his work at the Sydney 2000 Paralympic Games.

Mary Hums

Mary A. Hums holds a PhD, in Sport Management from Ohio State University, an M.A. in Athletic Administration as well as an M.B.A. from the University of Iowa, and a B.B.A. in Management from the University of Notre Dame. Mary was the 2009 NASSM's Earle F. Zeigler Lecture award and in 2008 was named an Erasmus Mundus International Visiting Scholar in Adapted Physical Activity at the Katholieke Universiteit Leuven, Belgium. In 2006, the USOC selected her to represent the United States at the International Olympic Academy Educators Session in Olympia, Greece. Hums was a co-contributor to Article 30.5 (Participation in Cultural Life, Recreation, Leisure and Sport) of the 2006 United Nations Convention on the Rights of Persons with Disabilities. She volunteered for the 1996, 2002, and 2010 Paralympic Games. In 2004, she lived in Athens, Greece, working both the Olympic (Softball) and Paralympic (Goalball) Games. Hums has co-authored or co-edited five books as well as 60+ refereed journal articles and book chapters, and is a frequent presenter at international conferences. She is a 1996 inductee in the ASA Indiana Softball Hall of Fame and a 2009 inductee into the Marian High School (Mishawaka, IN) Athletic Hall of Fame.

Patrick Jarvis

Patrick Jarvis is a Paralympian (Barcelona, 1992 – athletics) and is currently the Past President and CEO of the Canadian Paralympic Foundation. Prior to being appointed to this executive position, Patrick was involved with Canadian Paralympic sport as a volunteer for over 20 years including 13 years on the Canadian Paralympic Committee (CPC) Board; seven of those as president. With his extensive background in the Paralympic Movement, Patrick has served on a number of boards and committees including the Board of Directors of the Organizing Committee for the Vancouver 2010 Olympic and Paralympic Winter Games (VANOC); WinSport (Calgary); 2010 Legacies Now (Vancouver); the Board of Governors at the University of Guelph and is in his second four-year term as a Governing Board Member of the International Paralympic Committee (IPC).

Justin Jeon

Justin Y. Jeon, PhD, is currently an Associate Professor at Yonsei University, Seoul, Korea, teaching Adapted Physical Activity and Sport Medicine. Justin has been involved with the Paralympic Games since 1996 Atlanta Paralympic Games as a Secretary General of the Whang Youn Dai Achievement Award, and participating in a total of 8 Paralympic Games. He has been involved with preparing bid processes for 2014 and 2018 Pyeong Chang Winter Paralympic Games. He has been involved with Asian Para Games, and Paralympic Games as a member of the Development Committee. Currently, as chairman of the Sports and Development Committee of the Korean Paralympic Committee, he is promoting participation of sports for people with disabilities in elite and also non-elite levels. Justin is also involved with research into the areas of obesity, diabetes and cancer.

Phil Lane

Phil Lane was the Chief Executive Officer of the British Paralympic Association, Great Britain's second largest multi-sport organisation. He joined the BPA in August 2001, the organisation being responsible for leading and coordinating the development of Paralympic sport in the UK, and the funding, management and organisation of the Great Britain, Winter and Summer, Paralympic Teams at the Paralympic Games. Phil was the Chef de Mission for the GB Summer Paralympic Team in Athens 2004, and Beijing 2008 and Winter Paralympic Teams in Salt Lake City in March 2002, Torino 2006 and the recent Winter Games in Vancouver 2010. The former Essex head teacher and coach at Saracens rugby union club has been a tireless fundraiser and champion of Paralympic sport. He said recently that "involvement in sport has given me the privilege of working with and meeting elite performers, coaches and administrators from all over the world and in many sports besides rugby. The opportunity to extend this association through the Paralympic movement in Great Britain is one which inspires and challenges both my sporting and professional instincts." Phil was appointed an OBE in the New Year Honours list in 2008 for services to sport.

Jill M. Le Clair

Jill Le Clair PhD, is an anthropologist with a long term interest in the cultural framing of sport and physical activity, and in supporting opportunities for girls and women. She conducted a longitudinal study on the organizational changes in the Paralympic Games and in IPC swimming and has written about transformations in the lives of athletes through swimming. Recently her focus has been on the meaning of ableism, 'normalcy' and barriers to participation in the context of differing abilities in Canada, and globally. Jill is the founder of the *Global Disability Research in Sport and Health Network* with its aim of disseminating disability research, and supporting a global discourse on disability that includes low and middle income countries, while supporting inclusive national disability policy initiatives and good practices. Her hope is for the inclusion of ability and mobility as concepts in all aspects of curriculum, research and planning. She is a faculty member of the School of Liberal Arts and Sciences at Humber College ITAL in Toronto, Canada.

David Legg

David Legg, PhD, has spent the past twenty years actively involved as an educator, researcher and volunteer in sport management and adapted physical activity. At Mount Royal University, David coordinates the Bachelor of Applied Business and Entrepreneurship - Sport and Recreation Applied Degree. In 2004 David was a visiting professor at Dalhousie University in Halifax and in 2009 at Deakin University in Melbourne. As a volunteer David is currently the President of the Canadian Paralympic Committee. David also coordinates and teaches the sport management program for the Erasmus Mundus European Masters in Adapted Physical Activity at Katholieke Universiteit Leuven.

Travis Muschett

Travis Mushett is a writer based in New York City. In addition to producing short stories, plays, children's books, and works of music and cultural criticism, Travis is currently a PhD student at the Columbia University School of Journalism.

Gavin Poynter

Gavin Poynter PhD is Chair of the London East Research Institute (LERI) and Professor of Social Sciences at the University of East London. He has widely published on 'London 2012', the economics of the service industries and urban regeneration. He has completed several studies on the East London region, including for the London Assembly, central government and local boroughs. His most recent book publication (with Dr I. MacRury eds.) is 'Olympic Cities and the remaking of London' (Ashgate Press, September 2009). His 'From Beijing to Bow Bells' was published in Portuguese by the Ministerio do Esporte, Brazil as part of that government's analysis of major sporting events and their socio-economic legacies. He co-authored 'A Lasting Legacy?', a report for the GLA (2007) on 'London 2012' and is currently working on a new publication that focuses upon London's economy in the wake of the credit crunch and the global economic recession.

Fernando Telles Ribeiro

Fernando has academic training as a Civil Engineer and Physical Educator and is currently a Planning Specialist in Sport and Recreation Facilities. He works as an Architectural and Urban Technology Researcher at the University of São Paulo, Brazil and is a member of IAKS – International Association for Sports and Leisure. Fernando is Vice-President for Latin America of the American Association of Infrastructures for Sport and Recreation, Member of the International Committee for Latin America and Caribbean of IASLIN – International Association of Sport and Leisure Infrastructure Management and Director of the Brazilian Confederation of Aquatic Sports. He has co-authored several chapters on sport facilities and lectures on planning of sport facilities, legacy and sustainability of mega-events at international and national events. He is also the author of the site www.planesporte.com.br which aims to disseminate the most up-to-date knowledge about concepts, practices and policies adopted worldwide for planning of sports and leisure facilities. Finally, as a former athlete he was an Olympic Diving competitor at the Melbourne, 1956 and Rome 1960 Olympic Games and South American Diving Champion in 1958, 1960, 1962 and 1968.

Tony Sainsbury

Tony Sainsbury OBE qualified as a sport and recreation professional in the late 1960s. He had a successful initial career in Schools Physical Education before moving to local government sport and recreation management where he was Assistant Director of Sport for the Metropolitan Borough of Barnsley in Yorkshire and then Director of Sport at the University of Manchester where he completed this phase of his career. During the above period he conducted a parallel voluntary career as a leading sports manager in Paralympic sport, serving as Great Britain Chef de Mission five times between 1980 and 1996; initiating a ten year development programme for wheelchair basketball in the UK and helping to kick start the British Paralympic Association from its foundation in 1989.

After taking early retirement from the University Tony has worked professionally with many Organising Committees and Bid Committees for the Olympic and Paralympic Games - Sydney 2000; Salt Lake City 2002; Manchester Commonwealth Games 2002; Athens 2004 and Beijing 2008. After two unsuccessful Bids with Manchester Tony joined the successful London 2012 Bid Committee in 2003. Since that success he worked initially both as Head of Paralympic Planning and Athlete Villages Manager. He currently holds the post of Head of Athletes Villages. Throughout a successful career in sport Tony has written many articles on Paralympic sport and made informed contributions to other publications on this subject and Village operations. London 2012 will be the thirteenth Olympic and/or Paralympic Games in which he has participated in some organisational capacity. Tony was awarded the OBE (Officer of the Order of the British Empire) for his contribution to Paralympic sport in 1995.

Paul Smith

Paul Smith PhD, is a Senior Lecturer and an accredited Exercise Physiologist at the Cardiff School of Sport, UWIC. His main research interest lies within the area of upper-body exercise, and he has published extensively on methodological developments and physiological response to generic arm crank ergometry. In addition to his academic roles Paul is a trustee of the UK Handcycling Association, a national charity concerned with the promotion and development of this relatively new division of Paracycling. His work in this regard is targeted at both the recreational and competitive ends of the participation spectrum. Paul is the UK representative on the European Handcycling Federation committee, and has recently helped to organise and run a number of international, UCI-sanctioned road cycling competitions. He is currently exploring the development of a Centre for Disability Sport at UWIC, a project that will not only see the emergence of educational and sports science services for elite athletes, but one that will also strive to create new and lasting participation opportunities for people with disability from the wider community.

Robert D. Steadward

Bob Steadward PhD, is the founder and Honorary President of The Steadward Centre, a multi-disability fitness, research and lifestyle facility for people with disability at the University of Alberta. Founded in 1978 it was later renamed in Dr. Steadward's honour. For over forty years, Dr. Steadward has worked tirelessly to improve the health, fitness, and lifestyle, independence and sport opportunities for people with disability. Over the years,

Dr. Steadward's volunteer contributions have included posts in sport at all levels, from coach to administrator, from international to local, involving people with and without disability: Commonwealth Games, Universiade, World Championships, Olympic and Paralympic Games. He has been a passionate advocate for amateur sport. In 1989 he founded the International Paralympic Committee (IPC) and served as its President until his retirement in 2001. By that time the IPC had grown from 40 nations to over 175 member nations, resulting in expanding access to sport for people with disability, worldwide. He was also a member of the International Olympic Committee (IOC) and served on the IOC Commissions for Ethics and Reform; Peace and Truce; and Environment. Dr. Steadward created the idea and was the leader in mobilizing Edmonton's successful bid for the 2001 World Championships in Athletics. During this period of time he also served as a member of the Board of Governors for the 2005 World Masters Games in Edmonton.

Sun Shuhan

Dr. Sun PhD, is the Vice-President of the China Disability Institute at Renmin University in Beijing and has been the recipient of numerous national awards in research and teaching, while mentoring a large number of graduate students. As a highly ranked scholar she has headed up research teams that have addressed labour and insurance law while fulfilling her responsibilities as the Standing Director of the China Association for Labour Studies, and of the China Social Insurance Association. Dr. Sun has a passion for furthering the rights of women, and persons with disabilities and has played an important role in her country in conducting extensive research in the areas of industrial injury (migrants and miners), workers compensation, medical insurance, and labour law rights in health and safety. More recently she has addressed issues related to rehabilitation, accessibility in the built environment, and in sport focused on the impact and legacy of the Paralympic Games, as well as the development of recreational/leisure activities for the disabled.

Part I
The Paralympic Legacy Debate

Chapter 1
Conceptualising Legacy

Keith Gilbert and David Legg

Introduction

We first met over lunch at a restaurant in Melbourne, Australia on Monday 13th July, 2009 and since that time we have been working together to produce this book. The past two years have been a personal and exciting time period for both of us. In fact, we have grown to understand each other as individuals and academics so that in completing this book our friendship has grown along with our mutual understanding of the theory of legacy and the Paralympic Games. Throughout the arduous task of compiling this book we have been supported admirably by our academic peers, many of whom we class as friends, and they have intrigued us by offering a myriad of ideas, innovations and perspectives to support our themes without which there would be no book. We also discussed the development of the text with our postgraduate students who offered ideas as to what sort of content they would support for their courses and as an expansion to their skill and knowledge base. We realise that providing a description of our meeting and re ferring to the conception of this book is important in placing it into some context but we really need to get down to the main premise of the text and ask the question; What is Legacy?

What is Legacy?

There is little doubt that the notion of sporting legacy grew out of the Olympic Movements quest for further global recognition, self promotion and power. Indeed, Girginov and Hills (2008, p. 2091) refer to the IOC's quest for legacy in the following manner:

> '.....the concept of 'legacy', which together with the concept of 'sustainable sports development', has become an essential part of the IOC and the Organising Committee of the Olympic Games (OCOG) vocabulary'. As a result, the IOC, among other things, amended the Olympic Charter to include a particular reference to the creation of positive legacies from the Games and the promotion of sports for all in the host country'.

The birth of legacy, in reality, began in 2002 when the Olympic Studies Centre in Barcelona organised the International Symposium on Legacy of the Olympic Games, '1984-2000', (Chappelet, 2008, p. 2). The report from the Symposium exposed many new directions for Olympic legacy. However, delegates could not decide on a definition of legacy. Indeed, defining legacy is difficult as Gratton and Preuss (2008 p.1923) argue when referring to the outcomes of the Barcelona conference 'It attempted to define legacy, but the participants found that there are several meanings of the concept, and some of the contributions have highlighted the convenience of using other expressions and concepts that can mean different things in different languages and cultures'. When referring to legacy they go onto to argue that: 'Three legacy definitions can be identified: first, the degree of planned structure; second, the degree of positive structure; third, the degree of quantifiable structure'. They also provide 6 of their own event legacy structures and these are: [1] Infrastructure [2] Knowledge [3] Skill-Development and Education [4] Image [5] Emotions and [6] Culture (Gratton and Preuss, pp. 1926 – 1929). MacAloon (2008, p.2065) argues that the term Legacy as a general term is referential enough to seem substantive and readily hypostasized, yet it is open enough to attract the claims and particular attentions of paid specialists' and that 'in the name of legacy, every sport is now claiming the right to have a substantial venue and sports programming left behind after the Games are concluded' (p.2066). So what then is the definition of legacy?

We understand that there might be different cultural meanings for the term legacy and believe that the Barcelona delegates should have unpacked the debate; but we also believe that someone somewhere has to provide a definition in the context of sport as the open ended terms provided by the Symposium actually support the IOC stance. Because if no one can define legacy and what it is supposed to be achieving, then the IOC and or IPC can bend the term to suit themselves.

We accept that there are many definitions of the word and if we try to define the term 'legacy' it means 'something handed down or received from an ancestor or predecessor', (Macquarie Dictionary, 2006) 'an inheritance'

(Concise Oxford English Dictionary, 2008) 'a birthright or heritage',(Free Online Dictionary, 2010) 'a form of bequeath' or literally it means 'that which is left behind' (Merriam Webster Dictionary, 2009). For the purposes of this book we have chosen the latter 'that which is left behind' as our definitive open ended meaning. We feel that this definition is broad enough to cover most aspects of legacy as displayed in the academic narratives by authors such as Cashman (2003, p.32), Chappelet (2008, p. 3), Gratton and Preuss (2008, p. 1922), Girginov and Hills (2008, p.2092) and for the comments we make in the final chapter of this book. Having said this, many of our authors here have used their own definitions although they are similar enough to enable appropriate comparisons.

The Paybacks of Legacy?

Although Chapter 3 by David Legg and Robert Steadward provides an excellent perspective of the benefits of legacy what follows is a brief look at the paybacks of legacy in order to place the book in the correct frame of reference. Gratton and Preuss (2008, p. 2) list the positive characteristics of legacy as ranging from:

> '.....commonly recognised aspects (urban planning, sport infrastructure) to less recognised intangible legacies, such as urban revival, enhanced international reputation, increased tourism, improved public welfare, additional employment, more local business opportunities, better corporate relocation, chances for city marketing, renewed community spirit, better interregional cooperation, production of ideas, production of cultural values, popular memory, experience and additional knowhow'.

However, Richard Cashman et al (2003) have a more specific take on the benefits of legacy. They argue that legacies can be broken down into six categories which are: [a] economic [b] the built and physical environment [c] information and education [d] public life, politics and culture [e] sport and [f] symbols, memory and history. However, there are other legacies which appear just as relevant and the legacy of sustainability and the environment should clearly be taken into account. Perhaps the most important legacy, and one which is very difficult to put into place and sustain, as Girginov and Hills (2008, p.2092) argue when referring to the London 2012 bid, is to 'inspire the country's people to be more physically active'. We tackle this specifically in the final chapter.

It appears to us as outsiders looking into the Olympic legacy debate that everything which is positive coming out of the Games is classed as intended legacy but that there are also positive unintended legacies which occur as if by default such as changing attitudes and 'feel good factors'. Whereas we would not disagree that the above perspectives of legacy are important, we argue that there appears to be little research or idea as to 'planning for legacy' and what legacies are 'left behind' from the Paralympic Games. Hopefully this book will begin to address this void.

The Paralympic World

Understanding the Paralympic world is not just a question of understanding the reality of people with disabilities lives. It is also about reviewing and researching the policies which have been put into place by government, sporting authorities, and others regarding issues such as 'legacy' which has largely been ignored in the Paralympic empire. This issue is important as it affects the individual athlete, National Paralympic Committees, the International Paralympic Committee, future athletes and the public. We are not necessarily looking to be political but we have not shied away from the politics of legacy and in many ways we had a 'political awakening', a series of personal 'moments of truth' about ourselves, and each other, and about how the Paralympic world works. Some of these truths have left us dazed and it's no exaggeration to say that they were a cause of much reflection and angst regarding the lack of planning for Paralympic legacy. What we are manifestly unable to discuss in this book is how the culture and politics of a country can be hidden behind the development of globalisation and recent cultural shifts towards power, capital and control but argue that this is an area which requires further examination in order for us to understand more regarding the political climates involved in the Paralympic sporting contexts. This is interesting as the culture of the Olympics and Paralympics does get overlaid onto the culture of the host country and this, in turn, effects the way in which local legacy can be developed. Cultural contexts are thus important issues not to be undersold or forgotten in the development of the following chapters. Along with dealing with this cultural war between nation state and Paralympic legacies we experienced the problem of authors placing their own slant onto the chapter and approaching the work from a personal belief system. We understand that this is necessary as it is their perspective which we wanted but were wary of idealism and overzealousness as we fought hard to develop a text which was relatively 'apolitical'. However, when we looked at the content material of the book we realised that an 'apolitical' stance would be near impossible to achieve. This is a topic for another text perhaps? This book then is an attempt to place the legacy of the Paralympic Games into a framework to be further analysed and developed.

Anthology

This anthology of work in the area of Paralympic legacy plays a role in providing a no-nonsense and conjectural approach to the significance of the topics which contribute to the theoretical constructs at the core of Paralympic legacy. In actuality, when we first developed the concept of this book we were interested in understanding the notion of legacy across all concepts of sport. However, wherever we looked we could find little in the Paralympic context and consequently the chapters which follow are a first we believe for this area of research. Of importance is the manner in which the chapters which have been written by practitioners and academics. They are formulated into a serious analysis of the role of different parts of the Paralympic movement in developing legacy. This is achieved by developing some fundamental issues and discussions raised by the authors in their individual chapters without which we would not have been able to analyse the notion of Paralympic legacy as a whole. We have been very fortunate to gain the services of individuals who have had personal insider knowledge of previous Paralympic Games and this book details their thoughts, and as such, acts as a form of historical perspective of the Paralympic Games; albeit from a legacy viewpoint. In this manner we have used their thoughts to develop the area of legacy research within the university context and also to add to the literature so that managers, administrators, coaches, students and business people can better understand the notion of legacy in the Paralympic realm. It is hoped that the information in this book might be used to further develop bidding documents and other important projects which support the Paralympic movement.

This book has been divided into four distinct parts. The first part titled *The Paralympic Legacy Debate* places the book firmly into a historic-graphical contextual framework in order that the benefits of hosting a Paralympic Games can be discussed. These first three chapters highlight the nature of 'legacy' and its relationship to the Paralympics. The chapter by Legg and Steadward on the history of the Paralympics is really an interesting take on the history of the Games as almost every previous text has attempted to emphasise the historical beginnings of the Paralympic Games. This historical analysis takes into account the lived experiences of Steadward who of course is the Past President of the International Paralympic Committee. We therefore have an insider's account of how some of the major incidents affected the development of the Paralympics. They cover the issues of the foundation of the Games from 1960 to the modern history and particularly the influence that the Seoul and Sydney Games had on the movement. This chapter leads nicely into the themes further developed by Legg and Gilbert in chapter 3 on the 'Benefits of Hosting the Paralympic Games'. They argue that there are many advantages to the host city investing in the Paralympic Games and these include financial, tourism, cultural perspectives, and argue that host cities are prone to 'basking in the reflective glow' of the Games. Other important reasons for hosting the Paralympic Games include the total economic impact, cultural considerations, social debate, sporting legacy and political legacy. These two chapters set the scene for the main body of the book by offering some very important aspects of legacy and those are the influence of history and the benefits of the Paralympic Games.

The second part titled *Paralympic City Legacies* traces the effects of legacy of the Paralympic Games from Toronto to Rio de Janiero. The chapters in this section relate specifically to different Games and are organised from the point of view of a dateline from 1976 – 2016. The chapter by Ian Brittain on the 'Toronto Olympiad' is perhaps one of the most interesting in the book as it refers specifically to Toronto being the first multi-disciplinary Games and its impact on the 'naming' of the Paralympics. Of particular interest is the section on South African disability sport and their influence on Toronto while highlighting athlete reaction to political interference. Brittain highlights media coverage as an important aspect of legacy and credits the media with changing attitudes of Canadian sport and the rest of the world to Paralympic sport. This chapter is followed by the important writing of Justin Jeon and David Legg on the Seoul Games. They expand the notion of legacy from the development of KOSAD (Korean Sports Association for the Disabled) to the inherent social change which occurred in Korea prior to and during the Paralympic Games. They further argue that the Seoul Paralympic Games had more than just an impact in Korea but had worldwide influence. There was another important aspect of the Korean Games and that was in the development of the logo for the International Paralympic Committee. Patrick Jarvis has written an excellent chapter on the relevance and legacy of the Barcelona Paralympics. In his chapter he makes first reference to the social context of Games' legacies and provides a vivid account of the Games in Barcelona. He refers to the 'old adage' of urban renewal and of increased employment levels, increased public awareness and recognition, enhanced sport technical elements, implementation of functional classification, improved Games organization and perhaps most importantly the formalization of the transfer of responsibility for all things Paralympic to the International Paralympic Committee. On the other hand Travis Mushett and Ann Cody in chapter 7 argue that the legacies inherited from the 1996 Atlanta Games were not all positive. They discuss the problems which the IPC and teams had to endure on arrival to the Atlanta athlete's village and the efforts to make the village habitable. However, they are also very enthusiastic about the positive results which came out of the Atlanta experience. These include the number of records set, better media coverage, the introduction of the first Paralympic mascot and well performed opening and closing ceremonies. They complete this well written chapter by providing an excellent description of the founding of Blazesports which is an ongoing legacy from the Games. Sydney 2000 was the beginning of the legacy debate for the Paralympic movement so argue Simon Darcy and Lois Appleby in chapter 8. They found that perhaps the major legacy was the amount of people who attended the Games in Sydney and this started a new era of ticketing for the Paralympics. Branding, media coverage, sport delivery to athletes, education and increased IPC and NPC relationships and a strategic organizational vision including knowledge transfer were also important to them in their account of the legacy provided for and by the 2000 Games. In chapter 9 Mary Hums writes from a reflective and personal perspective about her work at the 2004 Athens Paralympic Games. This is a very detailed chapter and different from many of the others as it highlights her experiences in the management of people involved at the coalface during the actual event. Mary promotes the importance of the event to her own ideas of legacy and the Paralympic Games and further develops this theme by suggesting that she is a much better person because of her experiences. Her final section tells the tale of the effects of legacy on Athens itself and the muted promises from government and IPC as to the benefits of hosting the Games. Chapter 10 'Legacies and Tensions after the 2008 Beijing Paralympic Games' penned by Sun Shuhan and Jill Le Clair is a well written piece about the legacy of the Beijing Paralympic Games and relates specifically to the historical problems which Beijing and indeed China have had with people with a disability in communist society. They refer specifically to legacy issues which they directly relate to China's increasing economic power across the world and to its renaissance and political ascendency. More specifically they argue that a change in language associated with people with disabilities, and greatly improved world class facilities and training sites are important legacies from the Games. Also they discuss the celebration of disability sport in China and more specifically in Beijing as a lasting legacy from the Games. The following chapter by Dena Coward and David Legg is very important in the book as it highlights the notion of legacy in Vancouver which has boasted about its legacy perspective and leads the rest of the world in the Paralympic legacy debate. They argue throughout that Vancouver 2010 was responsible for a number of 'firsts' and that the Paralympic impact indicators should perhaps be applied to the Paralympics. Their main thesis relates however, to the 2010 LegaciesNow programme which is well documented and explained. Throughout, they highlight other specific legacy issues which arose in Vancouver and the important relationship between VANOC and their concept of legacy. Chapter 12 was written by Tony Sainsbury with his essay having as its premise that the historical relationship between the International Olympic Committee and the International Paralympic Committee is very important. He discusses the issue of the Paralympics being a distraction from the main event and offers pre Games/pre Bid analysis as an important tool in developing legacy from a sporting event. He argues that there is a "Purpose and Promotion" to any Games bid document.

Of particular interest is the final chapter of Part 2 by Fernando Telles Ribeiro a Brazilian academic who is interested in supporting the notion of Paralympic legacy in Rio de Janiero for the 2016 Paralympic Games. He provides a wonderful historical background to disability and Paralympic sport in Brazil and in particular the Brazilian Paralympic Committee. He goes further by highlighting some of their perceived issues relating to legacy. These include revamping the accessibility procedures, integrating planning and delivery of systems, comprehensive education and training and the importance of the media in the legacy plans of Rio de Janiero.

Part three of this book is titled *'Emerging Issues of Paralympic Legacy'* and here there are 5 chapters which are written by leading academics and practitioners in the field of Paralympic sport. They provide innovative and novel ideas to be taken forward in the legacy debate and offer solutions and areas to be included in future bid documentation. Chapters 14, 15 and 16 have been written by Ted Fay who is arguably one of the best known academics in the field of Paralympic Winter sports. Ted provides a sound historical basis to the chapters and highlights many significant legacy issues which need to be taken into account when organizing a Winter Paralympics. It is an important addition to the text and worth a careful inspection as to our knowledge there has been little written about the Winter Paralympics. Chapter 17 by Phil Lane provides an introspective viewpoint of a National Paralympic Committee. His main thesis is that he would like governments, and those responsible for legacy to target the area of 'social responsibility in respect of disability, ethnicity and gender, rather than the overtly economic, and politically expedient, one of health, education and crime'. Furthermore, Lane argues for more access to physical activity for people with disabilities and that there can be no better way to utilize future legacy. He argues that legacy should be lasting and not fleeting and that the only way to achieve long term legacy is by education. Chapter 18 by Paul Smith and Scott Fleming provides an excellent synopsis of the effects of legacy on health and fitness in society. They argue for increased exercise and raised levels of public awareness of public health and those local authorities, the NHS and various government agencies should be charged with the legacy and promotion of health and fitness across the UK. They write at length about health and disability and the barriers to physical activity for individuals with disability and the relationship between the Paralympics and health legacy. Natalie Campbell's work in chapter 19 revolves around the notion of physical education and Paralympic legacy. This is a well designed chapter which relates to individuals with an intellectual disability arguing many of the promises in the London 2012 document have not been met and have failed to reach an underrepresented group. She argues that a lasting sporting legacy to children with learning difficulties in schools is far down the list of priorities for LOCOG and other sporting authorities. Chapter 20 is the final chapter in this section and has been written by Gavin Poynter. He argues that any legacy from the London 2012 Games should include some examination of social legacy, social inequality and visions of social transformation. Poynter refers to the promises of Olympic legacies and the potential offered by such mega events for long lasting leagues both at the Olympic and Paralympic levels. He argues strongly for a lasting legacy of the engagement of young people in sport and physical activity but doubts that this will be the case in Paralympic mode. His final section refers specifically to legacy aspects of the London Games and in particular the London Sports Forum for Disabled People. It is an excellent chapter to complete this section of the text and leads nicely into part four of the book which is titled *'Reconceptualising Paralympic Legacies'*.

In this fourth and final part Chapter 21 offers a way to better understand the notion of Paralympic legacy and utilizes a metasynthesis approach to dissect the previous chapters and draw out the important perspectives of legacy in the Paralympic realm. Finally, in chapter 22 we offer an Epilogue which asks some important questions regarding the relationship between the International Olympic Committee and the International Paralympic Committee.

These four sections adequately reflect the areas of legacy which we felt required highlighting in the literature. While this book has been edited in order to support students in higher education it is also relevant for those for those working in the world of sport and those who wish to become involved in researching and working in this area. We also hope that the chapters herein will enable public and government eyes to be opened to the notion of Paralympic legacy and that the text will support the development of further research by academics into the Paralympics. To summarize, this book examines the relationship between the Paralympics and Legacy and the volume is attempting to achieve something new and innovative while opening up new areas of research. In achieving this we believe that we should challenge convention and not just live it.

References

Brown, L. (2008) *The New Shorter Oxford English Dictionary* (2 Vol. Set; Thumb Indexed Edition) p. 3647.

Cashman, R., C. Kennett., M. de Morgas., and N.Noria (2003) (Eds.) *What is Olympic Legacy? The Legacy of the Olympic Games, 1984-2002* pp. 31-42, IOC document, Olympic Museum, Lausanne.

Cashman, R. (2006) *The Bitter-Sweet Awakening: The Legacy of the Sydney 2000 Olympic Games*, Walla Walla Press, Sydney.

Chappelet, J-L (2008) Olympic Environmental Concerns as a Legacy of the Winter Games, *International Journal of the History of Sport*, Vol. 25, No. 14. pp. 1884-1902.

Free-on-line Dictionary (2010) http://www.thefreedictionary.com/ (accessed 12/09/2010).

Girginov, V. and L. Hills (2008) A Sustainable Sports Legacy: Creating a Link between the London Olympics and Sports Participation. *International Journal of the History of Sport*, Vol. 25, No. 14. pp. 2091-2116.

Gratton, C. and H. Preuss (2008) Maximizing Olympic Impacts by Building Up Legacies, *International Journal of the History of Sport*, Vol. 25, No. 14. pp.1922-1938.

MacAloon, J.J. (2008) 'Legacy' as a Managerial/Magical Discourse in Contempory Olympic Affairs, *International Journal of the History of Sport*, Vol. 25, No. 14.

Macquarie Dictionary (2006) Macquarie Library Publications; 4th Revised edition.

Merriam-Webster's Collegiate Dictionary, (2009) Merriam-Webster publications, USA.

Soanes, C and A. Stevenson (2008) *Concise Oxford English Dictionary:* 11th Edition.

Chapter 2
The History of the Paralympic Games

David Legg and Robert Steadward

Introduction

This book is based on review of the legacies of several Paralympic Games beginning in 1976 and envisioning potential legacies as far into the future as 2016. This chapter provides a background history to the Paralympic Games in order to place the book in the correct context and to provide a basic understanding of the Games and Paralympic movement as a whole.

The Olympic Games and Olympic movement's has a long history which began in 1896 with its original roots in 776 B.C., (Canadian Olympic Committee, 2009). The Paralympic Games, meanwhile only began shortly after World War II. Sport for people with a disability was initially considered and developed because of improved medical knowledge including the invention of penicillin and improved evacuation procedures regarding spinal cord and other previously fatal injuries. The reality was that persons with spinal cord injuries prior to the war did not typically live long enough for rehabilitation to be seriously considered. These health related changes translated into a longer life expectancy for persons with spinal cord injuries, which then created recognition for an increased emphasis on rehabilitation (Legg, Emes, Stewart & Steadward, 2002; Steadward & Foster, 2003).

The British Government recognizing this need opened a Spinal Injuries Centre at Stoke Mandeville Hospital in Aylesbury, England in 1941. There, under the direction of Dr. Ludwig Guttmann, sport was introduced to the war veterans in the form of remedial exercises and these evolved into ward versus ward competitions eventually culminating on July 28th 1948 with the organization of the first Stoke Mandeville Games. These Games included only archery and coincided with the opening ceremonies of London's Olympic Games. It was an apparent coincidence that the first Stoke Mandeville Games (referred to by Guttmann as a national festival of the paralyzed) were held on July 29th 1948 coinciding with the opening ceremonies as Guttmann alluded to this noting that this first gave him the idea that the Stoke Games would grow to become truly international. The Games were held every year following and in 1952 they did become international by including a small group of paralyzed ex servicemen from the Netherlands and by 1957 the Games had grown to include 360 athletes from 24 countries (Guttmann, 1964).

Following the slow and deliberate growth of the Stoke Mandeville Games in the 1950s Sir Ludwig Guttmann contacted the International Olympic Committee with the hopes of organizing the Stoke Games in Rome, which would follow the 1960 Summer Olympic Games. The IOC did not object and wheelchair events were held for 400 athletes from 23 countries (International Paralympic Committee, 2010). To many, these Games were the founding Paralympic Games because they were the first open to any person with a spinal cord injury which did not just include ex servicemen and women. It was in Rome that Pope John XXIII noted that the athletes were "the living demonstration of the marvels of the virtue of energy. You have given a great example, which we would like to emphasize: you have shown what an energetic soul can achieve, in spite of apparently insurmountable obstacles imposed by the body" (Guttmann, 1986). Pope Paul XXIII, further declared that Guttmann was: "...the de Coubertin [the founder of the modern Olympic Games] of the paralyzed" (Lomi, Geroulanos & Kekatos, 2004).

The Foundation of the Paralympic Games

Since 1960 the Paralympic Games have been held (with Winter Games starting in 1976) paralleling the Winter and Summer Olympic Games schedule. They have grown tremendously since then and one way to demonstrate this growth is the sheer number of athletes and participating nations. From 400 athletes representing 23 countries in 1960, the Games in 2008 included 3951 athletes from 146 countries in 2008 (International Paralympic Committee, 2010). It is also important to note that the Paralympic Games in 1960 were the first "Olympic style" Games for the Paralympians but many recognize the Modern Paralympic Games not beginning until 1988 in Seoul.

Returning to the history of the Games themselves in 1963 in Linz, Austria the 'First International Sports Meet for the Disabled' was held for those not having spinal cord injuries (Kasai, 2009) and in 1964, the Paralympic Games were held in Tokyo, which also hosted the Olympic Games. These Games were held in the midst of Japan's "economic miracle" and became a symbol of Japan's recovery from the war. As noted in the Tokyo 2016 bid website:

> "With the success of the 1960 Games in Rome, Sir Ludwig Guttmann was keen to stage the Games again at the same venue as the Olympic Games in 1964, in Tokyo. Support for his plan was boosted by the positive reactions of Japanese observers who visited the 1960 Games in Rome. Based on their reports upon returning to Tokyo, and with the agreement of the International Stoke Mandeville Games Committee, contact was established between Guttmann and the Japanese authorities" (Tokyo 2016).

The Opening Ceremony for the Tokyo Games was presided over by His Imperial Highness Prince Akihito and Princess Michiko and included 375 athletes (307 men and 68 women) from 21 countries. The largest delegation came from Great Britain, with 70 athletes, followed by the USA with 66 (Tokyo 2016).

The Games in 1964 were referred to as the International Stoke Mandeville Games and the Olympic Games of wheelchair sport, with Paralympics also being used arguably for the first time. Para was used as the prefix from Paraplegia and lympics as a suffix from Olympics. The combination apparently appealed to many and it was thus used in Tokyo's publicity for the Games (Kasai, 2009). At the closing ceremonies of the Tokyo Games the Mexican flag was presented to Dr. Leobarbo Ruiz, head of the delegation as from Mexico which was hosting the Olympic Games in 1968 (United Press, 1964). The assumption was that Mexico City would also host the Paralympic Games, albeit noting potential concerns with ill effects from the high altitudes expressed by Sir Ludwig Guttmann's in Reflections on the Olympiad for the Paralyzed in the Tokyo Games's final report. Also worth noting from the Tokyo Games was that it served somewhat as a precursor to the current Paralympic multi disability sport format, whereby following the Paralympic Games for those with spinal injuries the hosts also organized a domestic event (along with a few athletes from West Germany) in athletics, swimming and table tennis for multiple classifications. More specifically they included athletes with leg and arm amputations and all three sports and competitions were also held for athletes with visual impairments in swimming and athletics.

Guttmann himself articulated the legacy of the 1964 Games in Tokyo and remarked:

> "It is no exaggeration to say that the Games were a profound educational value to many thousands of Japanese people. They began to understand the meaning for rehabilitation of the severely physically handicapped through the medium of sport and to be aware that the severely disabled should not be considered as outcasts of society living on charity but should be assisted to live

within the community as respected citizens. In this connection, it is most encouraging to know that after the Tokyo Games the Ministry of Labor in Japan decided to build a factory for paraplegics in realization of the physical and psychological capabilities of their paralyzed countrymen" (Guttmann, 1964, p.7).

In 1968 the Paralympic Games were moved to Tel Aviv, Israel while the Olympic Games as noted earlier were hosted that year in Mexico City. As alluded to earlier officials in Mexico were apparently fearful that persons with spinal injuries would not survive in high altitudes and there were also no disability sport organizations operating in Mexico that could assist with planning and leadership. Israeli meanwhile and perhaps because of recent armed conflict recognized the need and importance of sport and rehabilitation and agreed to host the Games.

In 1972, the Summer Paralympic Games were held in Heidelberg, Germany while Munich was the host site for the Summer Olympic Games. Of note at these Games, was the inclusion of the demonstration sport of goalball and running events for athletes with visual impairments. Previously all Paralympic Games had been for only those with spinal injuries

In 1976, the Olympiad for the Physically Disabled or TORONTOLYMPIAD (as it was also then called) was held in Toronto only a few hours away from Montreal, which hosted the Summer Olympic Games (see chapter 4). The Toronto Games were unique in that they included those with visual impairments and amputation for the first time as official competitors and not only in demonstration status events. It was the addition of these athletes that encouraged the organizing committee to change the name from "Paralympics" to the "Olympiad for the Physically Disabled." The term Paralympics was avoided because of the perceived link to paraplegic Games (Legg, 2000, 2003).

The year 1976 was also significant in that the Winter Paralympic Games were held for the first time in Örnsköldsvik, Sweden (then called the Winter Olympic Games for the Disabled). In 1980 when the Summer Paralympic Games were held in Arnhem, the Netherlands, athletes with Cerebral Palsy were included for the first time. It would not be until 1996 when athletes with intellectual disabilities were included within the Paralympic Games with a separate Paralympic Games being held for them in 1992 in Madrid when the Paralympic Games were held in Barcelona (Legg, Emes, Stewart & Steadward, 2002; Steadward & Foster, 2003).

Modern History of the Paralympic Games

As noted earlier, in 1980, the Paralympic Games were held in Arnhem, the Netherlands while the Olympic Games were held in Moscow with Soviet officials, not offering to host Paralympic competitions. In 1984, the Summer Olympic Games were held in Los Angeles and the Winter Games in Sarajevo. At both Olympic competitions, athletes with disabilities where invited to compete in demonstration events; alpine for winter and wheelchair athletics for summer. The wheelchair demonstration racing events were then continued until 2004.

The 1984 Summer Paralympic Games, were held in two sites due to the intended hosts at the University of Illinois having to cancel plans only months prior. After the announcement, disability sport leaders then banded together and decided to host events for athletes with cerebral palsy, amputations and visual impairments in New York City while wheelchair events for athletes with spinal injuries were held at Stoke Mandeville.

During this time a number of international organizations specific to various disabilities were formed including those for athletes with cerebral palsy, amputations, and visual impairments. Eventually, they along with the Stoke Mandeville based organization that had been created for athletes with spinal injuries determined that there was a need to coordinate the Games and thus in 1982 created an International Coordinating Committee Sports for the Disabled (ICC). In 1984 Dr. Robert Steadward, on behalf of the Canadian Federation of Sport Organizations for the Disabled, circulated a proposal to every member nation in the ICC recommending a new organizational structure for disability sport, and in particular, the need for democratically elected governance. Other requests were also solicited and it was decided to host a seminar to review them in Arnhem where the ICC Secretariat was situated. (The secretariat had been created with the surplus funding from the 1980 Games). After two days of vigorous debate, 23 resolutions emerged, the most essential of which were as follows:

- To change the structure of the existing organization
- To include national representation as well as regional and athlete representation
- To reduce the number of classifications
- To implement a functional classification system
- To develop a structure by sport and not disability
- To work towards integration with the International Olympic Committee and other International Sport Federations. (Steadward & Foster, 2003).

Following the 'Arnhem Seminars', an Ad Hoc Committee was elected with the mandate to review the 23 resolutions and develop a new constitution and bylaws. Two years later disability sport leaders reconvened in Germany and here Dr. Steadward was elected as the International Paralympic Committee's founding President. For eight years the IPC operated almost solely on the benevolence of volunteers and it was not until 1997, that Bonn, Germany was selected as the host city for their headquarters, which officially opened an IPC office in 1999. In 2001 Dr. Steadward stepped down as President fulfilling three, four-year terms and since that time Sir Phillip Craven, a former wheelchair basketball player from the UK, has provided exemplary leadership as President. The International Paralympic Committee office in

Bonn now employs several full time staff, providing services for over 160 National Paralympic Committee's and several issue specific standing committees.

Returning to the Games themselves, as noted earlier the 1988 Summer Paralympic Games held in Seoul are now perceived by many as the start of the modern Paralympic Games, in part, because they were for the first time held in the same venues as those used for the Summer Olympic Games (see chapter 5). The 1992 Summer Paralympic Games were then held in Barcelona and these mirrored many of the initiatives begun in Seoul and are widely recognized as being hugely successful. Four years later in Atlanta the 1996 Summer Games were perceived by some as a disappointment (see chapters 6 and 7). Lois Appleby, CEO of the 2000 Paralympic Games in Sydney remembered being in Atlanta three days after the 1996 Olympic Games closing ceremonies and walking around the village and venues with colleagues from the Sydney Olympic Organizing Committee where she observed in her opinion total chaos. "Television cables to scoreboards required for the Paralympics had been cut; the garbage in the main stadium and other venues had been left for the Paralympic organizing committee to clean, the village needed to be refigured because the Georgia Tech University did not have an agreement for the Paralympic athletes; and keys from most of the rooms in the Athlete's Village had been thrown into a box unlabeled thus requiring all of the locks to be changed" (Appleby, 2007).

Following the Games in Atlanta, was the Sydney Summer Paralympics, which are what many consider to be a second benchmark Games after the 1988 Summer Games in Seoul (see chapter 8). The 2000 Games had a significant increase in the number of athletes and spectators and a dramatic rise in the organization of the Games. The Games in 2004 took place in Athens and in 2008 were held in Beijing (see chapters 9 and 10). Winter Games meanwhile took place in Geilo, Sweden in 1980 and Innsbruck in 1984 and 1988, Albertville in 1992, Lillehammer in 1994, Nagano in 1998, Salt Lake City in 2002 and Torino in 2006 (Steadward & Foster, 2003), (see chapters 14, 15 & 16).

In 2008 in Beijing (see chapter 10) the Paralympic Games were somewhat overshadowed by the inclusion of two athletes with disability in the Olympic Games; Natalie du Toit, from South Africa and table tennis player Natalia Partyka from Poland (Carter, 2009; du Toit, 2009). What is interesting is that the examples of du Toit and Partyka were not the first athletes with disability who had competed in Olympic Games (Legg, Burchell, Jarvis, & Sainsbury, 2010). As well, and possibly more noteworthy, to the media anyway, was the absence in the Olympic Games of another athlete with disability, Oscar Pistorius (Legg, Burchell, Jarvis, & Sainsbury, 2010). The notoriety was likely the result of his challenge to the International Association of Athletics Federation (IAAF) on their ruling regarding his eligibility to compete against non-disabled runners; which he won through an appeal to the IOC Court of Arbitration for Sport.

This brings us to the most recent Games held in Vancouver in 2010 (see chapter 11). These Games were the first to include several initiatives such as a joint marketing agreement with the host NPC and the first to integrate design and marketing of Olympic and Paralympic mascots. One can only imagine that these initiatives and vision will have a dramatic impact on Paralympic sport both nationally and internationally. Time of course will tell if this comes to pass.

Conclusive Statements

Reflecting on the history of the Games and movement it is easy to understand that as with any industry, with growth come challenges and opportunities. Consequences, unintended or not, are that expectations for the Paralympic Games have risen, in some cases without corresponding increases in sponsorship or infrastructure. Indeed, we ask the question: Are the legacies discussed in this book real or fantasy? In many ways this question is difficult to answer because there have been so few studies on individual's changed attitudes or other long term soft or hard legacy impacts emanating from a city which hosts the Paralympic Games. What is clear and what this book suggests is that when discussing sports legacy history has to be taken into account because what has happened in the past strongly influences future legacy plans. As such whether this book will fulfill the needs for the IPC and Paralympic sports to develop strong legacy perspectives for the future is to be tested but hopefully it can make a contribution by initiating and setting a benchmark in the development for future Paralympic bid legacy plans.

References

Appleby, L. (2007) 'Legacy of the 2000 Sydney Paralympic Games'. *Paper presented at The Sport Event Hosting Conference*, Taipei, Taiwan.

Canadian Olympic Committee (2010) *How the Olympic Games Began.* Retrieved from Carter, P. (2005) *Games Without Frontiers.* London, UK.

du Toit, N. (2010) Road to Beijing.

Guttmann, L. (1964) *Editorial Introduction: Reflection on the Olympiad of the Paralyzed.* the 1964 International Stoke Mandeville Games for the Paralyzed in Tokyo, 8th-12th November.

Guttmann, L. (1986) *Textbook of Sport for the Disabled.* Aylesbury, UK: HM + M Publishers Ltd.

A Brief History of the Paralympic Games, Retrieved from International Paralympic Committee (2010) Past Games – Summer Games Overview. Accessed from http://www.paralympic.org/ (27/10/2010).

Kasai, Y. (1964) Letter from President of the Organizing Committee in 1964.

Legg, D. (2003) 'Strategy Formation in Amateur Sport Organization: A Case Study'. *International Journal of Sport Management* 4, no. 3: 205-223.

Legg, D. *'Strategy Formation in the Canadian Wheelchair Sports Association (1967-1997)'.* PhD diss., University of Alberta, 2000.

Legg, D. Burchell, A. Jarvis, P. and T. Sainsbury (2010) The Athletic Ability Debate: Have We Reached a Tipping Point? Palaestra, Vol. 25 (1) 19-25

Legg, D. Emes, C. Stewart, D. And R. Steadward (2002) Historical Overview of the Paralympics, Special Olympics and Deaflympics. Palaestra, Vol. 20 (1) 30-35

Lomi, C. Geroulanos, S. & Kekatos, E. (2004) Sir Ludwig Guttmann - "The de Coubertin of the paralysed" Journal of the Hellenic Association of Orthopaedic and Traumatology 55 (1). (accessed 3/11/2012) from http://www.acta-ortho.gr/v55ti.html.

Steadward, R. and S. Foster. (2003) 'History of Disability Sport: From Rehabilitation to Athletic Excellence'. In *Adapted Physical Activity*, (eds.) R. Steadward, G. Wheeler, and J. Watkinson, 471-496. Edmonton, AB: University of Alberta, 2003.

Tokyo 2016 (2009) Tokyo's Hosting of the 1964 Paralympic Games, (accessed 12/10/2010) from http://www.tokyo2016.or.jp

United Press (1964) Paralympics Close, The Mainichi Daily News, November.

Chapter 3
An Overview of the Benefits of Hosting the Paralympic Games

David Legg and Keith Gilbert

Introduction

There have been a number of papers and reports reviewing the benefits of hosting major sporting events, and in particular the Olympic Games (Brown & Massey, 2001; Girginov & Hills, 2008; Malfasa, Therdoraki, & Houlihan, 2004; Preuss, 2006; Taylor & Edmonson, 2007). Alternatively there have very few specific to the Paralympic Games, which was, in part, the motivation for the development of this book. As an example Lois Appleby, who was the CEO of the Sydney 2000 Paralympic Games noted that the official Final Report for the Sydney 2000 Paralympic Games, did not have a section on the legacy of the Games and the Final report for the 2000 Olympic Games had only a small chapter titled 'Legacy and Opportunities'. These few pages noted that 'the Olympic Games were a catalyst for economic, cultural and social change,' but didn't expand on how, or what was to be measured.

Nevertheless, Olympic Games impact analyses have been carried out as early as the 1988 Calgary Olympic Winter Games (Ritchie, 2000). Indeed, the first concerted attempt to 'integrate' Olympic legacies was not made until 2002, when the International Olympic Committee (IOC) began framing the concept of 'legacy' after hosting their International Symposium on the Legacy of the Olympic Games (1984-2000) in Barcelona. As a result, the IOC, among other things, amended the Olympic Charter to include particular references to the creation of positive legacies (International Olympic Committee (IOC), Olympic Charter, New rules 2.13 and 2.14.) from the Games and they developed the Olympic Games Impact (OGI) project. This requires host cities to undertake a comprehensive longitudinal study designed to measure the economic, social and environmental impact of the Games (Girginov & Hills, 2008).

On the Paralympic side, meanwhile, there has only been one, third-party assessment of the Paralympic Games' legacy that we are aware of and that was completed by Cashman and Darcy on the Sydney Games in 2000. With the previous comments in mind this book was initiated to begin the process of providing a benchmark understanding of the Paralympic Games legacy and to identify future research opportunities. A legacy of Paralympic Games is difficult to define, as described in Chapter 1 and, in part, as only recently it has been addressed in any area and also because identifying legacies from any mega events is so difficult. The Olympic Symposium in 2002, referred to earlier, noted this second challenge pointing out that host organizing committees were typically time specific entities with multiple extenuating circumstances and factors. And as noted previously it was as a result of the IOC conference that legacy was formally introduced into the IOC vocabulary for potential bid cites during the 2012 bid process (Taylor & Edmondson, 2007). There is also a third potential argument that understanding legacy of a Paralympic Games is challenging in that there is still not a universally understood and accepted understanding of the nature and objectives of the Paralympic Games themselves, but discussion on that will be left for another time.

Regardless of these challenges, the London 2012 Summer Olympic and Paralympic Games organizing committee attempted to develop a definition of legacy which is the result of matching the needs of [a system] to the potential presented by [the event] resulting in a number of opportunity areas and turning these opportunities into actions and results (London 2012). Researchers assessing the legacy of the Olympic and Paralympic Games in Vancouver have further described legacy by using the analogy to a comet. "To assist the reader in understanding context impacts," they likened the related context impacts to a comet-shaped rock landing in a pond tail-first. The rock is the Games and the pond is the host region.

Regardless of what definition is used, we hope it is universally agreed upon that understanding legacies of hosting the Paralympic Games is important. One possible reason for this is that while the arrangement between Olympic and Paralympic Games being held in the same city has seen a number of advantages, there may be benefits for the Paralympic Games being held in different cities.

One bid one city

Cities are now bidding to host IPC Championships in sports such as swimming and athletics and perhaps they are doing so to prepare for other future bids but also we assume as standalone events. It is thus foreseeable that cities might be interested in bidding for the Paralympic Games not as a second rate Olympic Games but as a proud and worthwhile event on their own. Perhaps as a result of more formal assessments of the value and recognized legacy of hosting the Paralympic Games, city leaders may be encouraged to see these Games in a different light.

This may become more relevant as early as the 2018 Games. In 2001 the IOC and IPC agreed to the practice of "one bid, one city", meaning that the staging of the Paralympic Games would be automatically included in the bid for the Olympic Games. This Agreement came into effect beginning with Beijing and Vancouver although it was initially followed by the Organizing Committees in Salt Lake City, Athens and Torino. In 2003, the IOC-IPC Agreement was adjusted with the amendment aimed at ensuring that Organizing Committees for Games in 2008, 2010 and 2012 pay the IPC for broadcasting and marketing. In June 2006, the IOC and the IPC signed an extension to the agreement through to 2016 (International Paralympic Committee, 2009).

Most academics are not privy to the negotiations that have or will take place between the IOC and IPC but it is interesting to consider the possibility of one day having the Olympics and Paralympic Games held in different cities. The position taken by the authors of this book does not advocate for either position but simply suggests it might be worthwhile considering alternatives.

Smaller centre's for instance that are not able to bid for the combined two Games (either in Winter or Summer) may be interested in bidding for just one, particularly as it seems that global competition among city states has increased the pressure to brand through hosting sporting events. The potential financial benefit of branding, specifically to persons with disability, may also have appeal although the real financial power of persons with disability sometimes referred to as 'handicapitalism' is debatable.

Recent bids also seem to indicate an appetite for cities to host major events. As Don Lockerbie, COO of Cricket World Cup 2007, sums up "Other than Montreal," can you name a world Games city who would say afterwards, "Boy I wish we hadn't done that?" Even for Canada, Montreal may always be seen as the last financial disaster, but it hasn't discouraged them from bidding and hosting' (Whamsley, 2008). This interest continues even though hosting major events has also become increasingly expensive (Malfasa, Therdoraki, & Houlihan, 2004). The 1952 and 1956 Olympic Games attracted 16 candidates between them, while 27 expressed interest in hosting the 2016 Games alone. There are more than 300 cities in the US that employ at least one person dedicated to attracting sports events to their city. And today most cities are taking the long term view when bidding and not necessarily focusing on short term or immediate financial returns. Cities constantly try to differentiate themselves as world-class whether it is to attract tourism or civic pride. One way has been to host globally recognized sporting events and this practice is sometimes referred to as place branding. Recent examples include Dubai, Doha and Abu Dhabi in the Middle East, Shanghai and Singapore in Asia and Rio de Janeiro in South America (Legg, 2009). In a presentation titled "Levering the Impact of Mega Sports Events by Building up Legacy" Holger Preuss (2007) identified various stakeholders who would want to bid for major Games. Sport Governing Bodies like major Games because they create evidence that the event is good for the city, the sport is welcomed and the city can "bask in the reflected glow".

This approach to bidding and hosting followed Barcelona's success in hosting the 1992 Games and while the economic legacy was only a $5 million surplus the other legacies have been extraordinary. Thus, more and more cities are viewing their bids as a means of positioning their city, region or country as a place to visit, do business or invest in – in essence, as an act of place branding. China has several cities of 10-15 million people but they need to brand themselves and that is where sports events can help. As an example there were 23 major events stages in Chinese cities other than Beijing and Shanghai in 2007 and 2008 (Whamsley, 2008).

This interest is based in part on a number of assumptions regarding the legacies or benefits of hosting. The International Symposium on Legacy of the Olympic Games, 1984-2000 identified six tangible and intangible legacies to hosting Olympic Games and these included economic impact, cultural considerations, social debate, sporting legacy, political legacy and value of Olympic education.

Of these six, the one that is most typically referenced is economic which can be attained through improved tourism, external investment and infrastructure (Preuss, 2007). Political desire is also often a driving force and in particular to attract new investment in order to develop infrastructure such as telecommunications, transportation and housing and this has certainly been evident in Vancouver. Other reasons to bid and host Games are intangible such as international city branding, noted earlier, and emotional connection, sport development and social impact (Brown & Massey, 2001).

Social Impacts

Specific to social impact from a Paralympic perspective, is hopefully changing perceptions of persons with disability. This is addressed in many of the subsequent chapters in this book and this goal has also been mirrored by the Special Olympics. In a Sport Illustrated article written on the 40th Anniversary of the 1st Special Olympics Games held in Chicago in 1968, the editor presented a Legacy Award to Eunice Kennedy Shriver for using athletics to change the world for people with intellectual disabilities. In the accompanying article Chicago Mayor Richard Daley was quoted as telling Shriver in Chicago in 1968 – "you know Eunice, the world will never be the same after this" (McCallum, 2008, p.58). Other examples of where hosting the Special Olympics led to social change included in Ireland which rewrote its antidiscrimination statues after the World Games were held in Dublin in 2003. China, meanwhile, apparently routinely warehoused people with intellectual disabilities but at the 2007 Special Olympics World Games in Shanghai, a crowd of 80,000 cheered as a video on the stadium scoreboard showed the country's president Hu Jintao cavorting with a group of Special Olympic athletes.

A second socially related legacy, which is only now being recognized, is health. Major sporting events such as the Olympic Games can help host countries develop a "healthy legacy", as noted by the World Health Organization (WHO). China spent an estimated $40bn on hosting the Olympics in 2008, reports Reuters, with significant funds being used for public health projects, including attempts to reduce Beijing's notorious air pollution. A book entitled 'The Health Legacy of the 2008 Beijing Olympic Games: Successes and Recommendations' was launched by the WHO and the city of Beijing detailing the impact. "The Beijing Olympics experience showed that it is possible to advance a public health agenda by capitalizing on the attention generated by the Games among government agencies and the society at large," the WHO's China representative Michael O'Leary commented that: "The book's findings stress the need to plan well ahead and to establish clear roles and functions for the various agencies involved in partnerships" (sportcity.org, 2008).

Global Imperatives

As previously noted there are many reasons why a city would bid beyond this more altruistic rationale and in particular are economic benefits which to date have not been demonstrated from a Paralympic Games. Dunn and McGuirk (1999) claim that hosting a major sporting event have become a global imperative of competition between nations, regions and event individual cities, which try to attract international investment. More specifically they claim that place competition and place marketing are the effects of global competition and mobility in the contemporary borderless world (Malfas, Theodoraki & Houlihan, 2004). Hervey (1989), meanwhile, refers to mega events such as the Olympics as one of the main products of post modern society and a key means by which cities express their personality, enhance their status and advertise their position on the global stage (Malfas, Theodoraki & Houlihan, 2004). Indeed, Gratton (2000) argues that: "Increasingly sport events are part of a broader strategy aimed at raising the profile of a city and therefore success cannot be simply judged on profit and loss" (Gratton et al, 2000, p. 18). Thus there is justification for using scarce public resources to stage the event and it stimulates more future bids and therefore secures power and an ongoing existence of the sport.

Gavin Graham, Chief Investment Officer, with the Guardian Group of Funds in Canada suggests that the benefits (short term) to the host city go even further and can influence the host county's Gross Domestic Product (hereafter GDP). Research conducted by Scotia Capital Markets where they tracked the GDP's of all host countries of Olympic Summer Games starting in 1964 until 2004, recognized that GDP steadily rose from two years out, peaking the year the Games were held, and then decreasing the year following, returning to normal growth patterns three years after the Games ended (Legg, 2008). Graham suggested that this pattern takes place for several reasons. The first is the front end loading of construction that must be finished prior to the Olympic Games opening ceremonies. As the vast majority of work needs to be completed in advance and the host country wants to make sure to use the Games as an international showcase, costs for building are at a premium. Graham further noted that the Olympics, World Cup and United States Presidential Elections are the three largest media spends internationally and opportunities like these where countries can showcase themselves on the international stage are few and far between (Legg, 2008a).

Examples of infrastructure built for Olympic Games include Beijing's International airport which the Wall Street Journal reported on the opening as "with a simple flight from nearby Shandong, Beijing opened a $3 billion terminal Friday, bigger than the Pentagon and designed to evoke a mythological dragon (Legg, 2008b). It marks one more milestone in the city's transformation before this summer's Olympics Games" Graham suggests that without the Olympic Games these types of infrastructure projects get passed over as without a firm deadline, it is easier for leaders to pass on making the significant investment and inconvenience (Legg, 2008b). Whether these apply to Paralympic Games, however, is debatable.

Handicapitalism

Further complicating this understanding is the growing awareness of 'handicapitalism', a term coined in the 1990s that suggests that social acceptance of persons with disability will only occur when they gain status as consumers with enough buying power to command it (Russell, 2000). Consequently, while unemployment of persons with disability is still in many countries higher than those without disability and salaries are typically lower there is a large enough cohort with signifcant buying power that demands attention. Unlike other minority groups being tapped by business, people with disabilities appear to be undervalued and misunderstood. It appears as there is a boom waiting to happen in a competitive environment where population growth and tradition market growth may be currently slow. As the population ages, the number of people with disabilities will increase. For these reasons the economic benefits of hosting Paralympic Games may be extremely viable.

For instance potential benefits could accrue as evidenced by a survey in 1996 as part of Atlanta's Games Organizing committee that recognized that all households were more likely to purchase a product from a company that supported the Paralympic Games. This same study suggested that 52% of households paid more attention to advertising featuring people with disabilities with Bob Thanker, Vice President of Marketing for Target suggesting that incorporating persons with disabilities has been the single most successful consumer response they had ever received (Heller & Ralph, 2001).

Other indicators of the spending power of persons with disability were such that while the Royal Bank of Canada recognized that people with disabilities may only account for $25 Billion they influence an additional $75 Billion (Canadian Paralympic Committee, 2008). For example, David Legg's father had a disability and certainly whenever they traveled or went out for dinner accessibility was a huge determinant of where they went (and spent money). In Canada in 2005, 12.4 % of the population had a disability and this is expected to increase to 20.8% by 2026 (Statistics Canada, 2007). Furthermore, in 1995 according to Society for Accessible Travel and Hospitality people with disabilities spent $81.7 billion on travel and this did not include the significant expenditure on their families, friends and escorts. Accessible tourism in North America is estimated to be a $13 Billion a year industry and '2010 LegaciesNow' organization has created a program specifically capitalizing on this fact so that British Columbia could become the premier travel destination for people with disabilities, older travelers and those with accessibility needs (2010LegaciesNow, 2010).

It is also important to note that the economics above do not suggest that people with disabilities are on par economically with able bodied - as this is far from the truth and there is still a great deal of work that needs to be done to ensure greater equality and equity economically, socially and in many other facets. What this does suggest, however, is that as a cohort, people with disabilities may be a "minority group" that has also been generalized as being economically weak although there are many examples where this is not the case. Nonetheless, people with disabilities (perhaps an eight of the world population) remain the most impoverished and the last to rise above subsistence in every nation in the world (Russell, 2000).

Conversely, many people doubt the financial benefits of hosting major events at all (Canadian Press, 2007). There is recognition that bidding and hosting Games is not a panacea for all that ails a city and in particular the challenges in identifying true economic benefits (Preuss, 2006).

Questioning Legacy

The BBC reported that almost three out of four people believe that the 2012 Olympics will bring no real benefit to their area. Of the 2,000 adults questioned across the UK, just one in five mentioned that the Games would inspire them to take exercise (BBC, 2008). Many others question the legitimacy of figures used to demonstrate financial legacy and others suggest it is a colossal waste of finite public funds that could be better spent on those far more vulnerable, and some might argue this includes persons with disability.

Regardless, it would appear that future bid cities have accepted the legacy approach and have included this as key elements during their bid and preparatory phases for both Olympic and Paralympic Games. As an example, Tokyo when bidding for the 2016 Summer Games, reported that their Games would be an accessibility showcase. "Already regarded as one of the world's most barrier-free cities, Tokyo is making a series of major improvements for people with disabilities as part of its 10-year transformation plan, 'Tokyo Big Change'. Every Metropolitan subway station in Tokyo's transport system is already equipped with universally designed toilets. Indeed, 88% of stations are equipped with lifts and/or wheelchair access slopes, which will increase to 100% by 2016. Non-step buses will become standard issue for the entire municipal fleet and the principles of universal design will be applied to roads and other infrastructure" (Tokyo, 2009).

Madrid's 2016 bid also reflected on legacies from the Paralympic Games, which would use a transversal concept in design and building. The installations, accommodation and transport would all be designed for mass use. There was particular attention given to the high performance Paralympic Sports Centre, which would offer new opportunities not only to Paralympic athletes but also to all with any form of disability (Gamesbid.com, 2009).

Future 2014 Winter Games host Sochi, in Russia is also promoting the potential legacy of hosting the Paralympic Games. In April 2009 preparations for the Sochi 2014 Paralympic Winter Games were cited as helping initiate the work needed to bring Russia's national legislation into further alignment with international disability standards. For instance, Deputies from Russia's State Duma, together with representatives of leading public organizations, discussed Russia's ratification of the UN Convention on the Rights of People with Disabilities. Overall, the 2014 Paralympic Winter Games are perhaps accelerating social cohesion, giving access to winter sports and improving quality of life for 11 million people in Russia living with disabilities. In 2010 in a Sport Business report Russian President Medvedev was further quoted as stating:

> "A successful Paralympics will not be measured solely by ease of access at sporting venues. It will also be judged by the impact it has on the broader issue of social integration – both at home and in other countries. Sochi 2014 aims to break down psychological barriers and help assert those values enshrined by conventions on the rights of disabled people" (Sportfeatures.com, 2010).

In many cases cities are hoping that through planning they can avoid some of the pitfalls that have marked former Games such as the catastrophic failures of the 1976 Montreal Games, whose spiraling construction costs crippled taxpayers for almost 30 years. In the lead up to the Montreal Games, then mayor Jean Drapeau famously proclaimed: "The Olympics can no more have a deficit than a man can have a baby" (Sport-city.org, 2009).

Athens 2004 also serves as a stark reminder of the importance of legacy planning, having become associated with white elephants thanks to hastily built venues with no apparent post-Games planning or purpose. Six years after the Games, many of the Athens venues apparently remain fenced-off and bolted, awaiting private funding to be reopened, while the Greek government has spent hundreds of millions of Euros on maintenance costs and with their current financial woes are unlikely to continue. Beijing's iconic Bird's Nest stadium, the centerpiece of 2008's Olympics, faces annual 70 million Yuan (6.8 million pound) maintenance costs and 80 to 90 million Yuan interest payments. Revenue from 20,000 to 30,000 tourists currently visiting the site daily could cover those costs but the 2008 Olympic factor is not infinite so more cultural activities need to be planned to try to keep the numbers up with two special shows a day (Sport-city.org, 2009).

What future bid cites are hoping instead are to follow in the footsteps of cities such as Barcelona, which in 1992 used the Games as a platform to revitalize a Spanish Civil War-scarred city into a top European destination by overhauling everything from sewers to transport. Another example is from the United States, where Los Angeles hosted the first profitable Games of the modern era in 1932 and repeated the feat in 1984 with the help of big business sponsorship deals, making an estimated $220 million profit (Sport-city.org, 2009).

Conclusive statements

Many of the Chapters in this book make reference to legacies of past and future Games with most authors noting as we have done that a full understanding of this is still at a very nascent stage of evolution. Paralympic sport can be seen as a social agent that can raise a city's spirits and Paralympic memories can form lasting legacies. For example, in the Australian Sport Hall of Fame the following is posted: "A sporting moment happens once. Never to be repeated. A split second in time captured forever. They live in the minds of people: who competed, who were there, and who pass their stories from generation to generation. They shape our collective view of ourselves, and our country. They become a blueprint for what we value and inspiration for all. Moments that made us". We fully believe this to be true and have not recognized anything beyond sport that can impact such a broad legacy on the public. It is hoped that Paralympic sport can achieve similar results as to Olympic sport where the winter Games in Vancouver, Canada in 2010 it was reported that 80% of all citizens watched the men's gold medal hockey game where Canada defeated the United States. Our wish is for 80% of all Canadians and indeed eventually the majority of people across the world to experience or watch some form of Paralympic sport. If this occurs, it is hoped that this might be the way to create strong Paralympic memories, such as those which occur at the Olympics, and thus create further potential for Paralympic legacies and hence long term social benefits and impacts.

References

2010 Legacies Now (2010) Disability programs, Retrieved June 24, 2010 from http://www.2010legaciesnow.com/.

Appleby, L. (2007) Legacy of the 2000 Sydney Paralympic Games, (Paper presented at the Sport Event Hosting Conference, Taipei, Taiwan, 2007).

BBC (2008) People doubt Olympic benefit, http://www.sports-city.org/news_details.php?news_id+3873 (retrieved 12/10/2010).

Brown, A. and J. Massey (2001) *Literature Review: The Impact of Major Sporting Events – the Sport Development Impact of the Manchester 2002 Commonwealth Games:* Initial Baseline Research, Manchester Institute for Popular Culture, Manchester Metropolitan University.

Canadian Paralympic Committee (2008) Handicapitalism, Ottawa, Canada.

Canadian Press (2007) Report Says Winter Olympics brought benefits to cities: critics call it fluff. Available at: http://slam.canoe.ca/slam/othersports/2007/04/26/4132702-cp.html (accessed 10th October 2010).

Cashman, R. and S. Darcy (2006) *Benchmark Games: The Sydney 2000 Paralympic Games*, Sydney: Walla Walla Press.

Dunn, M. and M. McGuirk (1999) Hallmark Events, *In Staging the Olympics: The Event and its Impacts* (Cashman, R. and A. Hughes, Eds), Centre for Olympic Studies, UNSW, Sydney.

Gamesbid.com (2009) Madrid 2016 Prepares To Stage "Greatest Paralympics" (retrieved 08/05/2009).

Gratton, C. (2000) The economic Importance of Major Sports Events: A Case Study of Six Events, *Managing Leisure*, 5: 17-28.

Griginov, V. & L. Hills (2008) A Sustainable Sports Legacy: Creating a Link Between the London Olympics and Sports Participation, *The International Journal of the History of Sport*, 25 (14): 2091–2116.

Heller, B. & Ralph, S. (2001) Profitability, Diversity, and Disability Images in Advertising in the United States and Great Britain, Disability Studies Quarterly, 21(2). Available at: http://www.dsq-sds.org/article/view/276/301. (accessed 24th June 2010).

Hervey, D. (1989) *The Urban Experience*, Blackwell, Oxford.

Hiller, H. (1998) Assessing the Impact of Mega events: A Linkage Model, *Current Issues in Tourism*, 1(1): 47-57.

International Paralympic Committee (2009) Beijing Update. Available at: http://www.paralympic.org/release/Main_Sections_Menu/News/Current_Affairs/2009_07_24_a.html (accessed 10th October 2010).

International Olympic Committee (IOC). *The Olympic Games Global Impact*. Lausanne: IOC, 2003. Olympic Charter, Lausanne: IOC, 2007.

Legg, D. (2008a) The Global Economic Crisis and Sport, Sport Decision. Available at http://www.sportdecision.com/economics-and-law/news-921.htm?sel_lang=english (accessed 11th October 2010).

Legg, D. (2008b) The Olympic Effect, Sport Decision. Available at: http://www.sportdecision.com/economics-and-law/news--906.htm?sel_lang=english (accessed 11th October 2010).

Legg. D. (2009) The Economy of Sports: Are Sports Recession-Proof? *The Analyst*: Hyderabad, India.

London 2012, PA consulting (2007) *Pathway to Potential: Ensuring a sustainable Paralympic Legacy*, Author, London, UK.

Malfasa, M., Therdoraki, E. and B. Houlihan, (2004) Impacts of the Olympic Games as Mega Events, *Municipal Engineer*, 157 (3):209-220.

Preuss, H. (2007) Leveraging the Impact of Mega Sport Events by Building up Legacy, Presentation made to UTS – Sydney, September 3rd, 2008.

Pruess, H. (2006) Impact and Evaluation of Major Sporting Events, European *Sport Management Quarterly*, 6(4): 313-316.

Radio Free Asia (2008) Disabled Call for Protests During Paralympics, the *Epoch Times*, Sept 18-24, 2008.

Ritchie, J.R.B. (1989) 'Promoting Calgary Through the Olympics: The Mega Event as a Strategy for Community Development'. In Social Marketing (Ch. 20). Boston: Allyn and Bacon, 1989. *'Turning 16 Days into 16 Years Through Olympic Legacies'. Event Management* 6 (2000): 149–66.

Russell, M. (2000) Handicapitalism Makes its Debut, ZNet Commentary. Available at: http://www.zmag.org/Commentaris/donorform.htm (accessed 13th October 2010).

Schantz, O. & K. Gilbert. (2001) An Ideal Misconstrued: Newspaper Coverage of the Atlanta Paralympic Games in France and Germany, *Sociology of Sport Journal*, 18: 69-84.

Sport Business (2008) Bidding for MajorEvents.UK.

Sport-City.org (2009) Future Olympic hosts confident of promised legacies. Available at: http://www.sports-city.org/news_details.php?news_id=7760-&idCategory=1 (accessed 8th August 2010).

Sport-city.org (2008) Beijing spends $52 m on accessibility in 2007, http://www.sports-city.org/news_details.php?news_id+3102 (retrieved 8/8/2010).

Sportfeatures.com (2009) Sochi 2014 Paralympic Games bringing lasting benefits for people with disabilities. April 14th 2009. Available at: http://www.sportsfeatures.com/index.php?section=press-point-view&id=48992 (accessed 10th October 2010).

Statistics Canada (2007) Participation and Activity Limitation Survey. Available at: http://www.statcan.gc.ca/bsolc/olc-cel/olc-cel?cat-no=89-628-X&CHROPG=1&lang=eng (accessed 8th February 2009).

Suurballe, M. (2008) Selling the city of selling it out, *Playthegame magazine*. p. 12.

Taylor, M. & I. Edmondson (2007) Major Sporting Events – planning for legacy, *Municipal Engineer*, 160 (M#4): 171-176.

Tokyo 2016 can benefit people with perceived disabilities globally, Campaign Reports. Available at: http://www.tokyo2016.or.jp/en/news/2009/04/-tokyo_2016_can_benefit_people.html (accessed 12th October 2010).

Whamsley, D. (2008) Bidding for Major Events, *Sport Business International*, 134: 33-34.

Part II
Paralympic City Legacies

Chapter 4
The Toronto Olympiad for the Physically Disabled

'A.K.A.' the Fifth Summer Paralympic Games held in 1976

Ian Brittain

Introduction

The 5th Summer Paralympic Games held in Toronto, Canada from 3rd to 11th August, 1976 are best remembered for three facts. Firstly, they were the first Games to incorporate disability groups other than wheelchair users when both blind and amputee athletes took part in the Games in their own separate sections. Secondly, they were the first Paralympic Games to suffer from major political problems and interference centering (which spelling do we use – I assume we allow whatever makes sense for each author). on the participation of a fully integrated South African team at a time when South Africa had been ostracised from mainstream non-disabled sport due to the apartheid practices of their government[1]. Thirdly, perhaps partly as a result of the first two points, the Games, although dogged by organisational and financial difficulties, received widespread and on the whole very favourable media coverage and public support and were declared a big success. The combined result of these three facts was to have a huge impact upon the way disability sport and athletes with disability were viewed, organised and funded within Canada in the years that followed. In addition they paved the way for future editions of the Paralympic Games to successfully incorporate other disability groups into the Paralympic Games including athletes with cerebral palsy in 1980, athletes in the Les Autres group in 1984 and athletes with an intellectual disability in 1992. This chapter will, therefore, begin by outlining how each of the above three facts came about and then discuss their overall result in terms of the legacy they provided for disability sport in Canada and for the Paralympic Games themselves.

The first multi-disability games

According to the minutes of the International Stoke Mandeville Games Council meeting held at Stoke Mandeville on 24th July 1970 the Toronto Games were not the first attempt to make the Games a multi-disability affair. Sir Ludwig Guttmann in his capacity as President of both the International Stoke Mandeville Games Committee (ISMGC) who were responsible for wheelchair athletes and the International Sports Organisation for the Disabled (ISOD) who were responsible for blind and amputee athletes at the time, had attempted to get the Olympic hosts of 1972, Munich, to host a multi-disability Games. However, Munich declined to host the Games, citing accommodation problems, and although the German Sports Organisation for the Disabled (DVS) offered to host the Games in Heidelberg they stated they would only be able to accommodate the athletes of the International Stoke Mandeville Games i.e. wheelchair athletes (p. 2 item 3). In the minutes of the International Stoke Mandeville Games Federation (ISMGF) Council meeting held in Heidelberg on 8th August 1972 Sir Ludwig told those assembled that he had discussed with representatives from Canada the possibility of holding a joint ISOD-ISMGF Games in Canada in 1976 and that he was very much in favour of this in order that Canada should 'provide an example to the whole world in a combined international sports festival for as many disabled people as possible' (p. 7 item 8).

Impact on the 'Name' of the Games

Ironically, this decision to put on a combined ISOD-ISMGF Games in Canada had several knock-on effects upon both the venue and the name of the Games to be held in Canada. The increased size and complexity of the combined Games meant that Olympic officials in Montreal, already mired in spiralling costs of hosting the Olympic Games immediately declined a request to host the ISOD-ISMGF Games. Following some persistent lobbying by the Chairman of the Canadian Organising Committee, Dr. Robert Jackson, Toronto was eventually persuaded to host the Games. The four previous versions of the ISMGF Games had been officially known as International Stoke Mandeville Games, but as the Games in Canada were now to include blind and amputee athletes the name was no longer felt applicable. The previous Games had also been unofficially known as 'Paralympic'

Games, the name having derived from a shortening of the term 'Paraplegic Olympics' (Brittain, 2008) and so this term was also deemed unacceptable. In the end the committees of ISMGF and ISOD decided to call the games the Toronto Olympiad for the Physically Disabled, but which the organisers shortened to the 'Torontolympiad' for marketing purposes.

Organisational Issues

The increased size of the Games in Toronto, combined with a relatively inexperienced organising committee, the issues around South African participation and some computer issues at the beginning of the Games meant that things did not always run smoothly. On the very first day the computerised results system crashed, so no results were available to the media, the public or the athletes (McCabe, 1976). The participation of South Africa also led to a number of countries withdrawing at the last minute which in turn led to a large number of event schedules having to be reorganised. This led to communication issues around getting the new schedules to all the teams. McCabe (1976) reported that the Australian men's wheelchair basketball team thought they were due to compete at 6 p.m. and so failed to show for their rearranged time of 11.15 a.m. Organisers had to hastily rearrange the fixture. The mixing of the different impairment groups at the same event was also a steep learning curve for the organisers. Today blind sprinters run attached to a guide runner by a short rope that both hold. However, in 1976 blind sprinters were 'guided' by voice commands from someone standing at the end of their lane as they ran towards the finish line. This was not always successful and occasionally led to accidents. Sharon Myers, an American paraplegic athlete and swimmer, was injured when a blind runner veered off the track and ran into her. Sharon suffered a seven stitch cut on her cheek, a black eye and a knee injury when she was thrown from her chair (Torontolympiad Daily News, 1976[2]).

The influence of South Africa on disability sport

The issue of the impact of the South African team's participation in the 'Torontolympiad' upon the organisation of the Toronto Games is a complicated one. Given the space available for this chapter only a broad overview will appear here[2]. South African teams had competed at the Paralympic Games since Tokyo, 1964 and at all of the Games held at Stoke Mandeville in the intervening years with the exception of 1969. According to Guttmann (1976[1]) up until 1975 South Africa sent alternate teams of black participants and white participants to the Stoke Mandeville Games, although it appears to have been the all white teams that competed in the 'Paralympic' Games. Barrish, the Chairman of the South African organisation later pointed out that 'whilst the practice of the Association was one of non-discrimination, the environment within which it had to operate continued to be a discriminatory one. For this reason, the activities of the Association over a long period were a microcosm of the social battle that was going on in South Africa' (Barrish, 1992).

South Africa and the 'Torontolympiad'

With the next Paralympic Games due to be held in Toronto, Greig (2005) claims the first hint for the organisers that the participation of a South African team might cause problems came in May 1974 when the Canadian Minister for Health and Welfare released a statement informing all sports federations that it would not fund athletes travelling to South Africa because of its apartheid practices. As the Federal Government had promised funding of Canadian $500,000 for the Games the organising committee sought clarification from the Minister who in November 1974 wrote urging that South Africa not be invited as their presence would have embarrassing repercussions. South Africa was duly notified that it would not be invited. However, both the ISMGF and ISOD of whom the South African organisation was now a full member in good standing were against the expulsion and as such following a meeting in May 1975 the organising committee informed the South African organisation that a team would be welcome provided they had integrated trials and sent an integrated team (Grieg, 2005; p. 57), which may well have had some impact upon their decision to send their first ever integrated team to Stoke Mandeville in 1975. In the end South Africa sent a team of around thirty (Coetzee & van der Merwe, 1990; p. 83) including nine black athletes. The political ramifications of South Africa's participation impacted upon both the financial situation for the Games and also the number of countries participating. Eight countries withdrew either before or during the Games on the order of their governments. These were Kenya, Sudan and Yugoslavia who did so before the Games and Cuba, Jamaica, Hungary, India and Poland who turned up in Toronto, but either departed prior to the start of the Games or like Poland competed for several days (winning enough medals to place seventh in the medal table and withdrew. Jamaica for sintacen remainded and watched the Games. They even took part in the Opening Ceremonies but didn't wear the official hat). Poland finally pulled out after a failed appeal to the organising committee to have the South African team thrown out (Guttmann, 1976; p. 233).

Athlete reaction to political intrusion

Reports of athlete reactions to the intrusion of politics into their Games appear to show that, in general, the intrusion was resented and unwelcome. Indeed on Thursday 5th August, having won the class 3 discus event, Eric Russell, a university student from Brisbane, Australia, refused his gold medal in protest at the intrusion of politics into the Games. Russell claimed he was upset by governments, stressing he meant all governments, attempting to mix sport with politics (Torontolympiad, Daily News, 1976[1]).

However, following a press conference where Russell explained his actions to the media, and statements were made by Dr. Jackson and Dr. Guttmann, Russell finally accepted his medal from Dr. Guttmann.

Mixed messages from the Federal Government?

Despite the fact that the Federal Government stopped its funding from the Toronto Games and despite the withdrawal of several countries from the Games due to the participation of the South African team, there appears to have been no attempt by the Canadian Government to prevent the entry of the South African team into Canada. Whether this was as a result of the mounting media and public support for the Games and the integrated South African team's participation or whether it was merely a reflection of the low importance the Government associated with the Games themselves and their potential impact is hard to assess. What is clear is that the media and public support for the Games was sufficient to have a direct impact upon what the Federal Government did next as will be shown in the final section.

Pre-Games media coverage of disability and disability sport

The way the media portray people with disabilities and disability sport can have a major impact on how other groups and individuals within society view them (Brittain, 2009; p. 72). According to Greig (2005) prior to Canada being awarded the Games media coverage of people with disabilities, and athletes with disabilities in particular, was virtually non-existent within Canada 'confined to the lifestyles section or in a human interest area of the newspaper and rarely, if ever, could be found within the sports pages' (p. 97). In fact Greig goes on to claim that 'within the early to mid 1970s, persons with physical disabilities were seen as cripples and were generally pitied by the majority of society' (2005; p. 97).

Pre-Games/Pre-South Africa issue publicity

Despite the claims by Greig (2005), as mentioned above, regarding media coverage of disability in Canada; Guttmann (1976) claims that prior to the South African issue, which first arose in May 1974, the Canadian press, radio and television were apparently fully supportive of the Games in Toronto and were 'fully active in arousing interest in this venture of sport and humanity' (p. 226). Dr. Jackson and Dr. Guttmann apparently gave a number of lectures as well as a large number of press, radio and television interviews in order to both drum up support for the Games as well as make people aware of the existence of the Games.

The media appear to have almost entirely sided with the organising committee in its battle with the Federal Government over the participation of the South African team. It is possible this stemmed from a view that 'big brother' was picking on a section of the community that perception dictated was unable to defend itself, but whatever the reason it played a major part in allowing the Games to go ahead despite the withdrawal of the Federal Government funding. There was some media commentary that came down on the side of the Federal Government, mainly within the anti-apartheid lobby, but this was all but 'drowned out' by the overwhelming support from the majority of the media for the actions of the organising committee.

Games time media coverage in Canada and elsewhere

According to Greig (2005) newspapers such as the Toronto Star, Globe and Mail and the Toronto Sun all ran extensive coverage of the Games, the majority of it appearing on the sports pages. This coverage, supplemented by television broadcasts from the Games, was seen by Canadians nationwide. Greig (2005) goes on to claim that the widespread media coverage led to overwhelming public support for the Games by serving as 'an educational tool and an outlet for awareness for the Organizing Committee' (p. 97). These claims appear to be shared by Dr. Guttmann, founder of the Games, who wrote 'The Canadian press, radio and television media played a most active and very important part from the beginning and throughout the Games, and no praise is high enough for the support our Olympics received by these media' (Guttmann, 1976; p. 232). However, with regard to media coverage of the Games in other countries Guttmann bemoaned the considerable variance in the amount of coverage, particularly in relation to the coverage given to the recently finished Montreal Olympic Games, which Guttmann claimed revealed 'an astounding lack of appreciation of the value of the sports movement of the disabled in educating the public' (Guttmann, 1976; p. 232). Even in his own adopted country of Great Britain, where he had founded the Games, Guttmann described the coverage as 'miserable' and was particularly scathing of BBC television for continuing 'its previous policy of giving as little coverage as possible to our disabled athletes, who have kept the flag flying for Great Britain in the World of sport' (Guttmann, 1976[1]; p. 12).

Media Impact upon the finances of the Torontolympiad

Once it was known that the 'Torontolympiad' would have a half million dollar hole in the Games budget due to the withholding of the Federal Government finance the media coverage of the Games played an important role in helping to plug that gap. By making the public aware of the ongoing battle between the organising committee and the federal government and by raising public awareness of and interest in the Games the media helped in two ways. Firstly, by making the public aware of the financial problem they played their part in helping to persuade more than ten thousand people to donate funds in addition to the financial support and support in kind provided by the business community (Jackson, 1977). Secondly, by raising public support for the Games ticket sales which were far in excess of what was expected including the opening ceremony, which was a twenty thousand seat sell out. In the end the organisers were able to break even, despite the loss of the Federal Government funding.

The impact of this widespread media coverage of the Games and the effect it had upon the attitude of the Canadian public towards both disability sport and the way the Federal Government had acted in withdrawing its funding for the Games appears to have been enough to make the Federal Government feel the need to play down the negative publicity it had been receiving. The Federal Government took the decision that although it would not provide financial backing to the Games themselves it would, however, still provide the same amount of money to be used to promote disability sport and recreation and its organisation within Canada.

Games Legacy

The overall impact of the 'Torontolympiad' upon both future Paralympic Games and especially upon attitudes towards disability and disability sport within Canada was immense. Below are outlined just a few of the key impacts of these Games.

Change in attitude to disability in Canada

The lessons learned by both the media and the public in Canada following the 'Torontolympiad' appear to have been quite marked. Athletes with disabilities found themselves on page one of the sports section with bold headlines and large photographs, which was something not previously enjoyed. Jackson (1977) also claims the public learnt valuable lessons from the widespread media coverage. They apparently learnt that 'the physically disabled are human individuals with emotions, ambitions, fears, likes and dislikes, similar to anyone else' and also that they 'are capable of exceptional achievements if given the opportunity' (Jackson, 1977; p. 69). The overall message appears to have been the importance of removing the perceptual, attitudinal and architectural barriers present within Canadian society in order to allow the physically disabled to contribute to and partake fully within it.

Training of administrators, officials, volunteers, coaches for disability sport

The 'Torontolympiad' made use of over three thousand volunteers to help run all aspects of the Games. They worked as officials, administrators, translators, drivers and a whole host of other functions without which the Games would not have been unable to operate. In order to ensure the volunteers could do their jobs in the most effective manner possible the organising committee introduced training programmes and 'as a result of the initiative of the organizing committee in training volunteers, officials and administrators, the infrastructure was in place to promote and facilitate disabled sport in Canada' (Greig, 2003; p. 10). Perhaps the best testament to this fact is that many of these volunteers continue to be involved in disability sport in Canada today up until this very day. The author has even had the privilege of meeting one or two of them.

Federal money put into disability sport in Canada

Prior to the 'Torontolympiad' disability sport in Canada was not very highly developed or organised. Canada had first competed in the Paralympic Games in Tel Aviv in 1968, a year after the formation of the Canadian Wheelchair Sports Association (CWSA) in 1967. There had been little or no previous Government involvement in the running of disability sport in Canada, so the provision of nearly half a million dollars by the Federal Government not only provided the opportunity to better organise and support disability sport, but also provided it with a kind of legitimacy in terms of government and public support that had previously been absent. A Co-ordinating Committee comprising the Canadian Blind Sports Association, the Canadian Amputee Sports Association, the Canadian Associated of Disabled Skiing and the CWSA was set up in order to most effectively use the money in taking disability sport in Canada forward. This Co-ordinating Committee would eventually become the Canadian Paralympic Committee (CPC);(CPC Website, 2009).

Success of multi-disability games

Despite the few organisational difficulties outlined earlier the multi-disability nature of the Games was declared a huge success. The Games brought athletes with a variety of physical disabilities together in the spirit of sport and fraternity and showed the people of Canada, if not the world, what they were really capable of achieving if given the opportunity. Finally, they helped pave the way for the Paralympic Games to become the sporting mega-event that it is today, with the successful incorporation of further disability groups into the Games including athletes with cerebral palsy in 1980, athletes in the Les Autres group in 1984 and athletes with an intellectual disability in 1992.

Conclusions

Prior to 1976 the Paralympic Games were small, only attended by athletes in wheelchairs and relatively unknown and unheard of outside of the disabled community. Therefore, they were almost untouched by the kind of nationalist agenda and economic politics that plagued the Olympic Games. The Paralympic Games were all but ignored by the outside world. However, in 1976 events such as the Soweto riots, the New Zealand rugby tour of South

Africa, the African boycott of the Montreal Olympics combined with the fact that the Paralympics were to be a much larger multi-disability event for the first time and were to be held in Canada, whose Federal Government had co-sponsored a UN resolution against apartheid in November 1975, suddenly focused the world media spotlight upon the movement in a way never before encountered. Unfortunately, once the issue of South Africa's participation in international disability sport became an issue of media attention it became impossible to go back to the way things had been prior to the Toronto Games. In fact at one point Dr. Robert Jackson, Chairman of the Games organising committee in Toronto claimed the Games 'were a victim of worldwide media and had become a political pawn'. In the case of some of the countries that forced their athletes to withdraw from the 'Torontolympiad' this may well be true, but in terms of the media coverage the positive approach they took had a huge impact upon the outcome of the Games. The combination of the South African team's participation in the Games, the Canadian Federal Government's response to it and the positive media response to the Games impacted not only upon the success of the 'Torontolympiad', but also the future of disability sport in Canada and the future of the Paralympic Games themselves. Despite a rocky and uncertain build up to the Games the legacy that they left can still be seen today in the organisational structures of disability sport and the government and public support they still receive. It can also be seen in the success of the Paralympic Games today, which has almost trebled in size since the 'Torontolympiad' and has proceeded to become the second largest multi-sport event in the world after the Olympic Games.

Notes

1. Apartheid is an Afrikaans word meaning 'apartness'. It came about at a time when imperial rule was receding and enforcement of segregation was being relaxed. However, South Africa went against the world trend by strengthening barriers between blacks and whites and attempting to rationalise it in terms of ideas about racial purity (Cashmore; 1996). Whalley-Hammell (2006) claims that the function of this ideology was to preserve, protect and perpetuate minority white power and that ideology and power, in combination, served to maintain power and dominance with such effectiveness that the white minority group wielded the majority of power and the statistical majority was accorded minority status. Laws were often enforced through police brutality, thus using fear as a means of ensuring compliance. Where there was any form of attempt to protest or challenge the status quo it would often end up with the protesters being seriously injured or in certain cases with large numbers of protesters losing their lives such as in Sharpeville (1960) and Soweto (1976).

2. Readers wanting a more detailed account are recommended to consult Greig (2005) and Brittain (2011).

References

Barrish, M. (1992) *Letter from Menzo Barrish to Paul Luedtke dated 29th April 1992.* Stoke Mandeville, UK: IWAS Archives.

Brittain, I. (2011). South Africa, Apartheid and the Paralympic Games, in LeClair, J. (Ed.) Disability in the Global Sport Arena: A Sporting Chance, London: Routledge (in Press).

Brittain, I. (2009) *The Paralympic Games Explained*, London: Routledge.

Brittain, I. (2008) The Evolution of the Paralympic Games. In Cashman, R. & Darcy, S.(Eds), *Benchmark Games: The Sydney 2000 Paralympic Games.* (pp. 19-34) Petersham, NSW: Walla Walla Press.

Canadian Paralympic Committee Website, 2009, Organization History, (http://www.paralympic.ca/page?a=229&lang=en-CA) accessed 21-10-09.

Cashmore, E. (1996) *Making Sense of Sport (2nd Ed.)*, London: Routledge.

Coetzee, G.J. & Van Der Merwe, F.J.G. (1990) South Africa's Participation in the International Stoke Mandeville Games. In *South African Journal for Research in Sport, Physical Education and Recreation*, 13(1), 79-85.

Greig, D. (2005) *South African Apartheid and the 1976 Torontolympiad: A Historical Analysis of Influential Actions and Events Affecting the 5th Paralympic Games.* Unpublished Masters Thesis, Ontario, Canada: University of Windsor.

Greig, D. (2003) *Conflict, Perseverance, and Legacy: A Historical Analysis of the 1976 Torontolympiad.* Paper presented at the North American Society of Sports History, 23-26 May, Ohio State University, Colombus, Ohio.

Guttmann, L. (1976) Reflection on the 1976 Toronto Olympiad for the Physically Disabled. In *Paraplegia*, 14, 225-240.

Guttmann, L. (1976^1) *Report on the Olympiad for the Physically Disabled held in Toronto, Canada, from 3rd – 11th August, 1976.* Unpublished Report. Stoke Mandeville, UK: IWAS Archives.

Jackson, R.W. (1977) What Did We Learn From The Torontolympiad? In *The Canadian Family Physician*, 23, 586-589.

Minutes of the Interantioanl Stoke Mandeville Games Federation meeting held in Heidelberg, 8th August 1972, p. 7; item 8 (INAS Archives).

Minutes of the International Stoke Mandeville Games Council meeting held at Stoek Mandeville, 24th July 1970, p. 2; item 3 (INAS Archives).

McCabe, N. (1976) Olympiad for Physically Disabled opens amid state of utter chaos. In *The Globe & Mail Newspaper* dated Thursday 5th August (page number not known).

Torontolympiad Daily News (1976¹) Politics Interfere – Again, 1(4), 1.
Torontolympiad Daily News (1976²) Accidents will Happen, 1 (5), 1.
Whalley- Hammell, K. (2006) *Perspectives on Disability and Rehabilitation: contesting assumptions; challenging practice*. London: Elsevier.

Chapter 5
Seoul 1988

The first Modern Paralympic Games

Justin Jeon and David Legg

Introduction

Many people believe that the 1988 Seoul Paralympic Games influenced the development of the Paralympic movement not just in Korea but as a whole. Nationally, the hosting of the Seoul Paralympic Games left significant legacy in many different levels and areas. Dr. Minkyu Han, the director of Paralympic Sports for the Seoul Paralympic Organizing Committee (SPOC), noted that: "The Seoul Paralympic Games opens the new world of sports for the disabled and social perception of disability in general throughout Korea" (Jeon & Han, 2007). Indeed, internationally, many experts and scholars recognized the Seoul Paralympic Games as the genesis of the Modern Paralympic Games. Elaine Ell, a Canadian Wheelchair basketball player once stated:

> "In Seoul, you really felt like you were at the Olympics because the crowd was so well organized. We played in front of 20,000 people for the bronze medal match. At the opening ceremony, we marched in front of 75,000 people. There was great excitement among the athletes at those Games because of all the different disciplines were all together" (Steadward & Peterson, 1997, p. 45).

Along with this professionalism, the Seoul Games were different in their focus on sporting excellence, with Tony Sainsbury, a long time volunteer and professional leader in Paralympic sport, referring to them as "the line in the sand" which marked the end of disabled sport and rehabilitation and the commencement of the modern Paralympic Games (Sainsbury, 2008). What follows in this chapter, is the legacy of the Seoul Paralympic Games on national and international levels.

National level

While the 1988 Seoul Paralympic Games were recognized as an historical Games in the Paralympic movement, they were also important nationally and are an example of how hosting a Paralympic Games can leave a legacy for the host country. Dr. Youn-Dai Whang, former Vice President of the Korean Paralympic Committee (KPC), stated that the 1988 Paralympic Games accomplished significant improvement in the development of disability sports that would have otherwise taken decades to accomplish (Whang, 2008).

The first international Games attended by Korean athletes was in 1965 when they competed at Stoke Mandeville with the athletes being supported by the Korean Veterans Association. Three athletes competed in table tennis and power lifting. In 1967, Korea hosted their own Games called the Korean War Veterans Games and in 1968, Korea sent athletes to a Paralympic Games in Israel. In 1975 the Jung-Lip Polio Centre was opened in Korea which included a gymnasium, indoor pool, shooting range and archery field and it was here that they began hosting an annual 'Korean National Youth Games for the Disabled'. These were held from 1976 until 1990. In 1981, coinciding with the International Year of the Disabled, the 'Korean National Games for the Disabled' were held with over 1000 participants in 5 sport disciplines and 6 disability categories (Jeon & Han, 2007). Until the decision to host the 1988 Paralympic Games, only five different Paralympic Sports were practiced during the National Games for the Disabled (Whang, 2008). In 1985, SPOC (Seoul Paralympic Organizing Committee) took over the management of the National Games for the disabled and used them to prepare the host organizing committee as well as their own athletes. Very quickly this made an impact and the number of sports contested at the National Games grew from five to eighteen within three years. SPOC also invited Technical Delegates (TD) from other countries and organized workshops and seminars which further developed coaches, referees and most importantly athletes (both internationally but more importantly for Korea domestically). With vigorous efforts from SPOC, Korea was able to have their athletes compete in every sport during the 1988 Paralympic Games (Jeon & Han, 2007). Perhaps as a result of strong efforts to prepare Korean athletes and coaches they performed very well from 1988 as well as subsequent Games in Barcelona, Atlanta, Sydney and Beijing. In one case, Kumjong

Chung who won a gold medal in Power-lifting in Seoul won gold medals in four consecutive Paralympic Games and won silver and bronze in Athens and Beijing Paralympic Games, respectively (Jeon & Han, 2007).

KOSAD

A second important legacy from the 1988 Seoul Paralympic was the foundation of the Korean Sports Association for the disabled (KOSAD). After hosting the 1988 Games, Il-Mook Cho, the Secretary General and Kui-Nam Ko, the President of SPOC realized the importance of continuing support for Paralympic sports, athletes, the organization of National Paralympic Games, and sending Korean athletes to international sporting events. Therefore, they proposed to the Korean government the foundation of KOSAD under the Ministry of Health and Welfare and using the surplus resources which was approximately $5 million USD from the Paralympic Games. This was a marked departure from prior practice where disability sport had been the responsibility of only a few employees in the Ministry of Health and Welfare (Jeon & Han, 2007; Park, Lee, Cho, Hong & Whang, 1999). Many years later due to the strong desire of athletes with disabilities to have disability sports recognized as sports itself rather than welfare or rehabilitation, the governance was changed to the Ministry of Sports and Tourism. This change resulted in the creation of regional sports organizations, as well as sports federations for the disabled. This gew to 16 regional sports organization for the disabled and 31 sports federations under the direct and indirect supervision of KOSAD and KPC (Jeon & Han, 2007, Korean Sports Association for the Disabled, 1994).

Societal change

A third national legacy of hosting the Seoul Paralympic Games was the change of attitude of people with and without disabilities. Tony Sainsbury, reflecting on the impact in Korea from hosting the Games remembered that prior to the Games he suspected that having a disability in Korea was regarded as "some ordained travesty visited on a person or family for some long-past misdeed. Koreans were ashamed to have a disabled person in their family and did all in their power to hide the person and the issue" (Sainsbury, 2008). Sainsbury recounted that people with disabilities were not seen nor heard and instead left to socialize in medical settings. The society was like many at that time patronizing and overly focused on the disability. A story that demonstrated how this changed for Sainsbury was during the Olympic Games, when he found himself in the shopping centre of Itchewon. The pageantry of the Olympic Games was being removed and Sainsbury noted to his guide that this seemed odd with the Paralympics Games only weeks away. The guide's response was people with disability were not perceived as also being those that shopped and one suit maker noted "Paralympics! Bah! Not interested" (Sainbury, 2008) Once the Games began however this negative perception changed and "The same tailor had now employed four men to carry wheelchair athletes up the four flights of stairs to measure them for new suits. He was doing a roaring trade with those he had previously thought of only as beggars. He was amazed that these clients had jobs, University degrees, owned their own businesses and homes, were married and had children - that they lived 'normal' lives" (Sainsbury, 2008).

Society also changed or at least the way perhaps that people with disability viewed themselves within it. Prior to the Games approximately 90,000 people in Korea were registered as having a disability but following the Games this number rose to over 500,000 (Sainsbury, 2008). "A statistic so indicative of a nation who in a few short weeks had the blindfold of prejudice so irrecoverably removed" (Sainsbury, 2008). Hong-Jae Lee, Director of the Korean Paralympic Committee also recognized the impact of the Paralympic Games on the lives of persons with a disability. "They belonged and were valued and integral members of their community" (Hong, 2008). In Korea the legacy of societal change continues to evolve and twenty years later the Korean media sent correspondents from all four major television stations to cover the 2008 Summer.

International Legacy

Many pioneers in the Paralympic movement including former president of the International Paralympic Committee, Robert D. Steadward and current President of IPC, Sir Philip Craven have acknowledged that the 1988 Paralympic Games were the beginning of the modern Paralympic Games and movement. Many Korean Paralympians have also never forgotten the moment they walked into the stadium of the Seoul opening ceremony. An athlete who participated in two former Paralympic Games in 1980 and 1984 mentioned "I wept as I walked into the opening ceremony of the Seoul Paralympic Games and for the first time, I realized that I am an athlete who is representing my country. I am not a person with a disability but I am elite athlete with national flag on my shoulder" (Jeon & Han, 2007). Ljiljana Ljubisic, double medalist in discus and javelin at the Seoul Paralympic Games and who later became the IPC Athletes Committee Representative and governing board member of IPC recalled her feelings about Seoul.

> "In 1984, we were at least in decent accommodation. They were clean. The food was excellent. It was fabulous. The venues for competitions were of a standard that were equivalent to a State College in the United States, but the feeling, the camaraderie, the pageantry; that was where the essence of why we were there was intact. In Korea, we went another step higher. We had a Paralympic Village, and we were in the same city, in the same country as the Olympics. That was a huge step in our identity and our ability to raise money in order to do what we need to do. Seoul was a big step forward because we were now the true Paralympic Games and we were parallel with the Olympics" (Steadward & Peterson, 1997, p. 51).

Another international legacy of the Games in 1988 was the logo. The Seoul Organizing Committee chose to use five Tae Geuks, which are a traditional Korean symbol, in an alignment similar to the five Olympic rings. The International Coordinating Committee of World Sports Organizations for the Disabled (ICC), the precursor to the IPC decided to then adopt this logo for the organization and when the IPC was officially created in 1989 it was chosen as the logo for the IPC (Steadward & Foster, 2003). The Tae Geuks were replaced in 2003 with Agitos (from the Latin word "agito", meaning "I move");(International Paralympic Committee, 2009).

Conclusions

The 1988 Paralympic Games were very successful with a number of significant changes from prior Games which ultimately evolved into the model we see today. The Seoul Games were the first with the Olympic Games organizing committee (OCOG) having a Paralympic Games Department. Seoul's organizing committee also, for the first time, used the same venues for both Games and thirdly "Olympic style" opening and closing ceremonies for the Paralympic Games were held with the first day being declared open by Mr. Ro Tae-Woo, the President of the Republic of Korea.

Since 1988 every Winter and Summer Paralympic Games has been held in the same city as the Olympic Games. Prior to this only Rome (1960) and Tokyo (1964) could claim this honour. Tony Sainsbury (2008) recounted that "as many of the early leadership have now passed on from the early 1980s it is difficult to separate out truth from myth or legend. But the story goes that when asked 'what are the Paralympics?' by the Seoul Organizing Committee for the Olympic Games, the Government and the city of Seoul, the answer given to them was 'it's just like a smaller version of the Olympic Games.' The Korean delegation appeared to take this literally".

A final way in which the Seoul Paralympic Games left their legacy was through the Paralympic observer program. With over 20 people from the Barcelona Paralympic Games Organizing Committee participating in the program a precedent was set and the initiatives begun in Seoul have in many ways continued to this day.

References

DePauw, Karen., and S. Gavron (2005) *Disability and Sport*. 2nd ed. Champaign, Ill. Human Kinetics, 2005.

Han, M. (2001) Method Promotion of Sports for the Disabled in Korea through Analysis of the Paralympics Games, *Korean Adapted Physical Activity, 9*(1): p.p. 71-83.

International Paralympic Committee, (2010) About the IPC – IPC Symbol and Motto. Available at: http://www.paralympic.org/release/Main_Sections_Menu/IPC/About_the_IPC/IPC_Symbol_and_Motto (accessed 9th June 2010).

Jeon J. and M. Han (2007). *Paralympic Sports in Korea*, Presentation at the General Assembly of IPC, Seoul, Korea.

Korean Sports Association for the Disabled (1994) *Textbook of Adapted Physical Activity*, Seoul Korea, Taekun Publishing.

Park C, Lee J, Cho I, Hong Y, and Y. Whang (1999). *10 year history of Korean Sports Association for the Disabled (KOSAD)*, KOSAD, Seoul, Korea.

Sainsbury, T. (2008) Personal correspondence to author. February 12, 2008.

Steadward R. and C. Peterson (1997). Paralympics: Where heroes come, *One Shot Holdings Publishing Division*, Edmonton, Canada.

Steadward, R. and S. Foster (2003). 'History of Disability Sport: From Rehabilitation to Athletic Excellence'. In *Adapted Physical Activity*, (2003) (Eds). R. Steadward, G. Wheeler, and J. Watkinson, p.p. 471-496. Edmonton, Alberta: University of Alberta.

Whang, Y. (2008). In discussion with the author, Seoul, Korea, August 14, 2008.

Chapter 6
Barcelona 1992

The Coming of Age for the Paralympic Games

Patrick Jarvis

Introduction

Barcelona! Just the name evokes images of a unique and captivating city on the shores of the Mediterranean; a place steeped in history, strongly infused by the warmth of Spanish sunshine and the passion of the Catalan people. The urban area is abundantly adorned with magnificent manifestations of artistic and architectural achievement, often remarkably well presented including many of the greatest achievements of the famous yet controversial, Antoni Gaudi. The outline of one of his grandest aspirations, La Sagrada Familia with its delicate spires stretching for the heavens in the distance, remains an iconic image from the television coverage of the Olympic and Paralympic Games in 1992.

Barcelona is a metropolis of such strong cultural, architectural and linguistic appeal that a modern music legend, Freddie Mercury of the English rock group Queen, celebrated its existence not just in a single song but in an entire album of the same title. *"Barcelona... I had this perfect dream...."*[1]. Although not perfect, the Barcelona 1992 Paralympic Games, the IXth iteration of the Paralympic Games (Summer*), set new standards in the areas

53

of sport competition for people with a disability, public awareness, Games organization and the technical delivery of Paralympic sport. (*By general convention, within both the Olympic and Paralympic movements, winter is used as an adjective to distinguish the winter versions of Games, while summer is not required as a descriptor and is simply inferred when the title only includes 'Games'.)

I have chosen to approach this chapter from a fairly personal perspective, sharing thoughts and opinion based on my own experiences over the last two decades. The familiarity and knowledge has been drawn from my significantly diverse involvement with the Paralympic Games, complemented by my various roles within the Olympic Movement. Although Barcelona was my first and only Paralympic Games as a competitor, I have subsequently been involved in eight other versions of this celebration of athletic achievement, or more dramatically, the "triumph of the human spirit" that is manifested continuously by the athletes and those who facilitate their competitive outlet. From mission support (sport leader in Atlanta) to Chef de Mission (Nagano 1998); delegation leader (president of an NPC) to Games organization (Board Director with the 2010 Vancouver Organizing Committee - VANOC); serving on evaluation and coordination commissions (London 2012), to working with an organization specifically established to create Games legacies (2010 LegaciesNow director), I have had the privilege of a variety of viewpoints to witness first-hand the dramatic advancement of the Paralympic Movement over the last twenty years.

The perceptions and viewpoints I have acquired through my association with the Games include legacies, both those planned as well as the unforeseen. Even though my observations are based on a broad spectrum of Games experiences, I recognize that they may still be considered overly singular, perhaps providing less objective discernment and allowing the encroachment of personal bias. To balance this predisposition and personal bias, I have strived to draw upon other sources to supplement and corroborate my observations regarding definitive Games legacies.

The Context of Games Legacies

"Legacy" is a word that that has become very much in vogue within the realm of Olympic and Paralympic Games but what does legacy really mean? A common definition of legacy is that it's about the "gift that you leave to others", whether as a parent, a citizen, a corporation, or an organization. Legacy is about handing down or handing over; it is the residue of dreams, labor and capital, that is a lasting benefit to others, many of whom had no part to play in the actual events that spawned these contributions. Defined in this manner it has a positive connotation and for our purposes, we will restrict the concept of legacy to that of positive, lasting benefits.

It is important to note that even though people typically consider tangible legacies, many realize that most legacies are rather abstract by nature. Therefore, key legacy themes include both "hard" and "soft" forms, the former including 'Economic, Infrastructure, and Facilities', with the latter including Sport, Social, Cultural and the 'Intangibles' such as civic pride. Peel back the layers of any of these broad themes and the numerous opportunities presented from hosting a major Games clearly emerge. For example, sport legacy can involve technical improvements, programs, participation, coaching, officiating, purpose-built venues, sport presentation and even increased priority for subsequent funding. Examples of soft legacies include public perceptions and awareness, self-esteem, media attention, accessible facilities and personal networks.

There are numerous detractors of the Olympic Games and by association, the Paralympic Games. They question the money invested to stage the Games and call directly into question the idea of legacies, suggesting that the price paid far outweighs both the soft and hard legacies from hosting a "mega-event". On the other hand, there are those who see it as a once in a generation opportunity; the chance to generate numerous positive outcomes from a sport event. Where the skeptics see wasted resources, the proponents see opportunity across a vast spectrum of the abstract and concrete, both non-quantifiable aspects of human endeavor and measureable outputs, from intangible community pride to state-of-the-art venues and infrastructure.

Despite the politics, security issues, and financial concerns, it can still be argued that major Games are primarily about sports. Even though the case may be made that sport is the heart of the Games, it is certainly much more than just about sport. Even though major Games are about providing an opportunity for the world's best athletes to manifest their talents and skills upon a world stage, the Games are catalytic; they will cause changes and set things in motion that were often not thought possible, let alone planned for during Games preparations. Although in recent versions of the Games including even the bid process, far less has been left to chance and a great deal of effort has gone into deliberate legacies.

An example of deliberate planning for and implementation of legacy programs is the work that '2010 Legacies Now' embarked upon during the bidding phase of the 2010 Olympic and Paralympic Winter Games. Realizing that there were benefits to be gained even through the process of bidding, steps were taken to capitalize on the resources, general interest and support that the Games would generate, regardless of the outcome of the host city selection. In the end, Vancouver was selected as the 2010 host city by the IOC and the organization created solely to address legacies of the Games, was set fully into motion. Prior to the start of the Games in February, '2010 LegaciesNow' was "working with over 4,000 organizations and groups across the province to discover and create unique programs that strengthen sport and recreation, healthy living, arts, literacy, accessibility and volunteerism". As a single organization, their responsibility included 61 programs designed to be "lasting legacies resulting from the 2010 Winter Games that benefit communities in all regions of British Columbia" (2010LegaciesNow).

After the fact, it is relatively easier to inventory the clear, material legacies as the planned or unplanned benefits that emanate from specific efforts or events; assigning credit for the benefits, however, is often a far more contentious task. It is not unusual for different parties to dispute as to whom or what is singularly accountable for the root cause of the beneficial outcomes or long-term impacts. Even with legacies, "victories share a thousand parents while defeats are orphans". In the case of Barcelona, examining legacies is a looking-back exercise and even though there were likely strong considerations given to legacies, the purpose of this review is not to evaluate how well benefits were achieved based on what was planned, or even to assign specific credit for the 'gifts', but rather to simply present the most relevant legacies bequeathed to the Paralympic Movement.

The Games Begin – September 3rd 1992

As an athlete at the Games, I had the privilege of experiencing first-hand the incredible energy and enthusiasm of the Opening Ceremony on September 3rd 1992. The carefully planned display was designed to heighten emotion and immerse spectators, especially those in attendance, deep into the promise of the twelve days of competition. Over 3000 athletes from 82 countries that were gathered in Barcelona for the Games took in the dramatic splendor on that warm evening, along with 65,000 in the stands and millions via television. Watching the other athletes and in discussions with friends after, each of us in our own way filtered the sights and sounds of the grand spectacle, then blended them with their own thoughts of the athletic challenges that imminently awaited each of us on various fields of play.

Changes had been made to the sport program and these Games would see the start of functional classification with swimming applying this new approach, so the Barcelona Games were set to manifest the advancements in high-performance summer sport for people with a disability since the last Games in Seoul in 1988. Athletes, coaches and those intimately involved with the various sports on the program surely must have been anxious as to what the outcomes of the competition would be:

> "The 1992 Paralympics was to be the largest showcase ever of elite disability sport. The Organizing Committee of the Barcelona Olympic Games (COOB) was concerned that the large number of Paralympic competitions might reduce the credibility of the Games built up by increasingly superior athletic performances. Consequently, the Organizing Committee reduced the number of athletes by setting strict rules and regulations. This caused some controversy, but it also simplified and raised the level of competition, and allowed athletes with different disabilities to participate in the same events" (International Paralympic Committee, 2010).

Arguably the ultimate highlight of any Opening ceremony at an Olympic or Paralympic Games, is the lighting of the main cauldron and during the Barcelona 1992 Olympic Games, the Spanish archer Antonio Rebollo had mesmerized millions with his technical adeptness as he ignited the Olympic flame with a carefully aimed burning arrow. Although that proficiency would be subsequently called into question, the arrow streaking across the Catalonian sky with the Olympic cauldron bursting into flame as the arrow found its target, was seared into the memories of those who had witnessed the act.

> "Billions of people around the globe gasped in admiration as the archer bravely found his target with unerring accuracy. Or so it seemed. In reality, he had not actually landed the arrow in the middle of the cauldron - he had fired it way outside the stadium as instructed. Organisers dared not risk his aim falling short and landing into the grandstand and instead told him to fire it directly over the target area... some pyrotechnics-helpful camera angles would take care of the visual effect (BBC, 2010)."

A scant few weeks later, throngs once again gathered to watch another display of wonder on the hill overlooking the city of Barcelona. Sitting in the midst of the Montjuic Stadium that warm evening, I remember my emotions being rather amplified by each subsequent scene, with thoughts of my upcoming competition only barely suppressed by the on-going sense of awe. As we sat there, several of us chatted -- a part of the show yet detached -- about how they would light the Paralympic flame with none of us realizing that not only would Antonio Rebollo repeat his feat, but that he was actually a Paralympic archer. His deed once again captured the imaginations of on-lookers as he let loose, not a simple arrow set alight, but a flame representative of hope, dreams and inspiration. Looking back, an archer from our realm of sport being chosen to do the ultimate honor in the lighting ceremony, for both the Olympic and Paralympic Games seems even more symbolic: through the 1992 Games, Paralympic sport had attained new levels of competition and perhaps started to finally gain public recognition and credibility as a sporting event.

Everyone who has participated in an Opening Ceremony has powerful memories of the event; a shared moment of connection on a majestic scale, yet individual recollections becoming deeply personal and unique by nature. The ceremonies and other Games experiences are powerfully emotive with the potential to influence behavior and create legacies of the micro kind; participants are influenced and in the end, they influence others. Perhaps these small individual legacies, the ones resulting from participation in the Games, collectively are the most potent and enduring of all Games legacies. Paralympic Games are rich with drama and intrigue, magical moments that are created in and around the competition where sublime athletic achievements provide inspiration and cause for hope of better things from the world's collective human potential. Spectators create connections through this shared vicarious experience, be it a stellar performance or a crushing defeat, actually sharing moments of history, but is it simply sporting excellence that drives Games organizations or is it really more about the potential legacy opportunities that Games provide?

Barcelona Paralympic Games legacies

This brings us to the question of those items considered typically as legacies and specifically, the legacies of the 1992 Paralympic Games. What did the Barcelona Paralympic Games achieve in terms of leaving or establishing lasting gains for the Paralympic Movement, Paralympic sport or other associated groups? What do those involved with the Paralympic Games see as being tangible legacies from the Barcelona 1992 Paralympic Games? Are there reverberations still being felt by the hosting of the Games in Barcelona or has their impact long been diluted or even lost with the passage of time? Barcelona is often cited as an outstanding example of successful Games legacies and even London 2012 paid homage to the regeneration and urban renewal that was realized through the hosting of the 1992 Games.

> 'Barcelona is the city that, of the four (Atlanta, Sydney, Athens, and Barcelona), emerges with the strongest evidence of a Games legacy. Its economy benefited from a three-stage programme of transformation, with each phase addressing the omissions and negative impacts of the preceding cycle. The Games were a catalyst for urban renewal, which was driven by both hard (infrastructure) and soft (such as increased confidence) legacy successes. Redevelopment of the site was imaginative and generally positively received, and employment levels, after an initial blip, have risen' (Greater London Authority, 2010).

Given the high regard that Barcelona holds for achieving substantial regeneration of city infrastructure and facility benefits by hosting the Games, one could easily focus on their hard, physical legacies. However, as previously stated, for purposes of this particular examination of Games legacies, I have chosen not to look at this aspect of legacies in Barcelona but rather to restrict the scope to the overall important aspect of specific legacies to the Paralympic Movement. This being said, the lack of concrete documentation on the legacies from hosting Paralympic Games makes this a challenging undertaking and partly explains the dearth of substantive facts presented here, the balance of the reason being this author's desire to share a more personal perspective.

> 'However, partly due to lack of monitoring, Barcelona struggled as much as other cities to prove that it had achieved a lasting legacy in softer areas such as disability awareness and sports participation. However, the lack of information available on the legacy of the Paralympic Games more generally makes monitoring its impact very difficult. In Athens, there are no relevant papers whatsoever. This in itself gives an indication of the low priority attached to this aspect of the Games legacy' (Greater London Authority, 2010).

In the end, what are the most memorable or important legacies for the Paralympic Movement that one could acknowledge the Barcelona 1992 Games as having achieved? Based on conversations, informal interviews and existing literature, the case can be made that these include increased public awareness and recognition; enhanced sport technical elements; implementation of functional classification; improved Games organization; and the formalization of the transfer of responsibility for all things Paralympic to the IPC.

Awareness and Recognition

When Miguel Sagarra, Secretary General of the CPE (Spanish Paralympic Committee) and former Vice-president of the IPC, was asked directly about legacies of the 1992 Games, he cited several items but stated that the most significant Games legacy was increased public awareness, that is, the increased positive recognition and acceptance of people with a disability as being capable individuals. From his perspective, including that of having worked for the host Games organization, it was this "soft" legacy, one of a social nature that was one of the greatest benefits realized in Spain and in other nations. "The biggest change that came about after Barcelona hosted the 1992 Paralympic Games was the recognition of persons with a disability in Spain." Considering this was perhaps the most important legacy, it is important to note that he provided several other examples of important developments, other benefits gained by and through this event. Improved public perceptions of persons with a disability was a tremendous social gain but "there were other important legacies: accessibility across the spectrum (transportation, venues, facilities); and the competitions being promoted and treated as competitive sport events (sport presentation, level of competition, venues)".

In this sense, the Barcelona Paralympic Games raised public awareness but more importantly, moved public perceptions of Paralympians to a new level that have never been relinquished and continue to increase in stature. A sense of dignity to people with a disability was conferred through these Games as people could see what these athletes were capable of on the field of play and by inference, life.

Sports Technical improvements

"Every day throughout the Games, we noticed long queues of people who were excited about catching every event. It was the first time we experienced such overwhelming public support" (Steadward, 2002).

It can be argued that there were several reasons for this increased public support but a top contender for the primary reason was the fact that the competitions were treated and presented as top level sport. Spectators in Barcelona had expectations of sport; they had just witnessed the Olympic Games in their home city rife with incredible athletic achievements and Games organizers promised more of the same during the Paralympic Games. Although, not the most positive manifestations of these high expectations, spectators clearly demonstrated that they were not coming from a position of sympathy or would condescend to Paralympians. "There were incidents where coins were tossed on to basketball floor during competition as a protest and an athlete was 'booed' by spectators for his antics after a race, indicating 'equal' expectations around sport (Gonzales, 2009). They wanted to see sport of the highest calibre and when they did not, they demonstrated their disappointment.

To facilitate sport competition of the highest calibre, the organizers insisted that formal rules were finalized and documented by the respective sport federations, at this time, primarily IOSD's (International Organizations of Sport for Disabled) which were established based on disability. The result was that for the first time, published rule books were produced for all the sports where as prior to Barcelona, only two sports had rule books of any description *(Gonzales, 2009)*. Formalized rules and regulations are essential elements in any sport system. Without a fully developed sport technical system, sport languishes for recognition, advancement and even acceptance. In 1992, Barcelona provided a solid sport technical base from which Paralympic sports could advance.

Functional Classification

Paralympic sports were initially established for therapeutic reasons and as the years progressed, this medical model based on disability, gradually transformed through a recreation-participation model to one of competitive sport. With the establishment of formal rule books and a more robust sport technical approach, Barcelona accelerated Paralympic sport development along the medical-recreational-competitive sport continuum. This shift was further enhanced by the move away from disability based classification to a functional based sport classification system.

> "When the ISOD President Guillermo Cabezas informed me that Barcelona would take the Paralympic Games with the condition that classification would be by sport and not by disability, I hugged him. When I accompanied Her Majesty Queen Silvia of Sweden to a swimming event at the Barcelona Games, we both saw how perfectly everything was set up. I had to explain the tears in my eyes to Her Majesty, saying that I had never expected to see this true recognition of athletes with disabilities in my lifetime".(Lindstrom, 2002)

The Games Organization

> "Barcelona was, together with the Paralympic Games in Seoul in 1988, a turning point for the Paralympics, with a single triad for the first time: Same country, same city, same facilities as the Olympic Games. This seems very regular now, but it was a huge victory at the time". (Terranova, 2002)

It is often conceded that Seoul 1988 was the true emergence and firm establishment of the Paralympic Games as a mega-event on the international sports calendar but to many, perhaps especially the participants. Barcelona established the final elements of what is considered critical to the professionalization of Games delivery including the approach to ticketing. Following Seoul's lead, the Barcelona organizing committee took steps to firmly entrench Paralympic Games delivery standards that are still referenced when those involved in the Paralympic movement speak of benchmarks. The critical Games fundamentals have been subsequently protected through an agreement between the IOC and IPC, a public declaration by these two organizations on the prestige that has been achieved and needs to be managed. Indeed:

> "On 19 June 2001, an agreement was signed between the International Olympic Committee and the International Paralympic Committee aimed at protecting the organisation of the Paralympic Games and securing the practice of "one bid, one city", meaning that the staging of the Paralympics is automatically included in the bid for the Olympic Games. The agreement addresses the general scope and organisation of the Paralympic Games, with the aim of creating similar principles for the organisation of the Olympic and Paralympic Games. This agreement came into effect with the Beijing 2008 Paralympic Games..." (International Olympic Committee, 2010)

Transition to the IPC

The Games in Barcelona marked the end of an era; *"...the Paralympic Summer Games in Barcelona represented a historic milestone for the IPC with the official handover of the Games from the ICC to the IPC."* (Lindstrom, 2002).

It is further argued that:

> "It had been decided in 1987 that the ICC (International Coordinating Committee) must have a change in structure to recognize national, regional and athlete representation, whilst at the same time recognizing the representation and continuation of the existing International Federations for sports for Disabled (collectively known as IOSDs). An Ad Hoc Committee was formed in 1987 and worked towards establishing a constitution for a new body and in 1989 agreement was reached to found the International Paralympic Committee with transfer of Paralympic Games governance from the ICC to the IPC taking place in 1993".

(International Wheelchair and Amputee Sports Federation, 2010).

There had been several transitions and changes during the maturation of the Paralympic Movement and the Games in Barcelona and other than the Paralympic Games for athletes with an intellectual disability held in Madrid shortly after Barcelona, these were the last edition of the Games coordinated by the ICC (International Paralympic Committee, 2010). A true legacy for the IPC, the organizing committee of the Barcelona 1992 Games delivered an outstanding Paralympic Games and provided a model for the IPC to guide the development and delivery of all subsequent Paralympic Games. As argued by Elizabeth Dendy "In Barcelona, the Paralympics came of age. I have many happy memories: the professionalism and commitment of the organisers, the excellent facilities in a beautiful and friendly city and the enthusiastic support of the crowds. What more could athletes ask for"? (Dendy, 1992).

The Games End – September 4th 1992

"The Closing Ceremony on 14 September in the Olympic Stadium brought a spectacular end to one of the finest Games in the history of the Paralympics" (International Paralympic Committee, 2010).

Admittedly, my sport experience in terms of results on the track at Montjuic Stadium was profoundly disappointing but my Games experience in Barcelona was one of the highlights of my life. The Barcelona 1992 Paralympic Games were the only ones that I competed in as an athlete but only one of many I have participated in, yet I still hold a strong affection for the city, specifically the warmth and spirit of its people. For me, and many other athletes I have spoken with over the years, the Barcelona 1992 Paralympic Games established not only new standards in public awareness, sport technical aspects, classification, and organization, perhaps most memorably it is the benchmark they established for the emotive experience of the Paralympic Games. It was my experience at those Games that compelled me to become more involved with the Paralympic Movement and to give back in some fashion a part of what I was given through my experience in the Games. This along with my genuine gratitude to the citizens of Spain and the city of Barcelona is another type of legacy, one definitely of a personal nature.

Notes

[1] "Barcelona", a song and album by Freddie Mercury.

References

2010 'Legaciesnow (2010) Available at: http://www.2010legaciesnow.com/our-programs/ (accessed 15th October 2010).

BBC (2010) Sport on line: Available at http://news.bbc.co.uk/sport2/hi/olympics2000/926190.stm (accessed 15th October 2010).

Dendy, E. (2002) President CP-ISRA 1992, The Paralympian online-Newsletter of the IPC, No. 3, Available at http://www.paralympic.org/paralympian/20023/2002315.htm (accessed 15th October 2010).

International Olympic Committee (2010) International Olympic Committee Website, Paralympic Games, Available at http://www.olympic.org/en/content/Olympic-Games/Paralympic-Games/?Tab=1 (accessed 15th October 2010).

International Paralympic Committee (2010) Barcelona, Available at http://www.paralympic.org/Paralympic_Games/Past_Games/Barcelona_1992/index.html (accessed 15th October 2010).

International Wheelchair and Amputee Sports Federation (2010) Paralympic Games 1960 – 1992, Available at http://www.iwasf.com/iwasf/index-.cfm/about-iwas/history/paralympic-games-1960-1992/ (accessed 15th October 2010).

Lindstrom, H. (2002) The Paralympian online-Newsletter of the IPC, No. 3, Available at http://www.paralympic.org/paralympian/20023/2002315.htm (accessed 15th October 2010).

Greater London Authority (2010) Lasting Legacy, Available at http://www.london.gov.uk/assembly/reports/econsd/lasting-legacy-summary.pdf (accessed 15th October 2010).

Steadward, R. (2002) The Paralympian online-Newsletter of the IPC, No. 3, Available at: http://www.paralympic.org/paralympian/20023/2002315.htm (accessed 15th October 2010).

Sagarra, M. (2009) Kuala Lumpur, Conference Report, November.

Terranova, F. (2002) The Paralympian online-Newsletter of the IPC, No. 3, Available at: http://www.paralympic.org/paralympian/20023/2002315.htm (accessed 15th October 2010).

Steadward, R. (2002) Paralympian online-Newsletter of the IPC, No. 3, Available at: http://www.paralympic.org/paralympian/20023/2002315.htm (accessed 15th October 2010).

Chapter 7
Atlanta 1996

Trials and Triumphs of the Human Spirit

Travis Mushett and Ann Cody

Introduction

Despite the late summer Georgia weather, which was hot, humid, and sticky, a crowd of 65,000 gathered in Atlanta's Centennial Olympic Stadium to welcome more than 3,195 elite Paralympic athletes from around the world (*Daily News*, 1996). It was less than two weeks after the closing ceremony of the 1996 Summer Olympic Games, a hard act to follow by any estimation. But like Blaze—the phoenix mascot of these, the Tenth Summer Paralympic Games—the ceremony soared above anyone's expectations. United States Vice President Al Gore officially opened the Games before turning over the stage to actor Christopher Reeve, the master of ceremonies and himself a wheelchair-user. An all-star menagerie of American performers including Teddy Pendergrass, Aretha Franklin, Carly Simon, and Liza Minnelli entertained and, in a show-stopping moment of poignancy and pageantry, Mark Wellman, a paraplegic climber, scaled the 80-foot tower using little more than a series of climbing ropes and brute force to reach the cauldron and ignite the Paralympic flame (Disability Today, 1997, pp. 21-29).

Ten days of high performance competition followed. Gold medals were awarded and world records shattered. But the excitement and the sport and personal triumphs masked the behind-the-scenes struggles to pull the Games together. The Atlanta Paralympic Organizing Committee (APOC) faced unprecedented organizational challenges and yet assembled a high quality elite competition, one that included many firsts for a Paralympic Games. The Atlanta Paralympic Games proved to be a Games of transition, as its hard-earned lessons were assimilated into the structure of future Olympic and Paralympic organizing committees. Indeed, the legacy of the 1996 Paralympics lives on not just in the lessons learned by the disability sports community or in the records set and incredible performances logged. The Games also left behind a one-of-a-kind legacy organization in BlazeSports America, an organization that carries on the ethos of the Paralympic movement through its comprehensive approach to advancing the lives of youth and adults with physical disabilities through sport, education, and advocacy.

Atlanta was awarded the bid for the 1996 Paralympic Games in March of 1992 by the emerging International Paralympic Committee during the Paralympic Winter Games in Tignes, France. The Bid Committee was led by representatives from the Shepherd Spinal Center and officials from the United States (US) Disability Sport Organizations. The US Olympic Committee did not participate or lend any support to the Paralympic bid or participate in the process. Following the bidding procedure up to that time, a decision was made separately from the decision to award the Olympic Games to Atlanta, and the organizing committees were likewise completely separate. APOC and its Olympic counterpart, the Atlanta Committee for the Olympic Games (ACOG), had separate leadership, separate staff, and, it turned out, separate goals. These Paralympic Games were to be the largest and most complex yet, however, this separation of leadership would prove to be disastrous. G. Andrew Fleming was selected to serve as the President and CEO of the Atlanta Paralympic Games Organizing Committee (APOC), and from early on, he and his staff regarded funding as a potential stumbling block. "Our biggest challenges were financial", Fleming says. "We didn't know that we weren't going to lose millions until May of 96". These fears were deepened by the budget crisis that led to the shutdown of the US federal government in the winter of 1995-96, an episode that left the organization unsure of the level of support to expect from the U.S.A. Congress.

Negatives

In the face of such uncertainty, Atlanta pioneered the use of private fundraising to finance the Games. Fleming proudly pointed to the fact that two-thirds of APOC's revenue was raised through private channels. This focus on private rather than public funds reflected a change in philosophy from previous Games. "It was the first time that a Paralympic Games was approached as a commercial enterprise", says Xavier Gonzalez, APOC's

Vice President of Sports and the current CEO of the International Paralympic Committee. In a first for a Paralympic Games, the organizing committee secured substantial corporate funds. Coca-Cola, IBM, Motorola, Turner, the Home Depot, Bell South, and many companies were brought onboard. And while the funds secured were by no means insignificant—Gonzalez points to the $1 million grant and multi-million dollar sponsorship deal with Coca-Cola (Disability Today, 1997, p. 61) as a particular triumph—corporate sponsorship totals were far outpaced by those raised by the Atlanta Olympic Games. Mark Johnson, the director of advocacy for Atlanta's Shepherd Center—a world-renown rehabilitation hospital in Atlanta and founding sponsor of the 1996 Atlanta Paralympic Games—remembers the disability community's annoyance at the "sinful six" Olympic top sponsors that did not sponsor the Paralympic Games and yet made the unconscionable decision to prohibit APOC from soliciting support from other corporations by refusing to release the category to enable APOC to secure a broad range of financial support for the Games is but one example. In response to this slight, he says, "Shepherd issued a public boycott of the "sinful six" and did not use their products for years." The "sinful six" included John Hancock Mutual Insurance Co., Bausch & Lomb, Sara Lee, Anheuser-Busch, Visa and McDonald's.

However, the reconception of the Paralympic Games as potentially a moneymaking venture served as an inspiration for Games to come. In a similar vein, the 1996 Games were the first to successfully sell large numbers of tickets rather than simply offer free admission, and therefore proved that the public was willing to pay for the privilege of watching athletes with disabilities compete on an elite level. To take one amazing example, all 65,400 tickets to the Opening Ceremony—some costing as much as $100—were sold. Demand was so high that scalpers peddled tickets outside of the stadium. (*Daily News*, 1996).

As in Games past, the Atlanta Paralympiad was not solely a sports competition. For the four days before the Opening Ceremony, disability rights leaders and advocates from over 50 countries arrived at Atlanta's Marriott Marquis Hotel for the Third Paralympic World Congress on Disability. Expert speakers at the Congress presented on an array of topics ranging from community advocacy to performance enhancement to universal design. Chaired by American disability rights pioneer Justin Dart, the Congress also offered an opportunity for cross-cultural dialogue concerning both the common and distinct challenges faced by persons with disabilities. Joshua Malinga, President of the Pan African Federation of the Disabled and Mayor of Bulawayo, Zimbabwe, delivered the keynote address. Malinga, a polio survivor and wheelchair user, spoke firsthand about the lack of rehabilitation services and social invisibility of people with disabilities in less developed nations.

Under the insightful leadership of Barbara Trader the Congress sought concrete measures to offer opportunities to young people with disabilities around the world, and recommended the creation of a multi-agency global task force on sports opportunities for children. Additionally, students from less developed countries won tickets to the Congress to acquire skills that were directly implementable in their home communities. Film students with disabilities were given the opportunity to show their work alongside established filmmakers and in front of a panel of industry professionals at the Disability Film Festival, and all were invited to experience the latest in sport and accessibility technology at the Abilities Expo.

One first-of-its-kind cultural event was almost cancelled due to the financial strain on APOC and the uncertainty of revenue projections for the Games. APOC was forced to withdraw its support for the Cultural Paralympiad—an arts festival held in honor of the Paralympic spirit—but community groups stepped in to ensure that artists with disabilities had the opportunity to showcase their talents. Indeed, a coalition led by the Center for Puppetry Arts, Special Audiences, Very Special Arts Georgia, the Goethe Institute Atlanta, and the Georgia Council for the arts managed to raise more than $3 million for the exhibition of visual art, music, theater, and dance. (Disability Today, 1997, pp. 36-39).

And while APOC was well aware from the beginning that its financial situation would pose a challenge, the organization did not expect the callous treatment and degrading disregard it received from its counterparts at AOGOC. While quick to assert that some of the Olympic staff were indeed supportive, Senior Vice President & Chief Games Operations Officer for the Atlanta Paralympic Games, Mike Mushett expressed substantial frustration with the Olympic-centered myopia of ACOG. "There was not much enthusiasm for the Paralympics from the Olympic people", he remembers. "They wouldn't even allow us use of the International Zone—the athletes' social area—or the athletes' cafeteria". Instead APOC had to create an embarrassingly scaled-down dining area on top of a parking deck. Due to the less-than-ideal location and limited hours created by the displacement of athlete services, it was often difficult for athletes to eat meals in the makeshift cafeteria and still make it to their scheduled competitions. Mushett admits that the food and social services of the Games "were not up to Paralympic standards".

Gonzalez agrees with Mushett's assessment. "Not only were the Committees separate", he says, at Games time "we were going into a disaster zone in some venues". Gonzalez remembers ACOG locking away necessary equipment at sporting venues after the close of the Olympic Games that they had agreed to share, forcing APOC to spend precious time to procure equipment and repair damages instead of readying venues for Paralympic competition. Even the athletes took notice. Tim Willis—who took home a silver medal in the 10,000 meters and three bronzes in 1,500m, 5,000m, and 4x400m relay—noted, "Logistically you could see the difficulty in transitions ... the Olympic Games didn't see the value in a good transition to the Paralympics". Let's Get Together, an active disability rights group, at that time went so far as to give ACOG a grade of "F" on its Games report card, with the comment "support was token, shame on them". Astonishingly, ACOG workers tore through the entire Olympic Stadium and Track and Field venue literally cutting cables and stripping out the critical technology infrastructure needed for results systems, sport production, and essential communications. Again, Olympic Games officials had agreed prior to the Games to share this technology but apparently never communicated that commitment to venue supervisory staff.

Positives

Despite these difficulties—and the high standard set by Barcelona four years earlier—the level of competition had never been higher. Willis lauded APOC for "ensuring that there was a strong competition with opportunity". The statistics confirmed Willis' observation. An amazing 269 world records were set in Atlanta. Athletes competed in 508 events in 17 full medal sports and two highly successful exhibition sports—sailing and wheelchair rugby (International Paralympic Committee, 1996).

The Atlanta Paralympic Games are also considered a marketing triumph. In addition to the nearly 400,000 spectators who attended Paralympic events, more than 2,000 accredited journalists reported on the proceedings. Though the coverage, predictably, did not compare to the media surrounding the Olympic Games, it was substantial. CBS, for example, offered four hours of weekend coverage to a national audience, and cable's SportSouth and the Prime Network aired nightly one-hour highlight shows throughout the Games. The Atlanta Journal-Constitution—one of the nation's most respected and most read newspapers—created a special Paralympic section to cover each day's competitions (Disability Today, 1996, p. 94).

The popularity of the Games was aided by the evocative and dynamic visual design created for the event. Perhaps the most beloved symbol of 1996 Games was Blaze, the multi-colored phoenix mascot created by illustrator Trevor Irwin. Blaze merchandise sold at a remarkable rate and the mascot himself was received with near universal acclaim. As a phoenix—a mythical bird that rises from its own ashes—Blaze served as a potent symbol for both the city of Atlanta and the Paralympic spirit; Atlanta famously rose from literal ashes after being completely destroyed during the American Civil War, and Paralympians demonstrate that despite what some may see as physical limitations, they were capable of incredible feats of athleticism, skill, and prowess.

The Games' motto, "The Triumph of the Human Spirit", also proved popular amongst fans, athletes, and the media. The Starfire emblem, a simple and elegant design that incorporated a blue and white star, gold streaks, and the Paralympic flame, was ubiquitous on banners, clothing, pins, and other Games materials. And many of the promotional materials served the secondary purpose of raising public awareness of the abilities of people with disabilities, a prime example of which is the provocative "What's Your Excuse?" campaign. With a full array of television, print, radio, and billboard ads, the campaign featured Paralympic athletes alongside challenging statements like "What's changed most in my life since I lost my leg? I run more". and "I had a seeing eye dog once. He just couldn't keep up". always followed by the admonition, "What's your excuse?" The ads delivered a resolutely positive message about people with disabilities; rather than evoke pity such as the Jerry Lewis MDA Telethon frequently criticized by advocates within the disability community, they challenged audiences to rethink their preconceptions.

On August 25, the 1996 Paralympic Games drew to a close in spectacular fashion. Some 57,000 people attended the Closing Ceremony at Centennial Olympic Stadium and they did not leave disappointed. US Attorney General Janet Reno was on hand to praise the Games and its athletes, and then the real party began. Radio icon Casey Kasem served as master of ceremonies and the crowd was treated to performances by Chubby Checker, Bo Diddley, the Four Tops, and Jerry Lee Lewis. The night ended with recording of Aretha Franklin belting out "Climb Every Mountain" as fireworks lit up the skies above Atlanta. (Disability Today, 1997, p. 184)

Legacy

The effects of the Games did not end that night, however; the 1996 Paralympics left behind a multifaceted legacy both to the city of Atlanta and to the broader disability sports movement. In 2000 the International Olympic Committee and International Paralympic Committee signed an agreement setting out how organizing committees would organize both the Olympic and Paralympic Games. Beijing and Vancouver were the first host cities to organize both Games under the new IOC/IPC agreement. Gilbert Felli, Executive Director of Olympic Games for the International Olympic Committee, points out that it was the "fiasco" at the 1996 Atlanta Games, when Paralympic organizers arrived after the Olympics to discover that computers had been disconnected and telephone lines ripped out at the venues, that led to the IOC/IPC agreement and greater support for the Paralympics. Thus the blatant disregard APOC experienced is largely phenomena of the past. As Gonzalez puts it, "Sometimes you have to be sick to get better".

Additionally, APOC's innovative efforts to raise money in the private sector left them with the happy surprise of a multi-million dollar surplus, most of which was invested in its legacy organization the United States Disabled Athletes Fund, now known as BlazeSports America. BlazeSports is a nonprofit organization that advances the lives of children and adults with physical disabilities through sport, healthy lifestyles, and the prevention of chronic health conditions.

To provide an idea of BlazeSports' many and manifold efforts, below is a partial list of the successes of Blaze programming:

- The creation of a statewide and national network of community-based BlazeSports programs to ensure access to sport for people with physical disabilities.

- The establishment of the first continuous national conference on disability sport.
- The training of over 13,000 local sport service providers since 1999.
- The creation of employment and professional development opportunities for people with disabilities.
- The exporting of education and training programs to partners in less developed nations in Africa, the Middle East, and beyond.
- A partnership with US Paralympics to raise awareness and visibility of Paralympic sport nationwide.
- The creation of innovative web programming via webinars, the BlazeSports World Wide blog, BlazeSports TV, a source for multi-media information and instruction.
- The development of a publishing branch, TorchRunner Press.
- Has provided close to 2.9 million (2,868,991) hours of service to over 172,000 (172,353) individuals nationwide in the 14 years since the Paralympic Games.
- The establishment of a very active and successful BlazeSports Institute of Applied Science.

BlazeSports has earned the following designations as an organization:

- BlazeSports is the U.S. member of CPISRA, a founding organization of the International Paralympic Committee and as such sanctions and hosts major competitions, and selects and sends US teams to world and continental championships.
- BlazeSports is a member of the U.S. Olympic Committee's Multi-Sport Organization Council.
- BlazeSports is recognized by the U.S. Agency for International Development (USAID) as a Private Voluntary Organization for disaster and development support in the most needy parts of the world.
- BlazeSports is called on by the US Department of State to implement initiatives to advance human rights through sport and currently has active projects in 3 nations outside the US.
- BlazeSports has 2 active offices, Atlanta and Washington DC.
- BlazeSports is a certifying body for professionals in the field of disability sport and recreation.

Fleming, who once served as president of BlazeSports America, states the organization "filled a glaring need". Willis, a Georgia native who has noted the effects of BlazeSports in his own community, lauds its efforts. "You didn't see something like this happen with the Olympics", he says. "The Atlanta Olympics didn't evolve into anything in terms of youth programming".

The Paralympics also rendered Atlanta a more hospitable city for its residents and visitors with physical disabilities. The disability community successfully lodged complaints with the US Department of Justice to ensure that Olympic and Paralympic venues would be accessible to all, and the Department of Justice responded by offering oversight to ensure that the venues complied with US accessibility codes required by the Americans with Disabilities Act (ADA). Johnson also attributes the curb cut program—an effort to make Atlanta sidewalks safe and convenient for people in wheelchairs—and the increase in accessible parking in downtown Atlanta to the presence of the 1996 Paralympics. Local universities also benefitted. In order to meet the specifications required under the ADA and to house Paralympic athletes, several accessible dormitories had to be constructed. After the conclusion of the Games, these dorms were—and continue to be—used by students at Georgia State University and the Georgia Institute of Technology. In this way, the Games directly improved the quality of life for university students with physical disabilities.

Conclusive statements

The increase in awareness of disability sport in the US also helped to set the stage for certain provisions in the Ted Stevens Olympic and Amateur Sports Act amendments of 1998, which revised the Amateur Sports Act of 1978 to address changes in the domestic and international sport scene. BlazeSports worked closely with Senator Ted Stevens to craft the portions of the bill concerning athletes with disabilities, which included an expansion of the United States Olympic Committee to administer the Paralympic teams. "The Act gave parity to Paralympic athletes", says Fleming, "and it wouldn't have been possible without the credibility the '96 Paralympics gave athletes with disabilities".

In addition to such concrete effects, the Games also left a more intangible legacy in Atlanta and across the country. The visibility offered to both the Paralympics and people with disabilities more broadly is inarguable. "In a 1993 study with Georgia State University," Fleming remembers, "the Paralympic Games were at 3% recognition with the public, just behind the Georgia Youth Games at 4%. The thing was, the Georgia Youth Games didn't exist. After the Games in '96, the Paralympics were just behind the Olympics in terms of recognition".

In the 1996 Paralympic Games, the disability sports community dealt with the growing pains of a movement moving into maturity. The constant skirmishes between APOC and ACOG set the stage for a restructuring of the way Olympic and Paralympic Games are organized, a restructuring that has been advantageous for both sides. With its successes forging inroads into the corporate community, eliciting public interest as never before, engaging the media, and presenting a platform for some of the most amazing performances in the history of sport, the '96 Paralympics proved that the Paralympic movement deserved to be regarded and respected as an equal to its Olympic sibling. It had earned—and would insist upon—its place of prominence in the world of elite sporting events. Fleming remembers representing athletes with disabilities at a town hall meeting in the 1980s. "Some hammer thrower, a big guy, approached us and told us that we didn't belong here", he says, "that the Olympics was about the perfection of the human body". Through its insistence on—and demonstration of—its own worth, the Atlanta Games won a level of parity for the Paralympic movement that helped lay to waste such *misguided notions of the nature of disability*.

References

Daily News. (1996) *Paralympics Open in Atlanta: 3,500 Athletes with Disabilities to Compete at Olympic Venues.* Available at: http://www.thefreelibrary.com/PARALYMPICS OPEN IN ATLANTA : 3,500 ATHLETES WITH DISABILITIES TO...-a083959841

Disability Today Publishing Group Inc. (1997) The Triumph of the Human Spirit: The Atlanta Paralympic Experience. Oakville, Ontario, CA

International Paralympic Committee. (1996) *Atlanta* 1996. Available at: http://www.paralympic.org/Paralympic_Games/Past_Games/Atlanta_1996/index.html

Chapter 8
Sydney 2000

Moving from Post-Hoc Legacy to Strategic Vision and Operational Partnerships

Simon Darcy and Lois Appleby

The vision of the Sydney Paralympic Organising Committee was to inspire the world by successfully staging a Paralympic Games which set new standards in excellence to enable athletes to achieve their best performance (Appleby, 2007).

Introduction

The Sydney 2000 Paralympic Games demonstrated the transcendence of the Paralympic Games through a significant increase in the number of athletes, development of spectator numbers through marketing the event and media coverage. Yet, after what some described as the debacle of the 1996 Atlanta Paralympic Games, the major advancement for the Sydney 2000 Paralympic Games was the organisational partnership between the Sydney Olympic Games Organising Committee (SOCOG) and the Sydney Paralympic Organising Committee (SPOC), which effectively created a single administration to deliver the three month festival of the Olympics, Paralympics and cultural festival. Sydney redressed the substantial backward step of 1996 Atlanta by restoring the high standards set in 1988 Seoul and

1992 Barcelona. More importantly, the Sydney 2000 Paralympic Games went about setting objectives to improve on the two previous benchmarks. They did so by breaking previous ticket sales records with 1.1 million tickets sold and the Games attracted 360,000 organized school and community groups (Appleby, 2007; Cashman, 2006b; Cashman & Darcy, 2008).

Legacy

Before discussing the legacy of the Sydney 2000 Paralympic Games a number of preliminary considerations about the legacy need to be noted. Legacy is a reasonably recent area in the academic literature. As Appleby (2007) notes as late as 2007, with respect to the Sydney 2000 Games, most discussion had been anecdotal given a few notable exceptions (Appleby, 2007; Cashman, 2006b; Darcy, 2001; Darcy, 2003; Goggin & Newell, 2001). This, in part, is due to legacy being a recent inclusion within academia and major event considerations as part of the triple bottom line valuation processes where city states seek to broaden the inclusions for events evaluation beyond economic impact (Carlsen & Soutar, 2000; Preuss, 2007; Smith, 2009). However, there are two more important considerations that need to be acknowledged before we move forward. First, legacy by definition is an action that is planned for prior to the event and sustained into the future (Chalip, 2004; Preuss, 2007). There was not, by any stretch of the imagination, planning for a Sydney 2000 Paralympic legacy (Appleby, 2007; Cashman & Darcy, 2008). Any of the research into Paralympic Games legacy research prior to Beijing 2008 is post-hoc and quite simply, scholars use an historic lens to fashion a legacy arising from the Paralympic Games experience. Second, Paralympic scholars need to recognize the intrinsic link between the Olympics and Paralympics since Seoul 1988. In the introduction to this book, we recognize the connection of the Paralympic Games to the motivation of cities to host the Olympics. For whatever reasons that city states bid to host the Olympic Games, these are quite separate issues to the partnership agreement to host the Paralympic Games. The Paralympic movement should celebrate this partnership as the Paralympic Games is not yet of the same status, magnitude or gravitas as the Olympics or other major sporting events that host city's bid for. If this were the case, we are sure that the International Paralympic Committee (IPC) would be happy to 'go it alone' and put the Paralympic Games out to bid cities for competition in the marketplace. This in no way diminishes the Paralympic Games as an event, as an elite competition for athletes with disabilities or challenge the place it has as one of the largest sporting events in the world but it does recognize the harsh market reality of the city state, sponsors, the media and the public's perception of the Paralympic Games as a an attractive marketable commodity.

The perception of legacy is also affected by the stakeholder involved and their centrality to the event or phenomena taking place. While the Paralympic Games have primary stakeholders such - the IPC, National Organising Committees, National Paralympic Organisations, elite athlete participants, hosting city-state – there are also secondary stakeholders including the sponsors, volunteers, other facilitating government departments, the local community and people with disabilities. Stakeholder theory, developed from the field of strategic management studies, acknowledges that the conflicting perspectives of stakeholders need to be managed as part of organisational objectives (Freeman, 1983). Stakeholder theory has been used synonymously in relation to government management of environmental development processes and collaboration among key players as a 'fundamental ingredient in sustainable development' (Sautter & Leisen, 1999, p. 312). City-state redevelopment associated with the Olympic and Paralympic Games is a foundation of modern Olympic Games particularly in those cities where the Paralympics had been carried out within partnership. Stakeholders can be defined as, 'any individual, interest group, pressure group or corporation affected by a public policy issue, government action or inaction' (adapted from S. Davis, 1993; Hall, 1999; Mitchell, Agle, & Wood, 1997). The main contribution of such an analysis is to be able to identify from the perspectives of the stakeholders, the issues they regard as significant to the proposed changes and incorporate these views into management strategies. Stakeholder groups hold considerable power to influence the community and receive considerable media coverage. Certainly there are cases where the big cities have dropped out from contention because major stakeholders have protested at their exclusion or lack of consideration (e.g. Berlin). Historically there is a need for this understanding where citizen movements have had a major impact on the environmental landscape.

With these preliminary comments in mind, it is also recognized that the Sydney 2000 Paralympic Games has been well served by albeit post-hoc evaluation through an excellent yet poorly distributed post Games report (Sydney Paralympic Organising Committee, 2001), post Games access reports (Olympic & Paralympic Disability Advocacy Service, 2000; Olympic Co-ordination Authority, 2001), a number of disability critiques (Darcy, 2001; Darcy, 2003; Goggin & Newell, 2001), an historical review (Cashman, 2006b), an insider's perspective (Appleby, 2007) and the most comprehensive interdisciplinary examination of a single Paralympic Games (Cashman & Darcy, 2008).

Major Legacies

The chapter now examines the major legacies of the Sydney 2000 Paralympic Games through a re examination of the main legacy critiques of Appleby (2007), Darcy and Cashman (2008) and other sources, and by providing a fresh summary and interpretation as identified by the following Table 1. As evidenced by Table 1, what is interesting with the analyses by the two authors is that one presents an insider's perspective and the other a more interdisciplinary academic examination but both cover similar ground albeit in different ways and under different headings. Appleby acknowledges a more anecdotal approach where Darcy and Cashman limit their commentary to where research evidence can be presented. Both recognized that legacy should be split into international and domestic categories where as commentators have noted that both sport and disability have specific cultural contexts.

Table 1: Sydney Paralympic Legacy Literature

Appleby 2007	Darcy & Cashman 2008	This Chapter
International	**International**	**International**
IOC Recognition	Media benchmarks	IPC IOC relationship
Improved organization	IPC IOC relationship	Strategic Vision
Media coverage	Sport delivery	Branding/ Media Coverage
Athlete support		Sport Delivery and Athlete support
Education		Education
Moving beyond disability sport community		PostGames Evaluation/ Knowledge Transfer
Australia	**Australia**	**Australia**
Access issue	Community response	Community Response
Role Models	Disability education	AustralianParalympic movement (funding and mainstreaming)
Mainstreaming of Disability sport with NSOs	Legacy for Paralympians (funding and status)	Education/Role models
Greater sporting recognition		Infrastructure
Public recognition		

In presenting the following commentary it is acknowledged that many of these discrete headings are interdependent and overlapping.

International & Operational Partnership

The success of the Sydney 2000 Paralympic Games can in part be attributed to the operational partnership between SOCOG and SPOC to deliver the three month festival of the Olympics, Paralympics and cultural Olympiad (Darcy, 2003). The operational partnership established by SOCOG and SPOC alleviated many of the transitional problems that occurred between the Olympic and Paralympic Games in 1996 at Atlanta (Appleby, 2007; Heath, 1996). The importance of this operational partnership cannot be overstated as it meant that those responsible for delivering the Olympic Games were largely those responsible for delivering the Paralympic Games (Darcy, 2003, 2008a, 2008b; Darcy & Cashman, 2008a). This meant that there was an organisational continuity which embedded an understanding of Paralympic, disability and access issues across the organisational culture of SOCOG/SPOC. However, as discussed later, there were still tensions between the organising committees and other host city bodies responsible for the long-term planning, organization and management facilities and operations. In particular, the Olympic Coordination Authority had an important role to play in legacy as they were the ones that would be in charge of the access issues for perpetuity. The OCA in short did this through the production of *Access Guidelines*, implemented the Olympic Access Advisory Committee as central to process of planning for disability and access issues, produced an access guide for the Games and wrote a critical review of Games access operations (Olympic Co-ordination Authority, 1996, 1998, 1999, 2000, 2001). The Olympic Coordination Authority still plays a critical yet albeit reduced role in the NSW government through its successor the Sydney Olympic Park Authority, which recently released its master plan of the site to 2030 (Sydney Olympic Park Authority, 2009). SOPA has maintained the important role that the Olympic Access Advisory Committee played through the SOPA Access Advisory Committee.

IPC and IOC Relationship

The major international legacy was the closer relations between the IPC and IOC. Whilst the IOC had given some 'fatherly' support to the IPC it was after Sydney that contracts were exchanged positioning the Paralympics as part of the Olympic City Bid process. This has provided incredible status and security for the Paralympic Movement and the Games, which up until 1988 often was not staged with the Olympics and on occasions could not find a host city. The relationship between the two organisations was formalized by IOC President Samaranch and IPC President Steadward through two signed memorandums of understanding following the Games with a third signed by different Presidents in 2003 (Appleby, 2007). The first signed in October 2000 (International Paralympic Commitee, 2000) focused on IPC representation on IOC commissions while the second signed in June 2001 focused on formalizing the requirement where cities had to bid to host both Games – something that was understood but not enforceable through a bid document beginning as far back as the 1988 Summer Games in Seoul. It is difficult, however, to say that the 2000 Summer Paralympic Games were the catalyst for either of these agreements particularly when the relations between the IOC and Paralympic sport officials go back as far as when Sir Ludwig Guttmann hosted his first Stoke Games the same day as the opening of the 1948 London Summer Olympics. As well, meetings between Samaranch and Steadward started as early as 1988 when they met in Calgary and Samaranch attended the Paralympic Congress in 1992 in Barcelona just prior to their Games.

Strategic Organisational Vision

The legacy of the Sydney 2000 Paralympic Games could not have been achieved without the strategic organisational vision of SPOC. Dr John Grant, President of SPOC, in the foreword to the Paralympic Post Games Report (Sydney Paralympic Organising Committee, 2001) was rightfully glowing of his assessment of the success of the Games:

> 'The support for the Paralympic Games was outstanding. The 2000 Paralympic Games smashed all our predictions—the largest number of athletes and delegations ever to compete at a Paralympic Games, unprecedented media coverage and record crowds and ticket sales. More than 1.16 million spectators turned out in force to witness this spectacular international event showcasing some of the finest sporting talent in the world'.

Yet, operational success is not legacy as Appleby noted some six years later. In reflecting back on the vision of the Sydney Paralympic Organising Committee (SPOC) she could see that it was also a legacy statement (Appleby, 2007). Whilst recognizing that the Olympic and Paralympic Games had separate and unique identities, it was obvious to Appleby that economies of scale and efficiency in operations could be achieved by combining many of the operations of both Games, in effect delivering a 60 day sporting festival which would include the transition time between the two Games. Combining this operational planning allowed this transition to be seamless and highly effective, unlike what was experienced in Atlanta (Appleby, 2007).

As CEO she used her organisational skills to deliver the Paralympic Games seamlessly across the two organising committees. Importantly, the athletes were treated as elite athletes, in the same manner as the Olympic athletes and not as second rate athletes and to Appleby these are the two most important legacies of the Sydney Games. This closer link with the Olympics pointed the way to greater cooperation between Olympic and Paralympic movements and led to a succession of agreements between the IOC and IPC, which shored up the future of the Paralympic Games. This is not a legacy for the future of Paralympic Games is one in which Sydney is very proud (Appleby, 2007).

SPOC proved to the IOC in Sydney that the event was credible, professionally organized and could bring a softness to the often more calculated Olympic arenas. The Sydney model of close liaison and a constructive operating relationship between the two committees appealed to the IOC. Secondly, Sydney put the organization of this event on the same platform as an Olympics Games. This raised the expectation of athletes that all subsequent Games would be as well organized. This indeed seems to be evolving with joint organising committees for the Games. As well, Sydney expected the National Paralympic Committees to be professional, timely and organized. Many were not. The legacy here is that NPC's went home knowing that they had to improve their administration and management or get left behind (Appleby, 2007).

Appleby (2007) contends that there is a strong sense that Sydney contributed to the Paralympic movement being less dependent 'on its own people and networks', where there was a greater engagement with new relationships from areas of professional expertise that influenced development of the SPOC and the event itself. However, the SPOC organizers were not from the community of disabled people - there were only 3 staff out of 100 who had a physical disability. The CEO had no background with sport for the disabled but she had a background in running major sport events for example the World Masters Games. SPOCs apparent deficiencies in disability and disability sport expertise were balanced by the SPOC Board who were immensely experienced in these areas.

The philosophy taken was that this was an event for elite athletes who, happened to have a disability. SPOC didn't focus on the disability but instead applied the same philosophies and organizational systems to the Paralympic Games as the Olympics. The legacy here then is that people became passionate about these athletes. Many have gone on to other Paralympic Games and taken their passion with them. So an entire new group of people in Sydney became part of the Paralympic Movement. Sydney took the movement outside of itself introducing new ideas, new thought about how to present the athletes as speakers, ambassadors and heroes and new ways of marketing the event. Sydney set the benchmark for 2008 and 2012 Paralympic Games and those beyond (Appleby, 2007). Yet, this philosophy and the resulting organisational discourse also alienated the Sydney disability community who were not brought in as part of the community engagement process as school children and seniors were (Darcy, 2003).

Branding

Achieving this new sense of professionalization brought about by the strategic organisational vision of SPOC was closely linked to communicating this to external stakeholders. Before the Games Appleby noted that, while garnering greater recognition than any time previous, the Paralympic Games were still an event with no brand, little to no international sponsor interest, little public understanding and a high resistance by the public to watch 'handicapped people' or 'Supercrips in sexy chairs'. This was coupled with the fact that the Paralympics was up against the biggest sport brand in the world, the Olympic Games (Appleby, 2007). SOCOG and the SPOC took on this task and agreed that they must plan for a 60 day event, and with this, increase the international profile and marketing potential of the event. To do so required an organisational brand and media coverage in Australia and internationally.

Appleby has already noted the importance that Paralympic ambassadors played in portraying the event as one for elite athletes. The ambassadors were successfully used to create brand and develop the very successful community outreach programme. As the face of the Games the ambassadors provided the opportunity to leverage media coverage, ticket sales and merchandising. Iconic representation is always an important element of brand. As Darcy and Cashman (2008, p. 218) note, one of outstanding successes was the visibility and success of the mascot Lizzie in the Sydney 2000 Paralympic Games. The SPOC marketing group took the mascot to the community through its low cost pricing strategy and having the low-budget Franklins stores sell the product rather than the elite high end strategy adopted by the IOC and SOCOG for Olympic merchandise (see Cashman & Darcy, 2008, pp. 123-140). Where the Olympic mascots (there were three) never captured the imagination of the Australian public, Lizzie (Paralympic mascot) seemed to be everywhere and coupled with the highly successful community engagement programs became the iconic representation of the Sydney Paralympic Games. Subsequently, the APC recognised that there was a significant branding capital in the popularity of Lizzie that could be leveraged into the future. The Australian Paralympic Committee (APC) seized the opportunity that arose when SPOC disbanded to claim the rights to Lizzie and to develop the power of the brand over the coming years (Cashman & Darcy, 2008).

Media Coverage

The media benchmarks centred on the massive increase in coverage via the internet specifically as a result of coverage from US based WeMedia. WeMedia, however, was a casualty of the dot.com crisis and in 2001 and no longer exists. The coverage by WeMedia was regarded as first rate from a sport perspective and from the perspective of disability representation (Goggin & Newell, 2001). The concept of web-based delivery of content has subsequently been assumed by the IPC itself with www.Paralympicsport.tv but it is hard to ascribe that this was created as a direct legacy of the WeMedia precedent and not just as part of technological development. What can be linked, however, is the significant change in television coverage in Australia which may have translated to better coverage internationally. It is important to recall that only 4 years before the Sydney Games in Atlanta there was no US based network coverage and the organising committee actually had to pay for four hours that were shown after the Games (Cashman & Tremblay, 2008).

There was no doubt that media coverage of the 1996 Paralympic Games in Atlanta was disappointing in every sense (Schantz & Gilbert, 2001). In contrast to Schantz and Gilbert (2001), Darcy & Thomson (case study in Cashman & Tremblay, 2008, pp. 110-123) found the newspaper coverage by the Sydney Morning Herald to focus far more on the sporting spectacle, athletic performance, was gender balanced, sought to educate the public about Paralympic sport and presented the contrast between Paralympic and Olympics sports. The photographic imagery analyzed reinforced the importance of national medal count and ceremonies as part of the commercial media focus. However, unlike Schantz and Gilbert's (2001) analysis of

European coverage of the Atlanta Paralympics the Sydney Morning Herald images presented the full embodiment of Paralympic athletes and highlighted images of their athletic performance. In combination, the text and photographic representation had a much greater focus on athletic competition, while having a fascination for the technology body interface of Paralympic athletes.

Yet, the international transferability of these changes is questionable given other studies reviewed by Hardin (2003) that suggested the overall presence of athletes with disabilities in the mass media was still lacking in both quantity and quality. In particular a study by Golden (2002) noted that coverage of the 2002 Salt Lake City Paralympic Games was virtually nonexistent in US based media. In Golden's study a US reporter was quoted as stating 'It's a bone they throw to them to make them feel better. It's not a real competition, and I for one, don't see why I should have to cover it' (Golden, 2002, p. 13).

As well, in 2002 following Sydney, the Salt Lake organising committee signed a contract with A & E to broadcast eight hours, one per day, during the Games and NBC the Olympic broadcaster showed a one hour highlight of the opening ceremonies. In Canada, coverage too has improved with an announcement that the coverage for the 2010 Games was the highest ever with all coverage available in High Definition, marking the first time the Games was produced entirely in HD by a Canadian rights-holder (CTV Olympics, 2010). What is also of interest is that the coverage was delivered by Canada's Olympic Broadcast Media Consortium which is a unique relationship between leading media conglomerates CTV Inc. and Rogers Media Inc. which are both for profit ventures. Prior coverage was by the Canadian Broadcasting Corporation (CBC) which was a federally funded enterprise and thus was perhaps more inclined to showcase federally supported Paralympic athletes. Returning to Australia in particular was the significant coverage in 2008 from the Australian Broadcasting Corporation (ABC), which is Australia's government owned national television carrier. Having had the experience of covering the Games in 2000 they expanded their scope and televised three hours nightly in prime time hours. For their ongoing efforts the ABC they were awarded Paralympic broadcaster of the year for their coverage of the Beijing 2008 Paralympic Games (International Paralympic Commitee, 2009).

While these challenges continue, Sydney established the benchmark for media coverage and television production for this event. As Cashman and Tremblay (2008) note in their concluding comments, the Sydney 2000 Paralympic Games extended the television coverage and approach to Paralympic sport. This was evidenced through the record high ratings for the opening ceremony, the solid ratings for the daily highlights package which demonstrated public interest in Paralympic sport. Sydney provided baseline evidence of the media potential of the event. There is no doubt that this was linked to both SPOCs marketing and community outreach programs. The Secretary General of the IPC told Appleby that the coverage in subsequent

Games has built on what Sydney delivered. More countries are buying broadcast rights to the Paralympic Games. What is less well known is whether this increased profile translated into long term improved public perception, greater funding or other opportunities. For instance, only a few select athletes in Australia and abroad may now be recognized as elite performers but it is debatable whether this has transcended to all levels and whether the bias and prejudice of athletes with disability not being considered, at least publically, as true 'athletes' has changed (Appleby, 2007).

Sport Delivery to Paralympic Athletes

Linked closely to operational partnership between SOCOG/SPOC and the access culture fostered by the OCA was the phenomenal Games and sport competition experience delivered to Paralympic athletes (Cashman, 2008). Coupled with Appleby's (2007) approach of focusing specifically on the elite nature of the athletic performance, the Sydney 2000 Paralympic Games provided the entire infrastructure and support the athletes needed. The Paralympians used the Olympic village, venues, transport and planning overlay albeit with a slightly reduced number of venues due to different sports. As a result, performances hit a new level of excellence. The debate about the technology and the equipment used by athletes (wheelchairs, prostheses etc.) on the track, in tennis, wheelchair rugby and cycling engaged the public. The technology of prosthesis and wheeled equipment is advancing all the time and athlete performance are continuing to improve. Appleby was told that it was the athletes that were driving the need for greater advances in technology, rather that the technology driving the athletes (Appleby, 2007). However, a continuing issue with technology is that of the divide between the developed and developing world that creates further inequities for those athletes (Cashman, 2008).

As Cashman (2008) notes, what is not recognized by those outside of the Paralympic family is that the delivery of sport at a Paralympic Games is more complex and challenging than that of the Olympics. While there are 10 less Paralympic sports in 2000 compared with the 28 Olympic sports, Paralympic sports are then divided by as many as seven disability categories as well as by gender. With athletic classification, Paralympic sports are more complicated than for Olympic events through protocols, regulations and adaptations for disability. This was compounded with the introduction of the two new sports in 2000 of sailing and wheelchair rugby as well as the increase of 22 events for athletes with an intellectual disability. Yet, Sydney highlighted that with these challenges were efficiencies in having the same competition managers across the Olympics and the Paralympics. The other major innovation was the establishment of the SOCOG sports commission, which facilitated these efficiencies for sport competition delivery outside the politics of the organising committees (Cashman, 2008).

Education and Disability Awareness

A major legacy from Sydney 2000 was education and disability awareness and this was certainly what a great deal of media attention focused on in the lead up to, during and after the Games (Gare, 2000). The other component of education was about the Paralympics and Paralympic sport. The education legacy can be divided into: staff; volunteers; and the general public. All staff, volunteers and contractors working on the Games had disability awareness training that was facilitated through the production of a Paralympian specific disability awareness training video and program (Darcy, 2001). The aim of the training program was to introduce volunteers on how to live and work with people with a disability. They learned to focus on a person's abilities – the Paralympics was really about what people can do, not what they can't do. As Appleby notes, 'As able bodied people many of us would be out run, out swum by many of the athletes with a disability'. The real legacy in this area is that volunteers and staff took their education and, more importantly, their first hand experiences with them into the community and business where they will have an ongoing greater understanding of people with disabilities (Appleby, 2007).

As Cashman (2006a, pp. 237-239) notes, SOCOG organised an ambitious and innovative Olympic 2000 National Education Program for Australia's 10,500 school communities from 1997 to 2000. This included a Paralympic component and was well received by a post Games evaluation of the programs. The Secretary General of the IPC, Mr. Xavier Gonzalez, notes that:

> '......the IPC is getting more involved in the way the Paralympic Games education programmes are being planned and delivered. Our intention is to ensure that there is a quality programme that introduces the Paralympic values, Paralympic sport and Games to school children - not only a spectator programme. Sydney is the example we refer to'.

Further discussion of the education programme will be discussed later in the Australian legacy section.

Post Games Evaluation and Knowledge Transfer

The Sydney 2000 Olympic Games became the first Olympic Games where Games evaluation and knowledge transfer were a foundation to Games planning and on selling of knowledge (Halbwirth & Toohey, 2001). The same cannot be said for the Sydney 2000 Paralympic Games outside of what was common to the organising of the Olympics. Paralympic knowledge was not valued as much as Olympic knowledge. As such, the reports noted earlier became important documents for the IPC and future host cities. Sydney was the first Paralympic Games to complete a detailed post Games report (Sydney Paralympic Organising Committee, 2001) and an access specific Post Games Report (Olympic Co-ordination Authority, 2001). These reports were also supplemented through a third-party assessment of the Olympic and Paralympic Disability Advocacy Service (2000), which was a government funded project to assist and document any identified problems by the disability community with access to the Sydney 2000 Olympic and Paralympic Games. A full third party assessment related to legacy which was completed by Cashman (2006), and Cashman and Darcy (2008). These documents together with the disability education and awareness training became part of Beijing leading up to the Games but not so after the Games have ended.

The other knowledge transfer that occurred to Athens as part of education was courtesy of an 'Education Partnership' between SOCOG, The Greek Government and the University of Technology, Sydney. Some 100 Greek postgraduate students studied at UTS for a Master of Sport Management degree and simultaneously held operational roles with SOCOG and SPOC in preparation for Athens 2004. Most of these people went back to operational positions with the Athens Organising Committee with a significant number having positions with the Athens Paralympic Organising Committee. This in itself was an important legacy for Greece and Athens, which had very different cultural approaches to disability (Cashman and Darcy 2008). As Appleby (2007) identified, through opening up SPOC to people from outside of the Paralympic and disability sport communities, many staff also developed a passion and moved on to other disability related opportunities.

Australian Legacy: Community Response and Disability Awareness

The previously mentioned record television coverage and ratings, ticket sales and bumper crowds at many of the Paralympic events are all indicators of community response to the Sydney 2000 Paralympic Games. Arguably the most outstanding strategy devised by SPOC and the community development manager Donna Ritchie was the very successful *Reaching the Community Program* (SPOC 1998a) that targeted school children and seniors. It offered one of the greatest potential legacies of the Paralympics. Darcy (2003) reported that some people with disabilities noted that during the Games school children had openly approached them to see what sport they participated in (Stern 2001). Writing at the end of the Games, Australian Paralympian swimmer and swimming captain, Priya Cooper believed that:

> '......the Paralympics transformed Australia's perception of people with disabilities and added that this was a legacy that must be nurtured. She added that: 'the Games also left an everlasting social legacy for a generation of schoolchildren who witnessed first-hand the Games and athletes of all nations, and will grow up appreciating our sporting skills and be more accepting of all people with disabilities.'

Horin (2000) believed that the Paralympics had raised the nation's consciousness' and was a positive and possible life-changing experience for many Australians. About 320,000 school children attended the Games. They learned about disability in their school curriculum and they will never forget the achievements they saw performed (Appleby, 2007). Does the success of the attendance at the Paralympics equal improved disability awareness amongst the non-disabled public? Darcy (2003) identifies this as the outcome most discussed by politicians and the media. Yet, as Darcy (2003) and Appleby (2007) state, this can only be pointed to anecdotally as no research was conducted to affirm this before, during or after the Games. It was a lost opportunity. As previous research by Wilhite, Muschett, Goldenberg and Trader (1997) suggests that even school children involved in a Paralympic inclusive sports program may not have a positive attitude change towards people with disabilities. Certainly the case study by Darcy and Thomson (cited in Cashman & Tremblay, 2008) suggests that the positive images of athletes with disabilities competing in sport was an empowering image and one that challenged the stereotypes of disability that are portrayed in the media and film (Goggin and Newell 2001). In future Paralympic Games there is a need to research these and other aspects of legacy.

Australian Paralympic Movement

The Paralympians who competed at Sydney 2000, future Paralympians and the Australian Paralympic Committee have been the recipients of a lasting legacy. In 2006 and 2007 the APC in conjunction with Woolcott Research sought to monitor and analyse Australian attitudes towards the Paralympics and Paralympians (Australian Paralympic Committee, 2008). The key findings are:

- 93 per cent of Australians believed that Paralympic athletes were elite athletes who train as hard as able-bodied athletes and 87 per cent believed they should receive the same or more funding than Olympic athletes;
- 71 per cent of Australians would like to know more about the personal stories of the Paralympic athletes and 72 per cent think Paralympians do not receive the recognition they deserve in the media;
- 57 per cent of Australians followed the success of the Australian Paralympic Team in Athens; and
- Television and newspapers are the preferred media used by people to follow the Games (Australian Paralympic Committee, 2008).

As Darcy and Cashman (2008) suggest, the Paralympics have left a positive legacy as Paralympians continue to be highly regarded by the Australian public. Yet, there are questions as to whether these positive feelings translate into greater recognition for individual Paralympic athletes. What is not in dispute is the increased levels of Paralympic funding.

Increased Paralympic Funding

Higher levels of government funding to the Australian Paralympic Committee are a direct legacy of Sydney 2000 including coaching scholarships from the Australian Sports Commission to athletes with a disability. Now, national recognition is given to athletes with a disability in the national sports awards programs (Appleby, 2007). The Paralympics had a high level of political patronage, which has been converted into financial support (Darcy & Cashman, 2008, p. 222). Table 2 shows that the ASC grants to the APC more than doubled in the three years before the Sydney 2000 Paralympic Games and surged again before the 2004 Athens Paralympic Games. This table also shows the ASC regard for the Paralympics with an increasing proportion of funding (55%- 85%) compared to the 15% for 10 other disability sports groups.

Table 2: Grants to the Australian Paralympic Committee from the Australian Sports Commission

Year	APC/Paralympic grants	Grants other disabled groups	Total/ASC disabled grants	Percentage of APC grant to the total grants
1994–95	$650,000	$543,000	$1,193,000	54.5
1995–96	$1,000,000	$558,600	$1,558,600	64.2
1996–97	$837,200	$651,900	$1,489,100	56.2
1997–98	$995,000	$589,600	$1,584,600	62.8
1998–99	$1,975,000	$592,900	$2,567,900	76.9
1999–2000	$2,239,500	$571,000	$2,810,500	79.7
2000–01	$2,090,000	$1,009,700	$3,099,700	81.3
2001–02	$3,080,000	$710,323	$3,790,323	81.3
2002–03	$3,500,000	$720,123	$4,202,123	83.3
2003–04	$3,800,000	$813,000	$4,613,000	82.4
2004–05	$5,750,000	$719,593	$6,469,593	88.9
2005–06	$5,470,000	$864,000	$6,334,000	86.4
2006–07	$5,323,300	$894,905	$6,218,205	85.6

Source: Annual reports of the Australian Sports Commission (Cashman & Darcy, 2008, p. 223)

Mainstreaming Sport

Another important legacy in Australian sport has been the integration of disability sport with mainstream sport allowing for better training, coaching and officials. For example, Appleby was a Director on the Board of Basketball Australia and their responsibility covers all aspects of basketball in Australian including the wheelchair basketball teams. As Appleby (2007) notes, Greg Hartung, President of the Australian Paralympic Committee said in a 2006 newsletter:

> 'I believe that the mainstreaming partnerships between the APC and national sporting organizations are bearing fruit. The result is that athletes and their coaches are better supported and can focus on their preparation'.

This approach is administered through the Sport CONNECT program that seeks to partly tie National Sport Organisation (NSO) funding to their performance in disability inclusion (Australian Sports Commission, 2009a). The program is regularly evaluated with organizations gaining a hierarchal accreditation from green to platinum, with levels and funding being revoked based on performance. The program and NSOs have generally been quite successful. Yet, significant organisational constraints and cultural issues have been identified with certain NSOs, which suggests that there are still issues in mainstreaming disability sport.

The focus of government funding on one elite event, organization and sport development approach has also created great deal of concern as to access to disability sporting opportunities at the grassroots level. Quite simply, very little funding is available at the grassroots level and there are significant constraints that people with disabilities face if they want to participate in sport and recreation. People with disabilities in Australia have significantly lower participation rates than the rest of the community (Garber, Allsworth, Marcus, Hesser, & Lapane, 2008; Murphy & Carbone, 2008; Vanner, Block, Christodoulou, Horowitz, & Krupp, 2008). *The Crawford Report* made significant comment on these issues as part of a review of the funding of Australian sport (Independent Sport Panel, 2009). The ASC have commissioned research to better understand community sport and recreation needs of the Australian community people with disabilities (Australian Sports Commission, 2009b).

Education

As discussed in the international section on education, a *Disability Education Program* was delivered as part of the Olympic education programme with the objective to advance the discussion of disability, diversity and inclusion in the school curriculum. This program has continued and expanded since 2000 with the support of the Australian Sports Commission (ASC) and may provide the longest lasting legacy. As Table 3 indicates, from 1996 to 2008 the *Disability Education Program* has been delivered 1966 times to some 38,318 individuals including over one thousand people overseas predominantly from Asia and the South Pacific. The ASC has commissioned research to evaluate the impact of the disability education program, which will be due to report in mid-2010 (Australian Sports Commission, 2009b).

Table 3: The number of people involved in the delivery of the Disability Education Program 1996 to 2008

Australia	
Coaches:	5232
Students:	16,882
Teachers:	7130
Others:	8004
Total attendance:	37,248
International	
Coaches:	0
Students:	32
Teachers:	0
Others:	1038
Total Attendance:	1070
Overall Attendance:	
Coaches:	4626
Students:	16,323
Teachers:	6713
Others:	8645
Total Attendance:	38,318

Source: (Darcy & Cashman, 2008b, p. 220)

Infrastructure

One of the conventional wisdoms is that hosting the Paralympic Games will bring with it an improved level of accessibility for all those involved (e.g. Davis, 1996; Higson, 2000). Certainly one of the major motivations and legacy of the Olympics is generally urban regeneration and improved sporting infrastructure. Appleby (2007) was convinced that there was a steep rise in understanding about access issues for people with disability. Certainly Sydney had significant access issues, particularly with many of its sporting and cultural venues such as the Sydney Opera House (Darcy, 2003). As a result of the Games, many buildings made adjustments for wheelchair access and the main streets became access friendly for wheelchair and for those with visual impairments. The improvements that took place then helped the disability community long after the Games were over (Appleby, 2007). As previously discussed, the operational partnership between SOCOG and SPOC meant that there was the shared responsibility for planning and the operational delivery of the Games. As Appleby noted there was an emphasis on developing expertise from outside the disability sporting community so those within SOCOG and SPOC may not have given disability and access issues the prominence they deserved. However, these organizations are charged with an event focus rather than with a wider community and social sustainability agenda.

Others commentators regard the assertion that the Sydney 2000 Paralympic Games were the catalyst for the high level of access provisions as naïve. Access provisions and improvements could not have been made without a highly sophisticated approach requiring a human rights framework, building codes that include access considerations and Australian Standards for access and mobility (Darcy, 2003; Fox, 1994, 2000, 2001). Nowhere has the Paralympic movement benefitted from the political advocacy of the disability politic than the Sydney 2000 Paralympic Games (Darcy, 2003, 2008a, 2008b). In particular, the very lack of disability expertise within SOCOG and SPOC created a series of significant constraints for spectators, volunteers and employees with disabilities that culminated in a series of complaint cases and Federal court actions through the Australian Human Rights and Equal Opportunity Commission ("Maguire v SOCOG [HREOCA H pp. 99/115]" 2000; "Maguire v SOCOG [HREOCA H pp.99/115]," 1999; Olympic & Paralympic Disability Advocacy Service, 2000). It wasn't until the responsibility for the overall accessibility of the Games was handed over to the Olympic Coordination Authority that access was systematically included within operational planning (Darcy, 2008a, 2008b). What is certain is that the speed of access changes would not have been possible without Sydney's winning of the Sydney 2000 Olympic and Paralympic Games (Darcy, 2003).

It should be noted that one of the major contributors to the accessibility of the 2008 Beijing Paralympic Games was use of IPC accessibility consultants Nick Morris and Apostolos Rigas both of whom gained their experience through their positions with SOCOG, SPOC and as consultants (International Paralympic Commitee, 2008).

Summary

The above discussion takes the best available sources and research on the Sydney 2000 Paralympic Legacy and reinterprets legacy through the lens of the tenth year since the event. With the luxury of time, other sources and an insider's perspective Figure 1 suggests that the Sydney 2000 Paralympic Legacy can be conceptualised through an international and domestic construct and sport stakeholder and event/social/community stakeholder perspectives.

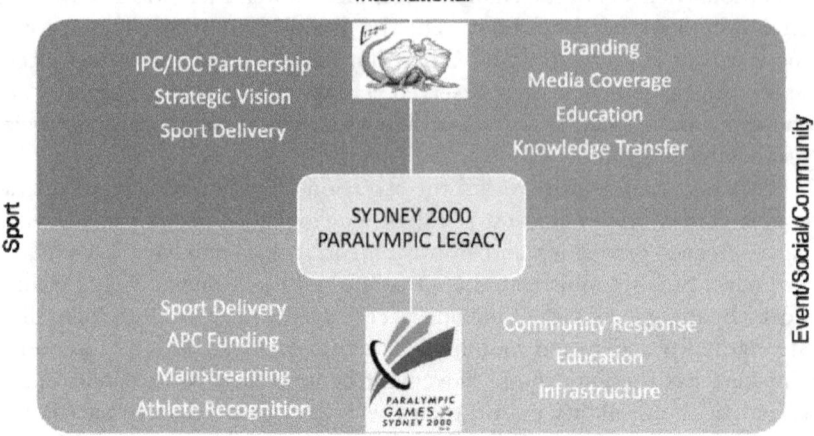

Figure 1: Legacy Matrix

As DePauw and Gavron (2005, pp. 241-256) note, there are a series of perennial and ongoing challenges for disability sport two of which were highlighted by the Sydney 2000 Paralympic Games and are still unresolved through to the conclusion of the Beijing 200 Paralympic Games.

Challenges

First, an area of ongoing concern for the International Paralympic Movement is the vexed area of classification and competition. This has implications for developing Paralympic sport as part of the global sport event calendar. Put quite simply, sport is a competition and competition should be easily understood and require little interpretation. Paralympic sports like wheelchair basketball require little interpretation as the game is similar to stand up basketball and the winner is the team that scores more baskets. While there is a complexity to the configurations of the team on the court based on an allocated point classification system, this is largely invisible to the spectating public. Yet, in swimming and other multiple classification races the results are delayed and there is not a simply understood result. This created confusion not only amongst the general public but also the sports journalists covering the events. Second, Sydney saw the controversial exclusion of athletes with intellectual disabilities due to a challenge with the classification system (Jobling, Jobling, & Fitzgerald, 2008). This critical incident raised many issues with regards to who is included within the Paralympic family from a disability perspective and what levels of ability should be able to compete. This question has a complex crossover between classification systems, sport development strategies and the way that the IPC will market the Paralympic Games into the future. The trend in Paralympic sport to become more sport specific rather than disability specific has occurred for a number of reasons. There are major administrative and logistics problems when, as DePauw and Gavron (2005) noted, there are over fifty 100-metre track events on the books to cater for gender and disability groups: this includes three for blind, eight for cerebral palsy, nine for amputee, six for Les Autres and seven for wheelchair users. Streamlining, based on a functional model, is an attractive alternative because it emphasises the elite athletic character of the Paralympic Games and, at the time, reduces the public confusion about a multitude of events. While streamlining is an attractive proposition, it will likely exclude the more severely disabled. There was no doubt that these issues of classification and sporting spectacle were some of the most challenging that were highlighted in the Sydney 2000 Paralympic Games.

Conclusion

Every event organising committee has a responsibility to improve the quality of the event from the previous one - to build on what has been done before and to make it incrementally better. From building the profile of the athletes, the brand, engaging the support from business, being financially responsible, taking the event to the people, the people to the event and to providing a legacy - all must be achieved. A successful event can mean different things to different stakeholders. Records broken are success. Coming in on budget with a surplus is success. Great athlete performances are a success. Extensive media coverage is success. A well thought out, planned, strategic and achievable legacy of the event is success.

So were the Sydney 2000 Paralympic Games successful?

By many criteria that can be applied, **yes**, the 2000 Games were a success. However, from a Legacy perspective there should have been a well thought out legacy strategy ownership of implementation and the sustainability of the legacy clearly articulated. As Figure 1 identified, the Sydney 2000 Paralympic Legacy can be conceptualised from an international and domestic construct and from a sport stakeholder and event/social/community community stakeholder perspectives.

Pleasingly, an ad hoc legacy from the Sydney 2000 Paralympic Games has happened to a degree but with more planning the legacy could have been powerful. Not only for an understanding of athletes with a disability as athletes and what they can do but for the community of people with disabilities. In some ways, there was an opportunity lost. We can only learn from each staging of an event and leave it to the Games organisers who follow to improve and grow the event and leave an enduring legacy.

What could others learn from the Sydney Paralympic experience about legacy?

From a domestic perspective, one part of that legacy responsibility should have been strategically bequeathed to the Australian Paralympic Committee and the National Sports Organisations. To do this would have required a well developed working relationship in the lead up to, during and after the Games had completed. This would have ensured that the organisations involved would have seen that they were going to be direct beneficiaries from their engagement. Similarly, at the international level SPOC and IPC could have been developing a knowledge transfer system of Paralympic documentation to rival that of Olympic movement. While there was knowledge transfer through the post-games documents and the movement of SOCOG/SPOC staff to future host cities, a great deal could have been done with the Paralympic specific knowledge legacy. While domestically there was a degree of legacy custody through the Olympic Coordination Authority and, its successor, the Sydney Olympic Park Authority, some 10 years post event even this body is only just beginning to consider Paralympic legacy where Olympic legacy has been much more consciously considered and celebrated (Hay & Cashman, 2008). Lastly, a great deal of what is regarded as the event/social/community legacy is without a research base and remains largely anecdotal. Future host cities have the opportunity to redress this situation through well-planned research programmes. We leave this challenge with them.

References

Appleby, L. (2007) *Legacy of Sydney Paralympics*. Paper presented at the Taiwan Olympic Committee Event Management Seminar for Deaf Olympics & World Corporate Games, Taiwan - Cities of Taipei and Kaohsiung.

Australian Paralympic Committee (2008) Did you know? (Available at: http://paralympic.com.au/Media/Didyouknow/tabid/448/Default.aspx (accessed on 15th April 2008)

Australian Sports Commission (2009a) Sport CONNECT, Available at: (http://www.ausport.gov.au/ http://www.ausport.gov.au/participating/disability/get_involved/pathways).

Australian Sports Commission (2009b) Sport CONNECT Research Update: Identifying the sporting needs of people with disability Available at: (http://www.ausport.gov.au)

Carlsen, J., & Soutar, G. (2000) Event evaluation research. *Event management*, 6(4), 247-257.

Cashman, R. (2006a) *The bitter-sweet awakening: the legacy of the Sydney 2000 Olympic Games*. Walla Walla Press in conjunction with the Australian Centre for Olympic Studies, University of Technology, Sydney.

Cashman, R. (2006b) Chapter 10: Paralympic Games *The bitter-sweet awakening: the legacy of the Sydney* 2000 *Olympic Games* (pp. 226-250). Petersham, NSW: Walla Walla Press.

Cashman, R. (2008) Chapter 8 - The delivery of sport. In R. Cashman & S. Darcy (Eds.), *Benchmark Games: The Sydney* 2000 *Paralympic Games* (pp. 141-160). Petersham, NSW Australia: Walla Walla Press in conjunction with the Australian Centre for Olympic Studies.

Cashman, R., & Darcy, S. (Eds.). (2008) *Benchmark Games: The Sydney* 2000 *Paralympic Games*. Petersham, NSW Australia: Walla Walla Press in conjunction with the Australian Centre for Olympic Studies.

Cashman, R., & Tremblay, D. (2008) Chapter 6 - Media. In R. Cashman & S. Darcy (Eds.), *Benchmark Games: The Sydney* 2000 *Paralympic Games* (pp. 99-122). Petersham, NSW Australia: Walla Walla Press in conjunction with the Australian Centre for Olympic Studies.

Chalip, L. (2004) Beyond Impact: A General Model for Sport Event leverage. In B. Ritchie & D. Adair (Eds.), *Sport Tourism: Interrelationships, Impacts and Issues* (pp. 226-252). on-line e-book: Channelview Publications.

CTV Olympics (2010) Record hours of coverage for Paralympic Games, Available at: (http://www.ctvolympics.ca/news-centre/newsid=11882.html)

Darcy, F. (2001) "The Best Ever" - Volunteering at the Sydney 2000 Olympics. *Australian Journal of Parks and Leisure*, 4(2), 15-17.

Darcy, S. (2001) A Games for Everyone?: Planning for Disability and Access at the Sydney 2000 Games. *Disability Studies Quarterly*, 21(3).

Darcy, S. (2003) The politics of disability and access: the Sydney 2000 Games experience. *Disability & Society*, 18(6), 737-757.

Darcy, S. (2008a) Chapter 5 - Planning. In R. Cashman & S. Darcy (Eds.), *Benchmark Games: The Sydney* 2000 *Paralympic Games* (pp. 74-98). Petersham, NSW Australia: Walla Walla Press in conjunction with the Australian Centre for Olympic Studies.

Darcy, S. (2008b) Chapter 9 - Infrastructure. In R. Cashman & S. Darcy (Eds.), *Benchmark Games: The Sydney* 2000 *Paralympic Games* (pp. 161-182). Petersham, NSW Australia: Walla Walla Press in conjunction with the Australian Centre for Olympic Studies.

Darcy, S., & Cashman, R. (2008a) Chapter 12 - Legacy. In R. Cashman & S. Darcy (Eds.), *Benchmark Games: The Sydney* 2000 *Paralympic Games* (pp. 218-231). Petersham, NSW Australia: Walla Walla Press in conjunction with the Australian Centre for Olympic Studies.

Darcy, S., & Cashman, R. (2008b) Chapter 12: Legacy. In R. Cashman & S. Darcy (Eds.), *Benchmark Games: The Sydney* 2000 *Paralympic Games* (pp. 218-231). Petersham, NSW Australia: Walla Walla Press in conjunction with the Australian Centre for Olympic Studies.

Davis, S. (1993) *Volunteering: Principles, Policies People*. Perth? Volunteer Centre of Western Australia.

Davis, T. (1996) The most accessible Games. *Paraplegia News,* 50(11), 40-42.

DePauw, K. P., & Gavron, S. J. (2005) *Disability and Sport* (8th ed.). Champaign, IL: Human Kinetics.

Fox, M. (1994) Access standards and legislation in Australia. *Quad Wrangle - the Journal of the Australian Quadriplegic Association,* 12(3), 10-12.

Fox, M. (2000) Housing for the Future - The Sydney Olympic & Paralympic Games Experience *Disability World,* 3(June/July), Available at: (http://www.disabilityworld.org/June-July2000/access/Housing.html.

Fox, M. (2001) *The Accessible Games.* Paper presented at the Centre for Accessible Environments.

Freeman, R. E. (1983) Strategic Management: A stakeholder approach. *Advances in Strategic Management,* 1, 31-60.

Garber, C. E., Allsworth, J. E., Marcus, B. H., Hesser, J., & Lapane, K. L. (2008) Correlates of the Stages of Change for Physical Activity in a Population Survey. *American Journal of Public Health,* 98(5), 897.

Gare, S. (2000, 14-15 December 2000) Awareness is the aim of the Games. *Weekend Australian,* p. 22.

Goggin, G., & Newell, C. (2001) Crippling Paralympics? Media, Disability and Olympism. *Media International Australia,* 97(November 2000), 71-83.

Halbwirth, S., & Toohey, K. (2001) The Olympic Games and knowledge management: A case study of the Sydney organising committee of the Olympic Games. *European Sport Management Quarterly,* 1(2), 91-111.

Hall, C. M. (1999) Rethinking collaboration and partnership: A public policy perspective. *Journal of Sustainable Tourism,* 7(3), 274-289.

Hay, A., & Cashman, R. (2008) *Connecting cities: Mega Event Cities, SOPA for Metropolis* 2008. Sydney, N.S.W.: Metropolis Congress.

Heath, J. (1996) 1996 Atlanta Paralympic Games. *Link,* 5(4), 16-23.

Higson, R. (2000, 11-12 November 2000) The Enabling Games. *Weekend Australian Magazine,* pp. 50-52.

Horin, A. (2000, 2 November 2000) After the Paralympics, priorities. *The Sydney Morning Herald,* p. 41.

Independent Sport Panel (2009) The Future of Sport in Australia (The Crawford Report) Available at: (http://www.sportpanel.org.au/internet/sportpanel/publishing.nsf/Content/crawford-report)

International Paralympic Commitee (2000). TheParalympian. *2000*(4), 3

International Paralympic Committee (2008) Paralympic planning for Beijing 2008. Available at: (http://www.paralympic.org/Media_Centre/News/General_News/2006_2009_-29_a.html) (accessed 16th January 2010).

International Paralympic Committee (2009) Paralympic Media Awards 200 Available at: (http://www.paralympic.org/IPC/Awards/-Paralympic_Media_Awards/Paralympic_Media_Awards_2009.-html?calendar.box.year=2010&calendar.box.month=0)

Jobling, A., Jobling, I., & Fitzgerald, H. (2008) Chapter 11 - The inclusion and exclusion of athletes with an intellectual disability. In R. Cashman & S. Darcy (Eds.), *Benchmark Games: The Sydney 2000 Paralympic Games* (pp. 201-216). Petersham, NSW Australia: Walla Walla Press in conjunction with the Australian Centre for Olympic Studies.

Maguire v Sydney Organising Committee for the Olympic Games (Internet) [2000] (Human Rights and Equal Opportunity Commission No H 99/115 2000).

Maguire v Sydney Organising Committee for the Olympic Games (Ticket Book) [1999] (Human Rights and Equal Opportunity Commission No H 99/115 1999).

Mitchell, R. K., Agle, B. R., & Wood, D. J. (1997) Toward a Theory of Stakeholder Identification and Salience: Defining the Principle of Who and What Really Counts. *The Academy of Management Review,* 22(4), 853-886.

Murphy, N. A., & Carbone, P. S. (2008) Promoting the participation of children with disabilities in sports, recreation, and physical activities. *Pediatrics,* 121(5), 1057.

Olympic & Paralympic Disability Advocacy Service (2000) *Final Report to the Department of Family and Community Services.* Sydney: Commonwealth Department of Family and Community Services.

Olympic Co-ordination Authority (1996). *Access Guidelines* (1st ed.). Sydney: Olympic Co-ordination Authority.

Olympic Co-ordination Authority (1998) *Access Guidelines* (2nd ed.). Sydney: Olympic Co-ordination Authority.

Olympic Co-ordination Authority (1999) *Access Guidelines* (3rd ed.). Sydney: Olympic Co-ordination Authority.

Olympic Co-ordination Authority (2000) *Sydney 2000 Access Guide to the Olympic and Paralympic Games.* Homebush Bay, N.S.W.: Olympic Co-ordination Authority.

Olympic Co-ordination Authority (2001) *Accessible Operations Post Game Report - Sydney 2000 Olympic and Paralympics Games.* Sydney: Olympic Co-ordination Authority.

Preuss, H. (2007) The Conceptualisation and Measurement of Mega Sport Event Legacies. *Journal of Sport & Tourism,* 12(3), 207 - 228.

Sautter, E. T., & Leisen, B. (1999) Managing stakeholders a Tourism Planning Model. *Annals of Tourism Research,* 26(2), 312-328.

Schantz, O. J., & Gilbert, K. (2001) An Ideal Misconstrued: Newspaper Coverage of the Atlanta Paralympic Games in France and Germany. *Sociology of Sport Journal,* 18, 69-94.

Smith, A. (2009) Theorising the Relationship between Major Sport Events and Social Sustainability. *Journal of Sport & Tourism,* 14(2), 109 - 120.

Sydney Olympic Park Authority. (2009) *Master Plan 2030.* Homebush Bay, N.S.W.: Sydney Olympic Park Authority.

Sydney Paralympic Organising Committee (1997) *Paralympic Games: Sydney 2000: information kit*. Sydney: Sydney Paralympic Organising Committee.

Sydney Paralympic Organising Committee (2001) *Paralympic Post Games Report (1 Vol)*. Sydney: SPOC.

Vanner, E. A., Block, P., Christodoulou, C. C., Horowitz, B. P., & Krupp, L. B. (2008) Pilot study exploring quality of life and barriers to leisure-time physical activity in persons with moderate to severe multiple sclerosis. *Disability and Health Journal,* 1(1), 58-65.

Wilhite, B., Muschett, C. A., Goldenberg, L., & Trader, B. R. (1997) Promoting inclusive sport and leisure participation: evaluation of the Paralympic Day in the Schools model. *Adapted Physical Activity Quarterly,* 14(2), 131-146.

Chapter 9
Athens 2004

Personal Reflections
Mary A. Hums

Introduction

In 2004, the Olympic Games showcased their heritage by returning to Athens, Greece which of course was the spiritual home of the Ancient Olympic Games. Exactly two weeks after the closing ceremony of the Olympic Games, the Paralympic Games kicked off, celebrating with their own opening ceremony which highlighted Greek culture, history, and the symbolic representations of air, water, and a large olive tree which covered the infield of the Paralympic Stadium. From a spectators' viewpoint the Paralympic opening ceremony was truly inspiring.

A Short Background

This chapter is written from the perspective of someone who has both practical and academic experience with the Paralympic Games. Particularly, though, this piece revolves around my experience working at the 2004 Athens Paralympic Summer Games. For my sabbatical from the University of Louisville, where I am a Professor of Sport Administration, I decided to move to Athens, Greece for five months and work at both the Olympic and Paralympic Games. Much of my early months there were spent as an Olympic volunteer with Competition Management for the Softball venue at the Helliniko Sport Complex. At the same time, I was also employed as a paid staff member by the Athens Organising Committee (ATHOC) as the Sports Information Manager for the sport of Goalball. In that capacity, I worked at offices both in the Paralympic Village and also at the competition venue at the Faliro Sports Pavilion, although my main responsibilities were at the competition venue.

I also have an interesting point of comparison for the Paralympic Games. From 1992-1994, I lived in Atlanta, Georgia and worked as a volunteer in Sports Information with the sport of Athletics at the 1996 Summer Paralympic Games. In addition to living in Athens for five months, I also had the good fortune to travel to Athens twice a year for five years from 1999-2003 to teach in the Masters program which my university offered in Athens with a local partner college. Hence, I had the ability to observe two cities, Atlanta and Athens, during Olympic and Paralympic Games preparation and operation. In addition, I also worked at the 2010 Vancouver Winter Paralympic Games as a volunteer Team Leader with Event Services at the University of British Columbia Thunderbird Arena, home venue to sledge hockey. As such, I will occasionally weave examples from those Games into this chapter.

Working the Athens 2004 Games – One Sport Manager's Daily Perspective

The Athens 2004 Games marked the first Summer Games which were fully staged by a unified organizing committee known as ATHOC and often referred to by the locals as 'The Company'. Up until that time, the Olympic Games and Paralympic Games, which took place in the same cities approximately two weeks apart, were operated by two different organizing committees. As one can imagine, from a managerial point of view, that was a rather bulky set-up, which at times resulted in redundancies, oversights, and communication issues in the host cities.

What was it like to work as a sport manager at the Paralympic Games on a daily basis? As those of us who work in the industry know, there is really nothing glamorous about working as a sport manager. The days are long and filled with tasks from the mundane to the sublime. So why do we choose to work in the sport industry? Because we love the atmosphere and the challenge. Why did I work the Paralympic Games? For me, from a sport management perspective, there is nothing more exciting than being part of an international event featuring elite athletes from around the world representing their countries at the highest level of competition. This is true of the Paralympic Games. Granted, as a sport manager, one never gets to be a spectator and watch the events, but being around people from all over the world and being a part of the management team that makes the event happen is beyond words. Plus, as a professor of Sport Management, working at the Paralympic Games provides me with an endless array of stories to pass along to my students in class. This way, they also learn about the Paralympic Games and the preparation and work that goes into making an event of this magnitude successful.

At Goalball, on a daily basis, we were in essence running two tournaments – a 12 team men's tournament and an eight team women's tournament. While that was true, there is really nothing quite like being around elite athletes representing their countries at the highest level in their sport. The excitement is hard to match, you meet incredibly interesting people, you work exhaustingly long hours, and if you are like me, you always hope to have the opportunity to do it all over again at a future event. Given that, what follows is a description of what was it like to work the Athens Games on a daily basis as a Sport Information Manager for the sport of Goalball.

Goalball, a sport designed by people with visual impairments for people with visual impairments, has been on the Paralympic programme since 1980. The competitions in Athens were held at the Faliro Sports Pavilion, which had been a competition site for Handball and Tae Kwon Do during the Olympic Games. One nice change for the Paralympic Games was the installment of a special strip of raised floor surface which led from the locker rooms down the hallway to the training and competition areas and also to the Competition Management Office. This was added so the athletes could navigate to those areas more easily. At Faliro, the Sports Information Office received daily results and information in Braille as well as paper form. Again, very useful for many of the athletes.

Interestingly, though, the sport was going to be relatively new to China for the 2008 Beijing Games. I had a conversation with one of the people from the Chinese Paralympic delegation who indicated this to me one day when we spoke at the Paralympic Village. At the 2008 Games, the Chinese men won gold and the women took silver, so their debut was quite successful.

The first few days at the Paralympic Village very few people were around. The delegations really started arriving a week or so before the Games opened. After a few days, with all the athletes and coaches and nations' officials on site, the place and its people really began to develop a great spirit. Oddly for Athens, during those first days the weather was so cold I imagine people thought that they had come to Athens for the Winter Games. The temperature could be almost 10-15 degrees Fahrenheit colder at the Paralympic Village than down by the seaside suburbs where I lived. Eventually it did warm up. You could really sense how the activity level picked up when people started arriving. During the first days before training started we had to hand out Team Leader Manuals, transportation schedules, training and competition schedules and other various memos the delegations needed from the federation. We also got a list of contact numbers for each team in case we had to contact them for some reason. This was a good idea because we used the list extensively. I also learned about the forms we had to use if anyone requested a change/cancellation in training times or transportation. You had to get signatures from a team official on the form and then take the forms to transportation desk and then to training desk. You had to get signatures at each of those locations, too. Then you had to bring back the signed forms and give a copy to the team and we kept a copy at the Sport Information desk. Teams were supposed to make all change requests before 17:00 of the day before. We received some late requests and some unique requests, such as when one team got invited to its country's embassy for a dinner and then only needed a bus to practice and then someone else was taking the team from training to the embassy and back. Sometimes teams wanted to stay at the facility longer (that was OK) or wanted to leave earlier (that was not OK). Sometimes only a few players wanted to stay and others wanted to come back. Sometimes non-team people wanted to ride a bus with a team. During the competition days, athlete/spectator buses also ran. So do you put the team on that and cancel its return bus? What if the team's coaches change their mind? Transportation may seem easy enough, but when you get into the details, it is a challenging, yet absolutely essential, task

The first day of training was pretty chaotic. This was to be expected until everyone got into a routine. We had some lost buses and some teams which did not show up for scheduled training times. Once a bus driver took one team to training, and while the team was in the facility training, the driver's shift ended so he literally took his bus and went home! Imagine the team's surprise when the coaches and athletes emerged from training - no bus! We had to get a new bus (never easy as there were no spare buses just sitting around). The team had to wait 90 minutes for a bus to arrive to bring them back to the Paralympic Village. The next day their driver got lost. Everything happened to this one particular team, but the coach was very good natured and never ever got angry. You could tell he was not exactly happy, but he didn't cause a scene, although personally I would not have blamed him. We still had buses get lost even during competition time. Apparently a number of the drivers were from outside of Athens, had not worked the Olympic Games, and did not get enough training before driving the routes. These issues were not unique to Goalball, as similar instances affected other sports as well. Eventually though, things ran smoothly enough. While transportation can be quite complicated, I was unaware of any issues with athlete busses at my venue in Vancouver, although apparently there were some issues at the Whistler locations with having sufficient busses to move people with disabilities.

Before the Games opened, each team had a familiarization session at the competition venue, Faliro Sport Pavilion. This session allowed every team an opportunity to train on the competition court for one hour. It took two days to have every team get its hour because of the number of them. Familiarization was an opportunity to get accustomed to the playing surface, acoustics, etc. of the competition field of play. On these days, the competition venue had to be fully staffed, just as if they were competition days.

Competition were long days. A colleague picked me up every morning at 05:55. It took about 20 minutes to drive to the venue. We would park on some back streets near a marina and walk in. One thing I remember was it was dark when we arrived and dark when we would leave. As workforce members we would go through security, check in at the staff check-in, get our meal vouchers, and then pick up our office keys at the Venue Management Office. The volunteer staff I supervised consisted of eight people, five of whom were from Greece, and the others were from Germany, Poland, and the Netherlands. Only the volunteer from the Netherlands had any previous experience with the Paralympic Games, as she had helped train a Paralympic athlete who competed in Sydney. The volunteer from Poland was a student majoring in Tourism and she was hoping to promote tourism to Poland after graduation so working this event was of interest to her. One of the Greek volunteers was a person with a disability and saw the Games as a great opportunity for people with disabilities in Greece. He shared some of the difficulties he had as a person with a disability living in Athens, and how he hoped the Games would be a positive influence. He particularly mentioned the difficulties of moving around the city and having enough access to public transportation. I had two shifts of volunteers, usually 2-3 people per shift. The first thing we would do is set the day's work schedule. We would determine who wanted to see which Games (for example, the Greek volunteers wanted to watch the Greek teams), and when people wanted to eat. This allowed me to determine who would be at the office at which times so that we always had someone visible at the Sports Information desk. Although there was work to be done, I wanted to make sure the volunteers had the opportunity to enjoy the event as well, so I built times for watching Games into their schedules. It was important that their volunteer experience be a good one and one on which they would look back with good feelings. The Greek volunteers felt especially proud because the Games are a chance to showcase their home country. When I was not at the desk, the volunteers had my mobile number and they would ring me and I could get back in less than 5 minutes to try and solve any problems. The first teams would arrive each day right at about 06:55a.m. for the first game at 09:00. We had eight Games a day, some men's and some women's Games. The shift would change around 15:00 and we would repeat the same schedule routine with the next group. I'm not sure they were always used to my management style, since it was quite democratic and they had choices about what they wanted to do, but I think they liked having some input. The last game usually ended at about 21:45. I had to wait for the final results from the day to be brought over from the results area. I had to distribute them to the team mailboxes and then also fax them to the Sports Information desk at the Paralympic Village. Then I could leave, check out, and walk out to the car. Next day – back at it!

In Vancouver, I also supervised teams of anywhere between 6-12 volunteers per shift. I had to make sure they got their breaks, were able to eat, and rotated positions while working to broaden their volunteer experience. Again, many of the volunteers felt proud about Canada's production of the

Paralympic Games. I worked with different teams of volunteers every day, and over the course of the Games, maybe only 5-6 volunteers were not Canadians, and all of my volunteers were from North America. This did not surprise me, however, with hockey being such a popular sport in Canada.

The facility in which I worked in Athens, Faliro Sports Pavilion, is one of the few Olympic and Paralympic venues which remain operative today in Athens. The Pavilion now serves as a multi-purpose indoor sport facility. The Olympic Sports Hall, which hosted wheelchair basketball, serves as home court for the Greek National Team and also Panathinaikos basketball club, while Helliniko Indoor Arena, home to wheelchair rugby, now is the home court for the Panionios basketball club. Some of the main Olympic venues, such as the canoe/kayak and softball facilities at Helliniko are not used at all, while others, such as the Karaiskaki Stadium (home stadium for Olympiakos football club) and Olympiako Stadio Athinas Spyros Louis (OAKA - home stadium for AEK football club) remain in full operation (World Stadiums, n.d.). However, both the softball and baseball venues are slated for use at the 2011 Special Olympics World Summer Games. Softball Games will be held at the softball stadium while football will be played at the baseball stadium (Organizing Committee Special Olympics World Games ATHENS 2011, n.d.a). The issue of what happens to Olympic and Paralympic venues after the Games end has been widely discussed. In Atlanta, the stadium for Opening and Closing Ceremonies and also Athletics, has become the home stadium for Major League Baseball's Atlanta Braves. The natatorium for swimming is now used by Georgia Tech. In Vancouver, the UBC Thunderbird Arena is now home to the hockey teams for the University of British Columbia. However, as we well know, other cities have not fared as well with venue use after the Games. For example, in Beijing, the Bird's Nest has become a tourist attraction and discussions continue about the future of the Aqua/Cube.

Around the City of Athens

While we were hard at work at Goalball, what was going on with promoting the Games in the city of Athens? Ticket sales for the event were quite strong, with approximately 750,000 tickets sold. The ticketing system was well conceived. A ticket for the day allowed the ticket-holder to attend several events. (This was a legacy from the Sydney Games.) For example, if one had a ticket for 25 September, s/he could go to swimming in the morning, tennis in the afternoon, and wheelchair basketball at night using the same ticket, which was in essence a 'day-pass'.

Every day, busloads of schoolchildren came to the Games to cheer on the athletes and get the opportunity to watch these elite athletes with disabilities compete. They brought quite a bit of enthusiasm to the venues. However, in an unfortunate incident, a bus accident involving children on their way to an event resulted in the loss of seven lives. In recognition of the children who died, the Closing Ceremonies were toned down a bit. The normal 'party atmosphere' of the event was replaced by a more somber tone as the Games came to a close. In the opening remarks, people were reminded of the tragedy. All the artistic entertainment elements of the ceremony were cancelled. Only the parts of the ceremony which included the protocol for the closing of the Games took place. While this was a tragic event, the idea of bringing school children to watch Paralympic events remained. In Vancouver, on some days we had 2000-4000 local school children bussed in to watch sledge hockey. Again, the children created a great atmosphere, particularly as these were Games at 10:00 in the morning when attendance would most likely have been quite slim. You could see how the teachers had worked with the students to prepare them. Groups of children came dressed in a country's colours and waving small flags from a particular nation. The students also had learned about the competing countries before they came to watch.

A legacy from the Athens Games was also the change from the old Paralympic logo with the five 'teardrops', to the new logo with the three 'agitos'. The official unveiling of the new logo occurred during the Closing Ceremonies. As a worker, all my uniforms and other kit were adorned with the old logo for the last time in Games history. When I worked in Vancouver, everything bore the new logo, which was first used at the 2006 Torino Winter Games. Workforce members' coats where designed for use at both the Olympic and Paralympic Games. On the front of the coats, there was space to attach a small Velcro-backed patch. Workers attached the Olympic logo for the Olympic Games and then replaced that logo with a Paralympic Games logo for those Games. The back of the jacket had a removable flap with the Paralympic logo. Underneath that flap were the Olympic rings. Other Workforce kit bore the words 'Vancouver 2010', and could be worn for either Games. This resulted in cost savings for Workforce uniforms. In Athens we were given a completely new set of kit with Paralympic logos when we worked those Games.

Around the city, Paralympic signage remained quite visible. During the Olympic and Paralympic Games, the designs, logos, and colors used in the venues and around a host city are referred at as 'The Look' of the Games. After the Olympic Games ended in Athens, much of The Look remained on streets, buildings, and overpasses and at the venues, and in many places the Olympic Rings and Athens 2004 Olympic logos were replaced with the logos for the Paralympic Games. This was in contrast to Atlanta, where after the Olympic Games ended, signage came down, leaving one relatively unaware that the Paralympic Games were even being held. In Vancouver, the venue for Opening Ceremonies displayed giant-sized Paralympic signs on the outside walls and streets leading up to the sledge hockey venue were festooned with Paralympic flags, banners, and logos.

Regarding transportation around the city of Athens during the Paralympic Games, the Olympic traffic lanes continued to be enforced so that athletes, officials, and the media would continue to move as smoothly as possible through Athens' congested streets. This same system was used in Beijing as well. Paralympic volunteers could ride public transportation for free by showing their credentials, just as Olympic volunteers could during the Olympic Games. This same system was used in Vancouver at the 2010 Winter Games. Once the Games ended, traffic patterns returned to their pre-Games status in Athens. While Athens traffic remains congested, the additional highway infra-structure as well as the expanded METRO system and tram lines built for the Olympic and Paralympic Games have helped in moving people around the city.

Another initiative which took place for the Paralympic Games was ATHOC's 'Accessible Business Guide', which according to the International Paralympic Committee (2004, p. 6), contained:

> 'E1,315 businesses in Athens, Thessaloniki, Heraklio, Magnesia and Achaia that were made accessible to persons with a disability in association with the 'Ermis - Accessible Choice Programme' and the ATHENS 2004 Paralympics. The businesses, including shops, restaurants and other service providers, were inspected by accessibility committees on criteria such as entrances, the provision of ramps, access to the ground floor, bathroom facilities and wheelchair friendly areas'.

Having personally visited Athens every year since the Games, I would be hard pressed to say I have actually noticed a significant change in accessibility in the main areas of downtown Athens. It is still quite unusual to see people with disabilities out and about on a daily basis.

In terms of media coverage, the daily English language newspaper, *Kathimerini* which is an insert in the *International Herald Tribune*, featured daily stories on the Paralympic Games. I am not sure about the local Greek language newspapers since I did not read those. I do not recall this in Atlanta's major newspaper, the *Atlanta Journal-Constitution*. However, during the Vancouver Games, every day the *Vancouver Sun* featured front page (not front Sports Page but front page of the whole paper) full color photos and headline stories from the Games. The Games were also broadcast on local television in Athens and on a selected basis in Vancouver. However, this was not the case in Atlanta. Even today, the Paralympic Games are not broadcast live on any networks in the United States.

After the Games – Life for People with Disabilities

What has happened since the Games? What legacies remain? Prior to the Games, Ioanna Karyofylli, Paralympic Games General Manager for ATHOC, stated, 'We put a major emphasis on accessibility issues, as accessibility will be a great part of our Games legacy. We have already raised the issue at ministerial level and requested specific programs and budgets from the Ministry of Culture and Transportation for the implementation of accessibility' (International Paralympic Committee, p. 5, 2002). The transportation system which was created and expanded for the Olympic Games included accessible buses and trains. The METRO system is quite accessible and has elevators and escalators. There are occasionally problems with all of these being in service, as often happens in many large cities. (I recently returned from a trip to Chicago where many of the downtown train stops are accessible only by steps. Curb cuts were added and a lift installed at the Akropoli. Parking places were designated for people with disabilities. However, anyone who has spent any amount of time in Athens realizes how difficult parking is in the city. And, similar to other major metropolitan areas, there will always be people who park in those designated places for people with disabilities who should not, and people who block areas where there are curb cuts.

The organization Disability NOW exists in Greece to aid people with disabilities. According to its website, 'The aim of Disability NOW is to produce and distribute all available disability related information, in respect of fundamental rights to independence and social participation' (Disability NOW Profile, rp. 1). According to this same website:

> 'Employment law and policy with regards to disability in Greece is one of the most active fields of action for social inclusion of disabled people. The law involves both mainstream approaches and special activation policies for the employment of disabled people, although the former has only recently been a reality by transposing EU directives for equal treatment and accessibility at work'. (Disability NOW, Employment Laws and Policies in Greece, p. 1).

Disability NOW provides a number of services for people with disabilities, including publishing the printed magazine Disability NOW, operating www.DISABLED.GR, organizing Autonomia EXPO in Athens, and editing several publications.

In terms of sport, there are glimpses that things have gotten better for people with disabilities in the city. For example, Athens will host the Special Olympics World Games in the summer of 2011 (Organizing Committee Special Olympics World Games ATHENS 2011). No doubt successfully hosting the Paralympic Games in 2004 helped make Athens a prime location for this major sporting event for people with disabilities.

A Personal Reflection of Legacy

How did working the Athens 2004 Paralympic Games create a legacy for me? I would see this in two ways – professionally and personally.

From a professional perspective, working the Paralympic Games allows me to experience managing an international workforce. As a Sport Management professor working in the United States, the vast majority of my students are from the United States. We have a handful of international students, of course, but they are in the minority. This is not reflective of today's global sport industry. Today the sport industry is part of an international marketplace and a country-specific skill set is not sufficient to be successful. Working the Games allowed me to experience the multi-cultural environment that is the sport industry.

Next, my work experience is valuable information to pass along to my students. I can use multiple 'real-life' examples of working in the sport industry. My lived experience with transportation, event management, and volunteer supervision, for example, bring stories to life in the classroom. Students always enjoy the information professors can bring from their experience in the sport industry. In this way, my students get the opportunity to learn about the Paralympic Games from someone who has been there. They also learn about what it takes to make a major international sporting event happen successfully. Hopefully they can apply some of those lessons to their lives as sport managers in the future.

From a personal perspective, I am always struck by the amazing athletic ability of the athletes competing in the Paralympic Games. I believe this is something which keeps me coming back to work at the Paralympic Games. I have had the good fortune to work the three Games I wrote about, as well as assisting the International Paralympic Committee Sports Department at the Salt Lake City Winter Games in 2002. Meeting and working with elite athletes and coaches from all over the world is inspiring to me. The athletes from developing nations are the ones I hold in highest regard. They have overcome barriers such as economic hardship, lack of training opportunities/equipment, war and conflict, and often significant discrimination in their home countries, and yet they compete and excel. These are the types of people we should admire as athletic role models.

On a different personal note, I think everyone should live in another country for at least a few months or longer. At times things are very challenging, but you always find a way to figure it out. The personal challenge is extraordinary and everyone should experience it, because you learn about another culture, another way of life, but more importantly about yourself. It is a lesson learned only by living it, not reading about in a textbook or listening to some professor drone on about it. There's a lot in life you never know, but I do know this. The time I spent in Athens working the Paralympic Games was an incredible experience. The people, the place, the Games. It was truly the experience of a lifetime. Five months seemed like five days. When I look back, what I experienced was amazing and I would do it all again in a heartbeat!!

References

Disability NOW. (n.d.a). Articles. Available at: (http://www.disabled.gr-/lib/?cat=5)

Disability NOW. (n.d.b.) Disability NOW profile. Available at: (http://www.disabled.gr/lib/?page_id=5772)

International Paralympic Committee. (2002) Ioanna Karyofylli: Athens will stage unique Games! Available at: (http://www.paralympic.org/paralympian/20023/2002313.htm)

International Paralympic Committee. (2004) Annual report. Available at: (http://www.paralympic.org/export/sites/default/IPC/Reference_Documents/2004_Annual_Report_web.pdf)

Organizing Committee Special Olympics World Games ATHENS 2011. (n.d.a). Sports venues. Available at: (http://www.athens2011.org/-en/premises.asp)

Organizing Committee Special Olympics World Games ATHENS 2011. (n.d.b). Welcome. Available at: (http://www.athens2011.org/en/-index.asp)

World Stadiums. (n.d.) Stadiums in Greece. Available at: (http://www.worldstadiums.com/europe/countries/greece.shtml)

Chapter 10
Legacies and Tensions after the 2008 Beijing Paralympic Games

Sun Shuhan and Jill M. Le Clair

Introduction

Transformations can take place at different levels and in the case of the 2008 Paralympic Games there was profound change at the national civic and personal levels for athletes, officials and the general public as disability was framed in new ways. Legacies have different meanings to both individuals and nations. The Beijing Olympic and Paralympic Games were based on the theme of 'One World One Dream.' Both were organizationally tied to three main themes; originally the 'Humanistic Games', but changed to the 'People's Games' (reflecting a harmonious society), 'Green Games' (man and nature and sustainable development), and China's innovative 'High Technology' (Price, 2008, p. 104). The Beijing Organizing Committee for the Olympic Games (BOCOG) and the National Government of China saw the Olympic and Paralympic Games as a means of demonstrating national pride, stressing its prosperity, order and economic status (deLisle, 2008) indicative of the economic importance of China on the world stage.[1] Many people in China had never seen athletes with disabilities compete in sport and the Paralympic Games held 'at home' allowed the population to see successful athletes in exciting sport events. At the same time, the Games were also a mechanism to awaken society by encouraging a greater understanding and respect for persons with disabilities. In the case of China, the aim to have a more inclusive society after the successful Games led to new programs and policies and have left an important legacy in a number of areas.

Legacy incorporates many different aspects; it includes the conventional meaning of the physical and the non-material left directly as an inheritance, as well as other contributions to national life including public discourse, policy, programs and technology. The Olympic and Paralympic Games were planned together and were seen as an impetus for profound change directly on the host city, on sport and the built environment, but in addition as an opportunity to shift the meaning of disability within the country, building on the principles of harmonious society and as part of the long term aims of the Chinese Communist Party to improve the lives of the Chinese people and 'raise all boats'. However, there were tensions between the old and new and the move from traditional collective to the individual. To help demonstrate this, the researchers[2] draw on the official policies of the national and provincial governments, and the English official newspaper the '*China Daily*' coverage in Beijing during the Games to outline some of these changes; however, it also needs to be recognized that the literature on some aspects of the Paralympic Games is very limited. The reports of the Vancouver City Council outlining plans to support economic, social and environmental sustainability were helpful in reviewing these issues (City of Vancouver, 2009, 2003).

Modernity, colonial humiliations, and the hidden disabled of the past

The history of China helps us in understanding the importance of the Games and their long-lasting impact. Overseas perceptions of China range from viewing it as a monolithic country with a repressive regime and an eco-

---

[1] It is important to remember that global technology also fundamentally changes how the Games themselves are framed and presented. What was new technology used by the media and general public at the 1996 Atlanta Games seems 'old fashioned' and 'primitive' compared with that in use in 2010 in Vancouver when one of the official legacies was the provision of funds to provide digital archives (Vancouver City Council, 2010). Also the non-accredited media internet, blogs, twitter, Skype, YouTube have changed the landscape (Miah, Garcia & Tian, 2008).

[2] Dr. Sun is a Professor and the Vice-President of the China Disability Institute, at the Renmin University of China, Beijing, China; Dr. Le Clair is the founder of the *Global Disability Research in Sport and Health Network* and a Professor on LTD from the School of Liberal Arts and Sciences, Humber College Institute, Toronto, Canada; and Yan Rui, is a PhD Candidate and Research Assistant to Dr. Sun Shuhan, at the School of Labour and Human Resources, Renmin University of China.

nomic powerhouse threatening world domination, to nostalgia about Chairman Mao and a romanticized rural countryside. At the same time, there are people who remember a country of the recent past where bicycles were the main form of transportation, and few households had televisions and consumer products. In the nineties, most people used bicycles for transportation, but economic change is reflected in the reality that "for many people, the bicycle has become history" in much of contemporary urban China (Xie, 2008, p. 7).[3]

The Beijing of the 2008 Games presented a very different reality from that of even ten years earlier with busy Beijingers fighting congestion and traffic on the six ring roads with high-rise buildings and construction everywhere, and teenagers and seniors chatting constantly on their cell phones. The vibrancy and economic activity reflectived a modernity and forward looking approach. The hesitancy to engage in the past was gone, as many Chinese both young and old seemed eager to meet visitors and communicate even if they knew no English. Varda Burstyn has called the Games the 'Circus Maximus of the planet Earth' (Lenskyj, 2000, p. ix) and hosting the Olympics and Paralympics "would mark China's transformation from outside to insider in the international community, and from underdevelopment to modernity" (Haugen, 2008, p. 159). The national government invested an enormous amount of money to present Beijing and China in its new form. The projected cost of the Beijing Games was $60 billion of public and private money, versus the $2,220 million Atlanta spent in 1996 (Shaw, 2008, p. 185). Surveys conducted after the Games showed this rebranding was effective as there was a positive shift in perspectives about China (Xin, 2008, p.3).[4]

Positive Shifts

Life for persons with disabilities before China became an economic powerhouse was difficult. Most of the country was rural with minimal technology and a strong body was key to survival; famines were common so families and individuals struggled to survive in the years before 1949 as a person with disabilities was seen to be the responsibility of each individual family, and often a source of shame and embarrassment (Gray, 2000; Jarvie, Hwang & Brennan, 2008). Persons with disabilities were regarded as a financial liability and most often hidden away, with no access to an education and if unable to do the manual labour of rural life condemned to poverty and isol-

---

3. Although the Chinese Cycling Association says at least 60 percent of Chinese people ride bicycles and there are 470 million bicycles in the country with 50 million electric powered (Xie, 2008, p.7). This reflects both the urban-rural divide and regional economic disparities.

4. It is expected that China will increase in popularity as a tourist destination with 137 m. tourists by 2020, but there was a 7.2% drop in the number of visitors in August 2008, thought to be due to tighter security and visa regulations (Xin, 2008, p. 3).

ation. The "New" China under Chairman Mao brought about change, and since the Reform and Opening Up policies began in the 1980s, government programs for persons with a disability were put in place and perspectives of disability as a whole changed.

The impact of disability was felt especially keenly in 2008 because of a major earthquake on May 12th in Sichuan, where many children were severely injured or died in their schoolrooms and the images of disabled children and their weeping parents became a part of the daily coverage by the media across the nation. The sponsor Lenovo chose four torchbearers who were survivors of the May Sichuan earthquake, one an amputee, as they were seen as heroes (Dan Na, 2008, p. 5).

China's 'Renaissance'

Historically, China felt the 'wounds' of colonialism and humiliation profoundly, and resented the stereotypes of despotism[5] (Wasserstrom, 2008). The Games were seen to be part of a Chinese renaissance where the country would host as it had done long ago in the Tang dynasty (Price, 2008, p.5), present its ancient history, and demonstrate a meeting of the East and West (Collins, 2008). In the past the Olympic and Paralympic Games were usually held in the hope of changing perceptions of the city on the world stage, but for China they were part of what is now viewed as a 'new Olympic internationalism with multidirectional flows' that operated in terms of a 'new global order' (Finlay, 2008, pp. 375-376). "Beijing's choice of logos, emblems, and slogans[6] for the Olympic and Paralympic Games all reflect the deep Chinese commitment to internationalization" (Xu G., 2008, p. 26). China in its attempts to have a successful bid went on what has been called by Joshua Kurlantzick 'China's Charm Offensive' to reframe its international image through sport using 'public diplomacy' to shape good will overseas (Cull, 2008, pp.117-118).

In moving to the world stage Beijing and China also came under criticism just as did the previous host cities of Atlanta in 1996 and Athens in 2004. There are many critics of the expense[7] and very premise of the Games (Lenskyj, 2000; Jennings, 2000; Simpson and Jennings, 1992) and China became subject to what has been called an 'anti-China campaign' as critics raised diverse issues. Others argue that the absolutist views of the west are

---

5. Wasserstrom argues that America has viewed China through a nightmare/dream framework for over a hundred years.

6. The five mascots were Beibei (a fish), Jingjing (a panda) Huanhuan (the Olympic flame), Yingying (a Tibetan antelope), and Nini (a swallow) and put together as Bei Jing Huan Ying Ni say 'Welcome to Beijing'. BOCOG Chair Lui Qi explained that the mascots "reflect the cultural diversity of China as a multiethnic country; they represent the enthusiasm and aspirations of our country" (Xu, 2008, p. 261).

7. Those opposed to the Olympic/Paralympic Games argue that the costs always overrun and the impact is rarely favourable to the taxpayer.

sometimes seen to be propaganda (Kidd and Donnelly, 2000) and that there has to be recognized that there is 'a deep divide' globally and often criticisms are 'normative and prescriptive' with a western bias (Jarvie, Hwang, & Brennan, 2008, pp.133-134).

It is interesting that political attacks were *not* directed at the Paralympic Games. Either they are thought to be the secondary event, or there is some discomfort in attacking Paralympians with disabilities, or perhaps both. Horton and Toohey argue that it is naïve to assume that the Paralympic Games will not become a terrorist target at some point as the sport 'matures' and receives more media attention (2008, pp. 194-195).

Economic and political legacy

China's government has overseen phenomenal economic growth in the past twenty years and positioning the country as a leading edge technological and business innovator was part of the Games' bid, and linked to disability. The marketing consultant Qiang Wei, stated in the *China Business Weekly* on the opening of the Games. "One of the three key themes of the 2008 Beijing Olympic Games is the People's Olympics. Thus support for the Paralympics is a channel for companies to showcase their love and care for the disadvantaged people and society." This takes place in the context that the Olympic Games had 63 sponsors whereas there were few for the Paralympic Games, but did include Lenovo Computers that provided computer equipment and access for Paralympians and the information system (Liu, 2008, p. 1).

One hundred and forty seven countries came to attend the Paralympic Games and to support their national athletes, but also to engage in furthering trade relations and diplomatic issues (Xiao, 2008, p. 2). During his visit President Horst Koehler recognized the huge challenges facing China by noting that the disabled population of China is more than 83 million which is the same size as Germany. He also praised the 2008 amendment to the 1991 disability act to promote the employment of the disabled, and the hosting of the Paralympics as important steps and illustrative of social inclusion (Koehler, 2008, p. 8; Zhao, 2008, p.8).

Language

As in the 'west' (Linton, 1998), the language around disability has changed over the last thirty years, parallel with national economic development and the improvement in standards of living and the expansion of education. In the past, people with intellectual disabilities were discriminated against and called 'crazy' or 'foolish', but the language used now is the non-judgmental 'mentally challenged' or 'intellectually challenged.' In Chinese, unlike in English, there is no differentiation between the terms handicapped, disabled and disabled people as they are all defined as persons.

The language used by Quan Wei above, in reference to disability, is similar to some of the other statements during the Games that often called for caring and consideration, that in English is reminiscent of the social welfare approach in post-war Europe (Oliver and Barnes, 1998), but also reflects a traditional focus on harmonious values, rather than on rights based demands. However, the social model of disability is increasingly becoming the norm as is the expectation of inclusion as discussed here. Also, it is not well known, but China ratified the UN Convention on the Rights of Persons with Disabilities in August 1st, 2008 (UN Enable, 2010), and this is almost two years before Canada. The Convention has strong statements about rights in sport and recreation, which sends a clear message of expectations about the future.

Linked to language, was the request to end prejudice and discrimination. Often comments were made by public celebrities or officials about the importance of changing attitudes. TV Anchor Liu Wenyan explained "I would like to take this opportunity as a Paralympic torch bearer to tell my friends with disabilities that love begins with respect and equality." (Chen Jia, 2008, p.2).

Legacy of Training and Facilities

China's National Games for the Disabled were held for the first time in Hefei, the capital of Anhui Province in 1984, but opportunities for participation since then have grown (Sun, Yan, Mao, Chao & Jin, 2011). In 2008, there were more than two million disabled athletes in China (Lan, 2008, p.3). These Games provided an impetus for supporting sport training. In 2007 the year before the Games in Beijing 3,000 athletes from across the country competed in Kunming, Yunnan Province. Chinese athletes trained in 188 provincial level sport centres and 1,264 city/prefecture centres and in 2007 838 city level sport competitions were organized for 51,975 participants. (*Xinhua News Agency*, 2008). In 2008, China sent an unprecedented number of athletes to participate in 44 international competitions in preparation for the Beijing Games and other international sport events. These included the Paralympic Games Trials, Special Olympics, and three types of deaf disability events including swimming, athletics, wheelchair tennis, wheelchair fencing, goalball, wheelchair basketball, sitting volleyball, archery, sailing, shooting, boccia for a total of 200 medals, 138 silver and 109 bronze medals (*China Disabled Persons' Federation*, 2008).

In addition to the legacy of a large number of athletes who have undergone training and experienced high performance competition a very important legacy is that of the China Disability Sports Training Centre. The government invested over $US 15 million in the construction of largest sports training centre for athletes with disabilities in the world. The CDSPC in Beijing's suburb Shunyi was used by Paralympians to prepare for the Games and will continue to be used by both Chinese athletes and foreign athletes in the future. It covers 238,235 sq metres and includes "a multi-sports training gym, a swimming hall, a goal ball hall, a cycling track, two outdoor football fields and two archery ranges" (Lan, 2008, p.3) and, athlete residences. The facility has also been designed to be fully accessible with accessible washrooms in the dorm rooms, telephones at different heights, elevators with Braille signage and so on, to ensure that athletes with diverse disabilities can access all aspects of the facility.

Growth of Paralympic sport: from being invisible to being celebrated

China's participation in the Olympic Games began in 1932 at Los Angeles with one athlete, but was absent from 1952 until 1984. China first participated in international disability sport at the 1984 Stoke Mandeville Games in New York with 24 athletes who competed in athletics, swimming and table tennis and China finished 23rd in the medal standings. (*Xinhua News Agency*, 2008a). Increased state support was provided and as is illustrated in Table 1 from a small team of 24 in 1984, participation grew to 334 athletes who competed in 2008. China from having no international standing in 1983 came first in the medal ranking in 2008 winning a total of 211 medals, with Great Britain and the USA in second and third place.

Table 1: *Participation of Chinese Athletes in the Summer Paralympic Games*

Year	Location	No. of athletes	Sports competed	Gold Medals	Silver Medals	Bronze Medals
1984	Stoke Mandeville, GBR & New York, USA	24	Athletics, swimming, table tennis	2	13	9
1988	Seoul, Korea	43	Athletics, swimming, table tennis, shooting	17	17	10
1992	Barcelona, Spain	24	Archery, athletics, boccia, cycling, equestrian, football 5-a-side, football 7-a-side, goal ball, judo, power lifting, sailing, shooting, swimming, table tennis, volleyball, wheelchair basketball, wheelchair fencing, wheelchair rugby, wheelchair tennis	11	7	7
1996	Atlanta, USA	37	6 sports	16	13	10
2000	Sydney, Australia	87	Athletics, swimming, table tennis, goal ball, judo, powerlifting	34	22	16

| 2004 | Athens, Greece | 200 | Track and field, swimming, table tennis, weightlifting, judo, shooting, archery, cycling, fencing, wheelchair tennis, sitting volleyball | 63 | 46 | 32 |
| 2008 | Beijing, China | 334 | Archery, athletics, boccia, cycling, equestrian, football 5-a-side &7 a-side, goalball, judo, powerlifting, rowing, sailing, shooting, swimming, sitting volleyball, wheelchair basketball/fencing/rugby/ tennis | 89 | 70 | 52 |

Note: The IPC reduced the number of eligible athletes with integrated disability teams. Sources[8]

Athlete development and gender

Historically, few Chinese women participated in sport and the profound change in the current extensive inclusion of female athletes reflects a huge change in the role of women in Chinese society (Fan, 1997; Jinxia, 2003; Brownwell, 1995). In the early days of disabled sport there were few competitors and very few women. However, the official IPC records indicate that in 2008, 147 countries participated with a total of 4,011 athletes, 2,628 male and 1,383 female and 2,500 coaches and officials; this was the largest number of countries and regions in the history of the Games.

The Games had a wide impact as the Chinese delegation had 547 members with a total of 334 athletes, which included 199 male athletes and 135 female athletes who participated in all 20 competition categories and nearly all classification categories (IPC, 2010). The Chinese team won a total of 211 medals with 89 gold, 70 silver and 52 bronze (2008 Beijing, 2008). This meant that another legacy was a considerable number of female athletes, coaches and officials who have international experience and can train and support upcoming athletes. The successes of Chinese female athletes also

---

8. 2008 Beijing Paralympics.Medal Tally. *Paralympic Games September 6-17*, 2008. Retrieved from http://www.china.org.cn/paralympics/node_7052638.htm
China's Paralympic History. (2008). Retrieved from http://www.china.org.cn/paralympics/2008-09/03/content_16378772.htm

were a source of great pride and were covered extensively in the media, raising awareness across the country of the potential leadership roles for girls and women in sport.[9]

Athlete transformation through sport

Participation in sport can often reframe the meaning of disability both within sport and outside it and this has been found in different cultural and national settings, globally, (Le Clair, 2009a; Legg & Steadward, 2011) and in Canada (Le Clair, 2009) and this was the case for Chinese athletes. The Games as spectacle with Jumbotrons, press interviews, television coverage, and sometimes even YouTube notoriety had significant impact of the meaning of being a Paralympian and on the daily lives of individuals. Athletes found that the Paralympic Games had special significance for them in that they obtained new opportunities, greater independence and social recognition as athletes.

Gold medallist and visually disabled, Li Yansong competed in the 4 × 100-meter relay. Li explained what the Paralympic Games meant to him:

> "Sports have changed me a lot, whether material or spiritual, it has completely changed my life. Sports have also opened a window for me, because I am a blind athlete, this way, I seem to grow wings, fly even higher."

The women's judo champion Yuan Yanping also described the impact of sport on her life outside sport which gave her increased independence.

> "We were looked after by others before, and now I'm going to care for others. Sport really has changed my life and my destiny. I am grateful to sport, it gives me motivation."

Beijing's female shooting champion, Lin Haiyan, reflected on the wider impact of the Games as being an impetus for inclusion and how the Games increased the appreciation of training and work engaged in by high performance athletes.

> "Now there is more inclusion and better accommodations for persons with a disability. People recognize us and our contributions. I participate in a number of activities as an equal after the Paralympic Games (Kooning, 2009)."

Volunteerism

The Games could not be held without the essential support of volunteers. There were 40,000 volunteers at Sydney, and 120,000 expressions of interest for the Athens Games, but the research focus has been the Olympic Games and there has been "no literature that examines the experiences and motives of volunteers in the Paralympic context" (Kellett, 2008, p. 176).

---

9. The gap between female and male participants in the Paralympic Games has been narrowing because the IPC has worked hard to increase the opportunities and training for female athletes, coaches and officials as seen in the IPC Women in Sport Committee reports (IPC 2008; 2001).

Kellett found anecdotally that that volunteers liked to learn about other people, understand the performances of the athletes and learn more about the Games themselves *and* learn a new set of skills related to the logistical matters associated with persons with disabilities as well as specific sport and equipment requirements of elite athletes (2008, pp. 176-179). There were 908,334 applications to become Beijing Paralympic Games volunteers and 44,000 Games-time volunteers were recruited from 27 nations and regions (All Access, 2008, p. 3; Nilsson & Lei, 2008, p. 1). Some employees volunteered at their own workplace as 10,000 of the 20,000 volunteers in the subway stations worked for the Subway Managing Company of Beijing. The other half consisted of student volunteers from the 28 universities in Beijing (Wang R., 2008, p. 8). To include persons with hearing impairments or Deaf visitors sign language volunteers provided support (Cheng X., 2008, p.8; Lin, 2008, p.1).

Volunteerism was not part of traditional Chinese culture as in the past support and assistance usually came from the extended family. The Games, however, brought a new volunteerism to Beijing and interestingly also included persons with disabilities themselves as volunteers. Foreign tourists found there were energetic and smiling volunteers at all the venues, eager to help. 400,000 people with a disability came to the Games venues and experienced the 'Happy Paralympics.' 5000 volunteers with a disability, disabled actors, and technical experts with a disability directly served in the venues for the Olympic Games and Paralympic Games (Two Olympic, 2009, p.1).

This volunteering allowed thousands of Chinese to come in contact with visitors, practice their English and other communication skills, and meet Paralympians and spectators with disabilities. In addition their hopes to learn about the Games were fulfilled. Some volunteers and spectators saw sports they had never seen before. Some were familiar, such as wheelchair basketball, but others like sitting volleyball or goal ball were often unknown, with different rules and requirements such as being quiet during competition so the athletes competing in a sport like goal ball could hear the ball to locate it (Li Xiaokun, 2008, p.6).

Urban Renewal and Accessible Built Environments in Beijing

Significant changes took place to shape and support the Olympic and Paralympic Games, many leaving a long term legacy, such as the highways and subway system. The profound physical change in Beijing is almost unimaginable for those who have not seen it. Historically Beijing consisted of quadrangle houses and multifamily compounds built on strict grids and lanes with strong social connections (Xu C, 2001). Starting in the 1990s some 'Old City' neighbourhoods changed and high rises and private ownership appeared alongside and sometimes replaced the traditional *hutong* and courtyard houses and subsided work-unit assigned government housing (Li, Dray-Novey, & Kong, 2007).

An accessible built environment was a very important aspect in the planning for the Beijing Games, not just for the sport facilities, but also for 'the mega spaces' that continued the spatial sophistication of the Emperors and elites of the past (Marvin, 2008). Accessibility was part of the planning of the well-known Aquatics Centre (the Water Cube) and the National Stadium (the Bird's Nest), and of the public washrooms, the transportation system and the city itself, making parks and tourist destinations like the Summer Palace more accessible.

These initiatives continued after the Games and on December 23rd, 2009 a second meeting of a specially created government committee took place in Beijing to draft 'barrier-free building regulations.' The regulations promoted and effectively protected persons with a disability; the elderly and other special interest groups, to improve accessibility to China's urban and rural buildings, services, and support policies that made a significant contribution to promote equity and support inclusion. Tang Xiaoquan, the Executive Vice-President of BOCOG and a senior official of the China Disabled Persons' Federation explained that this legacy of accessible buses, subway stations, taxis and hotels was not just for the Paralympic Games, "We mean to get the city's nearly one million handicapped population more involved in public life" (All Access, 2008, p. 3). Accommodations were made to allow access by tourists attending the Games and for Beijingers, recognizing that shopping is an important part of social integration and important for customers to access stores such as the Silk Street Market and tourist destinations (All Access, 2008, p. 3).

Repeatedly, inclusion was described as an indication of 'social progression' and a need to be more inclusive linked to surprise at the extensive changes tied to the Games; "The improvement or installation of such accessible facilities was beyond the imagination a few years ago even in Beijing, not to mention other less developed regions" (Yang, 2008, p. 4).

Transport in Beijing

Beijing is now equipped with 2,835 low-floor accessible buses and many bus stations have pathways with raised tiles within sidewalks to mark the way for the blind or those with limited vision, as well as ramps, wheelchair waiting areas, and accessibility signage. Eight of the city's subway lines were designed to make at least one of each station entrances and exits accessible for wheelchair passengers, and at least two entrances and exits to meet the accessibility needs of passengers with visual disabilities. Beijing also provided 70 barrier-free taxis for wheelchair users. Compared with Beijing in the past, it can be said that these accessibility changes to make travel for persons with a disability more accessible and more convenient were earth-shaking (Chen-Chen, 2008). However, some buses have not retained the open spaces with removable seats to allow wheelchair access, and some parking lots still do not have disabled spaces.

Fitness programs for everyone: After the Games

The National Health Regulations were passed on October 1, 2009, and August 8th was declared as National Fitness Day and a national fitness program was introduced to further support "an overall improvement of the nation's physique and health and a basic establishment of a national fitness system with Chinese characteristics" (Chinese Olympic Committee, 2005). They further recognized the importance of students, the elderly, the disabled and the special needs of rural residents. It stated that public sports facilities should be made available for the masses to participate in physical fitness activities, and services in the rural areas and also take into account local work and cultural values.

Specific examples include the opening of 139 provincial disabled sports centres, 1053 city (prefecture) level sports venues; 174 provincial disabled sports training bases, 533 city (prefecture) disabled sports training bases. 645 coaches were hired in permanent positions at the provincial level, 1301 coaches at city (prefecture) level. Ninety-six sport activities were developed for persons in the hope to provide opportunities for people with a wide range of disabilities. There are provincial Games for the Disabled that include 57 sport events that led in 2008 to the participation of 11,964 people. 784 disabled sport events were held and recreational sport activities, involving more than 62,107 athletes (China Disabled Persons' Federation, 2009a).

National Disability Policies and Social Accessibility

Television, radio and the printed press raised issues related to increasing respect for persons with disabilities and supporting accessibility and inclusion and thus the Games left a legacy of awareness about these issues. A common theme of those active in disability movements or in the Paralylmpic Games is that argued by Xiong Lei (a council Member of the China Society for Human Rights Studies) in a *China Daily* editorial the first week-end of the Games (September 6-7). He states his concerns clearly:

> "Just look around, you rarely see (in Beijing) a person with a disability, although statistics show that there are more than one million disabled people in Beijing. That means one in 15 citizens. Yet on the streets you hardly see any such persons. This fact indicates the lack of facilities to make them more mobile. ...We must learn to be more considerate, and take the needs of disabled people into account when planning buildings, streets, and other infrastructure."

Recognizing this lack of universal design in the past, BOCOG ensured that during the Games '*The Guide to Barrier-Free Services*' that included everything from Paralympic venues, transportation, hotels and shopping (BOGOC, 2008) was made available at information desks across the City.

The possibility of participating in sport events needs to be founded on support for individuals and families with disability, so that they can be included in all aspects of social life. If much of the family effort needs to be spent on the activities of daily living – using the bathroom, food preparation and so on - in addition to struggling to get in and out of the home itself, it is very difficult to participate in wider social activities like sport. In the summer following the Paralympic Games (June 18, 2009), Beijing issued a new proclamation "Specific Practices to Promote Disability Policies to provide basic social assistance, social services, a basic disability pension, compulsory education, basic medical care and employment opportunities and protective policies by 2010". By 2015 it is expected that social security and service systems for people with a disability will be more complete, the health gap between urban and rural areas significantly reduced, with rehabilitation available, support at home and more accessible transportation (Li-Wen & Le-Yahong, 2009, p.1).

There are more than 18 million people with intellectual and mental disabilities of working-age in China. With the increased awareness linked to the Paralympic Games a new interest in this issue led to approximately 30,000 families of persons with a disability being built barrier-free homes in Beijing and more than 5,000 households were remodelled in 2008. Also 12,860 household families of persons with a disability had their homes transformed in 2009.[10] These modification expenses were paid by the municipality of Beijing with an average of 4,000 Yuan being spent on each home. (City provides 2009).[11]

Cultural Impact

The cultural component of the Games includes many different aspects of dance, art, photography and music, and disability was also reframed in these events. Most spectators had not seen any performances by artists or entertainers with disabilities and so there were discussions about the unexpected skill and beauty of their performances and work. The spectacular video of amputee ballet dancers Ma Li and Zhai Xiaowei went viral globally" (She without, 2008). In the Opening Ceremonies 109 hearing impaired dancers performed 'Non-stop Dance Moves' with ballet shoes on their hands, particularly moving for the Chinese audience as one of the performers had lost a leg because of the Sichuan earthquake (Lin, 2008, p,1). Not all cultural interaction was in the formal context of performances and museums. The

---

10. The accommodations or remodelling focused on improving the activities of daily living for those with physical disabilities and improving accessibility; these included modified and accessible baths and showers with benches, squat toilets and modified kitchens, installing ramps, anti-slip surfaces, handrails, benches and anti-slip surfaces. For the deaf and blind modifications included voice activated equipment, intercoms, flashing doorbells, flashing bottles and other assistive devices.

11. From 2009 to 2011, the central government will provide 200 million Yuan each year for a total of 6 million Yuan in special funds, and to focus on care and grants to support group homes, and to support families receiving at least 500 Yuan per person each year. In addition support was provided in subsidized education and training in the workplace, but will not be addressed here.

Mid-Autumn Festival on September 15 with its special pastries called 'moon-cakes' (Ye jun, 2000, p.5), when everyone sits outside to observe the moon and drink wine or tea, was a new and special event to visitors, although Chinese athletes missed their families.

Future Challenges and Tensions

China at the national, provincial and municipal level has been influenced by the impact of the Paralympic Games. Historically, it was accepted that persons with a disability were hidden or isolated both physically and socially because of their disabilities and because of negative attitudes towards them. Now, there are diverse legacies from the Games; not only are there the obvious public indications of change such as the global symbol of the wheelchair on new disability signage indicating accessible routes on public transit, but there have also been fundamental changes in other less immediately visible aspects of society. The government has built on the high profile impact of the national pride of the successful feats of Chinese athletes at the Paralympic Games and celebrated their accomplishments to introduce policies in all aspects of society, including those related to the workplace, education, the built environment and in all aspects of sport management and organization.

With the economic boom there have been considerable resources available to support disability sport policies and programs and it is to be hoped that this continues. There are also other ongoing challenges specific to persons with a disability, some of which we suggest might be of interest for further research. Service organizations to support persons with a disability, at all levels of care, support only a small percentage of the total population in China, so the hope is that support service capability will develop. There are gaps in the literature about the Paralympic Games and disabled sport in such areas as volunteerism, grass roots training and athlete development, and research in these areas would further understanding of ongoing challenges.

China was one of the first countries to sign the UN Declaration on the Rights of Persons with Disabilities on May 3rd, 2008, but disability activists such as the Director of Handicap International China, Jean Van Wetter, have suggested a need for direct government support and for more support of NGOS with better professional training to better address the needs of disabled communities (Wang Z., 2008b, p. 6). Some activists may be impatient wanting more immediate action on all fronts, but as we have discussed, considerable change in policies and practices have taken place already and important legacies have resulted, both directly and indirectly, from the Paralympic Games.

References

All Access. (2008, September 8-14) *China Business Weekly.*, p.3.

Beijing Organizing Committee for the Games of the XXIX Olympiad. (2008 April) Guide to barrier-free services. Beijing 2008 Olympic and Paralympic Games.

Brownell, S. (2008) *Beijing's Games: What the Olympics mean to China.* Lanham, MD: Rowman & Littlefield Publishers, Inc.

_____ (1995) *Training the body for China: Sports in the moral order of the People's Republic.* Chicago: University of Chicago Press.,

Chen, J. and Lan T. (2008, September 6-7) Torch began 2-Day journey in Beijing. *China Daily*, p. 2.

Chen Chen, X. (2008) Paralympic Games in Beijing will bring change. *Shenzhen Special Zone Daily* (September, 12). Retrieved from http://sztqb.sznews.com/html/2008-09/12/content_335489.htm

Chen X. (2008, September 8) Watch my hands, read my lips. *China Daily*, p. 8.

China Disabled Persons' Federation. (2009) 2008 Statistical Bulletin of China Disabled Persons Development. Retrieved from http://www.cdpf.org.cn/sytj/content/2009-04/23/content_302-43391.htm

China Disabled Persons' Federation. (2009a, May 25) China Paralympic sports management center for media and communications department. Retrieved from http://www.cdpf.org.cn/zcfg/content/2009-05/25/content_30245191.htm

China Disabled Persons' Federation. (2008) Communiqué on major statistics of the second China national sample survey on disability. Retrieved from http://www.cdpf.org.cn/english/contactus/content/2008-04/14/content_84989.htm

China's Paralympic History. (2008) Retrieved from http://www.china.org.cn/paralympics/2008-09/03/content_16378772.htm

Chinese Olympic Committee. (2005) An outline of the national fitness programme: Goals and tasks. Official Website of the Chinese Olympic Committee. Retrieved from http://en.olympic.cn/sport_for/nfp_project/2005-06-08/121886.html.

City provides funding to thousands of families with disabled members to provide barrier-free homes (2009, April 1) *Beijing Times*, p.1. Retrieved from http://www.mof.gov.cn/

City of Vancouver, Administrative Report. (2009) Olympic and Paralympic legacy reserve fund and archives on the 2010 Winter Games. March 24. L. Mobbs, pp. 1-4. Retrieved from http://vancouver.ca/ctyclerk/cclerk/20090324/documents/a10.pdf

City of Vancouver Administrative Report. (2003) Implementation plan for Olympic legacy C. Edwards, Retrieved from http://vancouver.ca/ctyclerk/cclerk/20031021/a5.htm

Collins, S. (2008) The fragility of Asian national identity in the Olympic Games. In M.E. Price and D. Dayan (Eds.), *Owning the Olympics: Narratives of the New China*, pp. 185-209. Ann Arbor, MI: University of Michigan Press.

Cull, N. J. (2008) The public diplomacy of the modern Olympic Games and China's soft power strategy. In M.E. Price and D. Dayan (Eds.), *Owning the Olympics: Narratives of the New China*, pp. 117-145. Ann Arbor, MI: University of Michigan Press.

Dan, Na. (2008, September 8) Lenovo IT effort continues with Paralympics passion. *China Daily*, p. 5.

deLisle, J.. (2008) One world, different dreams: The contest to define the Bejing Olympics. In M.E. Price and D. Dayan (Eds.), *Owning the Olympics: Narratives of the New China,* pp. 17-66. Ann Arbor, MI: University of Michigan Press.

Fan, H. (1997) *Footbinding, Feminism and Freedom: The Liberation of Women's Bodies in Modern China*. London: Frank Cass.

Finlay, C., J. (2008) Toward the future: The new Olympic internationalism. In M.E. Price and D. Dayan (Eds.), *Owning the Olympics: Narratives of the New China*, pp. 375-391. Ann Arbor: University of Michigan Press.

Gilbert, K. & O.J. Schantz. (2008) Reconceptualizing the Paralympic movement. In K. Gilbert & O. Schantz (Eds.), *The Paralympic Games: Empowerment or Side Show?* pp. 8-18. Maidenhead, UK: Meyer & Meyer (UK) Ltd.

Gray, J. (2000) *Rebellions and Revolutions: China from the 1800s to 2000*. Toronto, ON: Oxford University Press.

Guan X. (2008, September 13-14) Number of homeless centers to double. *China Daily*, p. 3.

Haugen, H. O. (2008) "A very natural choice": The construction of Beijing as an Olympic city during the bid period. In M.E. Price & D. Dayan (Eds.), *Owning the Olympics: Narratives of the New China.* pp. 145-163. Ann Arbor, MI: University of Michigan Press.

Horton, P. & K. Toohey. (2008) It comes with the territory: Terrorism and the Paralympics. In K. Gilbert & O. Schantz (Eds.), *The Paralympic Games: Empowerment or side show?* pp. 190-200. Maidenhead, UK: Meyer & Meyer (UK) Ltd.

Howe, D. P. (2008) *The Cultural Politics of the Paralympic movement: Through an Anthropological Lens*. New York, NY: Routledge.

IPC. International Paralympic Committee. (2010) Participation numbers: Beijing 2008 Paralympic Games. Retrieved from http://www.paralympic.org/Sport/Results/reports.html?type=participation&Games=2008PG&sport=all.

IPC. International Paralympic Committee. (2008) Women in Sport Committee WIPS Network Update. July 2008 Report. Bonn, Germany: International Paralympic Committee.

IPC. International Paralympic Committee. (2001) Women and Sport Progress Report. Bonn, Germany: International Paralympic Committee, 2001.

Jarvie, G., Hwang, D.J., & Brennan M. (2008) *Sport, Revolution and the Beijing Olympics.* Oxford, UK: Berg.

Jennings, A. (2000) The great Olympic swindle: When the world wanted its Games back. London, UK: Simon and Schuster.

Jinxia D. (2003) Women, sport and society in modern China. Holding up more than half the sky. London: Routledge.

Kellett, P. (2008) Volunteerism and the Paralympic Games. In K. Gilbert & O. Schantz (Eds.), *The Paralympic Games: Empowerment or Side Show?* pp. 176-184. Maidenhead, UK: Meyer & Meyer (UK) Ltd.

Kidd, B. and P. Donnelly (2000) Human Rights in Sport. *International Review for the Sociology of Sport.* (35), 2, pp. 131-148.

Koehler, H. (2008, September 6-7) Helping the disabled a play a bigger role. *China Daily*, p.8.

Kooning. (2009 September 8) "Beijing Paralympic passion never fades: Sport opens a window." *The Beijing Evening News.*

Lan T. (2008) China's Paralympians get a good head start. *China Daily.* May 23, p.3

Le Clair, J.M. (ed) (2011) *Disability in the Global Sport Arena: A Sporting Chance.* London: Routledge. In press.

_____ (2009) Water, senses and the experiences of the pool: Paralympic athletes and swimming. Proceedings: *Third International Sensory Therapy Conference*, October 21-25, Toronto, Canada.

_____ (2009a) Sport and health: Global challenges to biomedical definitions of disability. *Vis-à-Vis: Explorations in Anthropology.* 9 (2) pp. 203-219.

Legg, D. & R. Steadward. (2011) The Paralympic Games and 60 years of change (1948-2008): unification and restructuring from a disability and medical model to sport based competition. In *Disability in the Global Sport Arena: A Sporting Chance.* (ed) Jill M. Le Clair. London: Routledge. In press.

Lenskyj, H.J. (2000) *Inside the Olympic Industry: Power, Politics, and Activism.* Albany, NY: State University of New York Press.

Li, L.M., Dray-Novey, A.J. & Kong, H. (2008) *Beijing: From Imperial Capital to Olympic City.* New York, NY: Palgrave.

Li-Wen & Li-Yahong. (2009, September 6) Paralympic Games: Statistics illustrate the changes in Beijing. *Beijing Daily*, p. 1.

Li, X. (2008, September 10) Silence golden for goalballers. *China Daily*, p. 6.

Lin Qi. (2008, September 10) For her, sign language is a great art form. *China Daily*, pp. 1-2.

Linton, S. (1998) *Claiming Disability: Knowledge and Identity.* New York: New York University Press.

Liu J. (2008, September 8-14) Handle with care: Paralympics a great platform for firms to showcase their social responsibility. *China Business Weekly* in *China Daily*, p. 1.

Marvin, C. (2008) "All under heaven": Megaspace in Beijing. In M.E. Price and D. Dayan (Eds.), *Owning the Olympics: Narratives of the New China*, pp.229-260. Ann Arbor, MI: University of Michigan Press.

Miah, A, B. García, & Tian Zhihui. (2008) "We are the media": Non-accredited media and citizen journalists at the Olympic Games. In M.E. Price and D. Dayan (Eds.), *Owning the Olympics: Narratives of the New China*, pp. 320-346. Ann Arbor, MI: University of Michigan Press.

Nilsson, E. & Lei Lei. (2008, September 6-7) Excitement reaches fever pitch. *China Daily*, p. 1.

Oliver, M. and C. Barnes. (1998) *Disabled People and Social Policy: From Exclusion to Inclusion*. New York: Longman.

Price, M. E. (2008) Introduction. In M.E. Price and D. Dayan (Eds.), *Owning the Olympics: Narratives of the New China*, pp. 1-13. Ann Arbor: University of Michigan Press.

_____ (2008) On seizing the Olympic platform. In M.E. Price and D. Dayan (Eds.), *Owning the Olympics: Narratives of the New China*, pp. 86-117. Ann Arbor, MI: University of Michigan Press.

Shaw, C. (2008) *Five Ring Circus: Myths and Realities of the Olympic Games*. Gabriola Island, BC: New Society Publishers.

She without arm, he without leg: ballet 'hand in hand'. (2008). YouTube video. http://www.youtube.com/watch?v=LnLVRQCjh8c

Simpson, V. & A. Jennings. (1992) *The Lord of the Rings*. Toronto, ON: Stoddard.

Sun Shuhan, Yan Rui, Mao Ailin, Chao Liu, Jung Tang. (2011) China and the development of sport for persons with a disability, 1978-2008: A Review. In *Disability in the Global Sport Arena: A Sporting Chance*. (ed) Jill M. Le Clair. London: Routledge. In Press.

Thomas, N. & Smith, A. (2009) *Disability, Sport, and Society: An Introduction*. New York, NY: Routledge.

Two Olympic and Paralympic Games have had an Effect on the Protection of the Disabled in China? (2009, September 3) *People's Daily*, p.1.

UN Enable. (2010) Ratifications. June 14. Retrieved from http://www.un.org/disabilities/countries.asp?id=166

Wang R. (2008, September 8) Pointing the way to Olympic glory. *China Daily*, p.8.

Wang, Z. (2008, September 16) Disabled charities call for more help. *China Daily*, p. 6.

Wasserstrom, J. N. (2008) Dreams and nightmares: History and U.S. Visions of the Beijing Games. In M.E. Price and D. Dayan (Eds.), *Owning the Olympics: Narratives of the New China*, pp. 163-185. Ann Arbor, MI: University of Michigan Press.

Xiao Yang. (2008, September 6-7) Games offers opportunities to boost ties. *China Daily*, p. 2.

Xie Fang. (2008, September 12) Life on bicycles. *China Daily*, p. 7.

Xin Dingding. (2008, September 13-14) Olympics set to boost tourism. *China Daily*, p. 3.

Xinhua News Agency (2008a) China's Paralympic history. Retrieved from http://www.china.org.cn/paralympics/2008-9/03/content_1637-8772.htm.

Xinhua News Agency (2008) Participation in sport by disabled people in China. (2008) Retrieved from http://www.china.org.cn/paralympics/2008-08/29/content_16355692.htm.

Xiong Lei. (2008, September 6-7) Paralympics offers opportunity to learn. *China Daily*, p. 4.

Xu Chengbei. (2001) *Old Beijing: People, Houses and Lifestyles*. Beijing: Foreign Languages Press.

Xu Guoqi. (2008) *Olympic Dreams: China and Sports: 1895-2008*. London, UK; Cambridge, MA: Harvard University Press.

Yang Li. (2008, September 8) Society needs to care more for the disabled. *China Daily*, p.4.

Ye jun, (2008, September 8) Society needs to care more for the disabled. *China Daily*, p.4.

You Nuo. (2008, September 8-14) In with the new. China Business Weekly in *China Daily*, p. 1.

Zhao Shijun. (2008, September 6-7) German Ambassador: Sports enable all to shine. *China Daily*, p. 8.

2008 Beijing Paralympics. Medal Tally. Paralympic Games. (2008, September 6-17) Retrieved from http://www.china.org.cn/paralympics/2008-08/27/content_16341893.htm

Chapter 11
Vancouver 2010

Dena Coward and David Legg

Introduction

On July 2nd 2003, Vancouver, Canada was awarded the 2010 Olympic and Paralympic Winter Games and this presented the Paralympic Movement in Canada with opportunities not seen in the country since 1976 when it hosted the Torontolympiad. The Vancouver Organizing Committee for the Olympic and Paralympic Winter Games (VANOC) identified early that the hosting of the tenth Paralympic Winter Games would be a tremendous vehicle to raise awareness around the Games, the athletes and the Movement in Canada. As many organizing committees prior, VANOC saw as its responsibility to raise the bar for the Paralympic Games, to initiate a number of significant changes within the history of the Paralympic Games and to pass the Games onto to future organizing committees stronger than Canada received them.

In particular, VANOC recognized that the Paralympic Winter Games wasn't about capturing the hearts of Canadians. It was about changing their minds (Levitz, 2010). And this lofty goal wasn't precluded to just Canada. For some, 2010 was to be another step along a long line of benchmark Games. The 1988 Games in Seoul may have marked the transition from rehabilitation to sport but Vancouver may be seen years from now as the defining moment when the Paralympic Games moved from being about athletes with disability to simply about ability.

"In China, the (Paralympic) Games were really a transformation tool for changing attitudes across the board in China towards people with disability, to building accessible facilities in the city, to changing laws to allow people with a disability to be part of society," said Xavier Gonzalez, the chief executive officer for the International Paralympic Committee (Levitz, 2010). Vancouver had "a different goal and consequently . . . here it is more about presenting sport as sport and to showcase these are athletes and nothing else" (Levitz, 2010). Ticket sales may have supported this idea with all of Team Canada's sledge hockey Games being sold out and one of the authors recalling with fondness being approached by scalpers in a preliminary match. After all, said Keith Baulk, the venue manager for the sledge hockey events, to Canadians "hockey is hockey" (Levitz, 2010).

Firsts

With the lofty goal of being the first Games to focus on ability the host organizing committee was also first for many initiatives. VANOC was the first organizing committee to include Paralympic Games in its official name, the first to have a joint marketing agreement with the host National Paralympic Committee (NPC), the first to include a member from the National Paralympic Committee on its Board of Directors, the first to include a Paralympian on one of its subcommittees, the first to have a separate Paralympic Games countdown clock, the first to fly the Olympic and Paralympic flags side by side, the first organizing committee to create and implement a Paralympic School Day program, and the first to depict Paralympic sports on Games circulation coins (Qualtrough, 2009; VANOC, 2009;). For Vancouver, the mascots announcement was also a first as those for the Olympics and Paralympics were introduced together and travelled together. The posters for the two events were also linked with each representing half a maple leaf (the Canadian symbol) that only becomes whole when they were put together (Levitz, 2010).

While there were many firsts in how the Paralympic and Olympic Games worked together there were also subtle differences that were purposeful and hopefully from the organizer's perspective will have a lasting impact on legacy. One example was the torch relay. While the Olympic torch relay was a 106-day, cross-country odyssey, the Paralympic relay was a 10-day event that jumped from city to city, culminating in a 24-hour relay in downtown Vancouver. The education program for the Paralympic Games was also run separately which brought Paralympic athletes to dozens of schools. "They make the word impossible look like it's just a distraction, frankly," said John Furlong, chief executive officer of the Vancouver organizing committee. "Kids are in disbelief when they look at what these men and women are able to do so it has a lot of power on its own," he added.

"It has a huge impact on children. This is why there is specifically school programs that take place around the Paralympics that don't exist as much around the Olympics" (Levitz, 2010).

The 2010 Games were also the first to have a dedicated group responsible for ensuring legacy and was also the first to include Paralympic Legacy as part of the Olympic Games (Global) Impact study. The OGGI is assessing 'global impact' = 'total' or 'holistic' impact of the Games on the host city and region, and not 'worldwide' impact of the Games. It is a major research program commissioned by the International Olympic Committee (IOC) to the International Academy of Sport Science and Technology (AISTS) in Lausanne, Switzerland with the goal to measure the impact of the Olympic Games economically, socially, and environmentally; to create a comparable benchmark across all future Olympic Games, and help cities that are bidding for an Olympic Games, and future organizers, to identify potential legacies to maximize Games' benefits. There are 126 indicators (social + environmental + economic) and they now include four specific to the Paralympic Games (Legg, 2009). Paralympic indicators were added to the OGI in 2007 following formal requests from representatives of the Canadian Paralympic Committee and 2010 LegaciesNow. The four items included employability of persons with a disability, perceptions of people with disability in society, support network for persons with a disability and professional sport education for persons with a disability. A fifth indicator included in the Paralympic "bundle" was facility accessibility of Games and public venues, which had already been included in previous studies.

In part, due to the Paralympic Movement's relative infancy as alluded to in other chapters in this book was the dearth of research pertaining to the legacy of hosting Games, which is why the inclusion of Paralympic indicators in the Olympic Games Impact Study was so important and welcomed. As noted by the International Working Group on Sport and Development "while sport has value in everyone's life, it is even more important in the life of a person with a disability. This is because of sport's rehabilitative influence, and the fact that it is a means to integrate the person into society… sport teaches independence" (Legg, 2009).

Impact indicators

One of this chapter's authors was asked to assist with the OGI study and helped prepare an overview of the five indicators, which is reviewed here (Legg, 2009). The final OGI report, including the five Paralympic indicators, is scheduled for publication in December 2011 but already some results are being shared. An online survey as part of the OGI study was conducted by Synovate Research in December 2009 with more than 1,600 Canadians participating. The survey measured changes in public and personal awareness and attitudes since the Olympic/Paralympic Games were awarded to Vancouver/Whistler in 2003. Results showed that 41-50% of respondents believed the Games enabled additional accessibility of buildings, sidewalks and public spaces as well as specialized programs and training for athletes with disabilities and government support for disabled individuals. Also, 32-40% of respondents believed both the Winter Olympic and Paralympic Games increased their knowledge of sports for people with disabilities and their overall acceptance of people with disabilities. Among employers, about one-quarter said their willingness to hire people with disabilities has gone up due to the Games (UBC, 2010). The specific results to each of the five indicators are also noted below.

The first OGI indicator, Employability of People with Disabilities hoped to reflect how the Games' would have an impact on the able-bodied populace to see people with disability as employable. In 1968, the President of the Canadian Wheelchair Sport Association who would subsequently go on to chair the organizing committee for the 1976 Torontolympiad, Dr. Robert Jackson noted that "it was hoped that persons who were able-bodied would begin to understand that if a paraplegic could race a mile in seven minutes, or lift 472 pounds in a bench press, that the same individual should be able to work a full eight-hour day" (Legg, 2000). Jackson clearly saw the link between performance and employability in 1976 and for many this potentially positive correlation continues to exist.

As noted earlier, in June, 2010 the results from the first pre and post Paralympic Games impact study were circulated as part of the OGI report with the data collection completed by Synovate Research (Yuen & Winram, 2010). In the areas of employment less than half of Canadians believed that the Games had a positive impact on employment opportunities for persons with a disability but the Games had led to increased willingness to hire people with disabilities.

The second OGI indicator, Perceptions of People with Disabilities in Society, was created to identify any changes in how able-bodied persons viewed persons with disability. More specifically this indicator was assessing attitudes towards social inclusion and perception. As noted earlier in this book the introduction of sport for people with a disability in late 1940s enabled the transformation of patient to athlete to citizen; thus this second indicator was intended to judge how this evolution continues. According to the Canadian Attitudes Towards Disability Issues; 2004 Benchmark Survey Canadians were most likely to point to prejudice on the part of individuals and society-at-large as the most significant barrier to inclusion facing persons with disability (49%), a view shared by citizens with and without disability (Environics Research Group Limited, 2004).

One the ways to improve public perception is through media. Television coverage in Canada for the 2010 Games, while still not perfect, was certainly a step in the right direction. In Canada 65 hours (the total includes both those in French and English) (this was up from the 50 hours they originally committed to) were shown across the country with all sledge hockey Games shown live. Unfortunately (for Canada) they did not play in the gold medal match, which likely would have set a record for Paralympic television audience, particularly as it fell in a convenient Saturday afternoon time slot. Interestingly, the CTV-Rogers consortium that held the television rights to the Games in Canada was forced into broadcasting the opening ceremonies live in British Columbia (the Province where Vancouver is located) after strong demand when they had originally planned to only show the ceremonies on a tape delay across the country the following day during the afternoon. Even though the ceremonies were shown in the host Province live the remainder of the country was outranged that they were not given this same opportunity. As a result the closing ceremonies were broadcasted live across the country in all five time zones and were watched by 1.5 million viewers. At the end of the Games, it was reported that a record 165 Canadian media were accredited by the CPC for the Vancouver 2010 Paralympic Winter Games and using the 10-days of the Games, 13.6 million Canadians tuned in to support Canada's Paralympic athletes (Canadian Paralympic Committee, 2010).

"As a result of the coverage of these Games more Canadians with a disability than ever before are aware of the opportunity to play sports. This legacy of greater awareness will lead to greater participation and inclusion in local, provincial, and national sport programs—critical if Canada is to continue to create Paralympic champions," said CPC President, Carla Qualtrough. "And, the benefits of greater awareness will be seen far beyond sport. Seeing Paralympians compete in high performance international sport has challenged preconceptions of disability, and will change attitudes for the benefit of persons with a disability in all walks of life" (Canadian Paralympic Committee, 2010).

Results from this improved media coverage may in fact already be felt. In a survey conducted one week after the Paralympic Games ended, to 987 respondents, results suggested that Canadians viewed the Paralympics and Paralympians extremely favourably, 69.2% of respondents agreed that the Paralympics Games were one of the best showcases of the power of the human spirit. Additionally, 3 out of 4 Canadians (76.1%) agreed that the athletic performance of Paralympic athletes was truly amazing and this same percentage also agreed that Paralympic athletes deserved the same emotional, corporate, and financial support as our Olympic athletes (Canadian Paralympic Committee, 2010b).

At the 2010 Paralympic Games Closing Ceremonies, John Furlong, CEO for VANOC also reflected on how Canadian's views of Paralympians had changed. "Paralympians – you have dazzled us with your agility, your strength, your endurance and your sportsmanship. You have demonstrated great courage, skill and determination. You have given us drama and thrills we will never forget. You reflect the best kind of human character, integrity and focus" (Canadian Paralympic Committee, 2010). The Synovate research corroborated this view and noted that the majority of Canadians in all regions believed that the Games led to more positive portrayals of people with disabilities in the media and increased their social status (Yuen & Winram, 2010).

The third OGI indicator, Support Network for People with Disabilities assessed government's support towards people with disability such as the rate of persons with disability acessing financial support. According to a report completed in 2004, Canadians looked to government to take a lead role for persons with disability in such areas as health care, transportation, and providing specialized equipment; although specific to recreation they also cited the importance of non profit organizations (Environics Research Group Limited, 2004). This indicator will hopefully note any changes to these support services, which are achieved in light of the 2010 Games. The short term results, however, don't look promising as the Synovate research noted that while the majority of Canadian believed that the Games themselves did not result in improved social support or integration (Yuen & Winram, 2010).

The fourth OGI indicator is Professional Sport Education for People with Disabilities referring to the quantity of adapted physical activity courses in higher education in Canada. Lack of awareness and misperceptions from able-bodied physical educators and sport and recreation administrators is viewed as one of the most significant barriers to participation in sport and physical activity for persons with disability. Goodwin, Gustafson and Hamilton (2006) noted, however, that in education specifically, teacher's perceived competence in working with disabled athletes typically rose through academic training and this was a strong indicator of a positive attitude. The implication then is the need for increased educational opportunities for all practitioners in sport and recreation and not just educators. In Australia, a legacy of the 2000 Summer Games were a series of disability education programs that were geared towards coaches, teachers, and students with the Australian Sport Commission planning to commission research to evaluate their impact in 2009 (Cashman & Darcy, 2006).

One caveat to this, however, has been to some the hope for disability related issues to be infused within the entire academic curriculum and not to have just one or two courses specific to persons with disability. Anecdotally this ambitious goal has appeared to not taken root in the various institutions they have taught at.

A fifth OGI indicator was Accessibility of Public Services, intended to capture changes in buildings such as City Hall and post offices. One example of a program addressing this was the 2010 Vision for British Columbians with Disabilities. This was started by the City of Vancouver Council in 2003 in order to create a rating instrument to help municipalities determine how they could make their communities more accessible. The Province of BC was brought in as a partner and the idea was then distributed to every municipal council in BC and over 40 municipalities have endorsed the motion. In 2005, 2010 LegaciesNow assumed responsibility for AICCP and in 2007, the Government of BC would provide a one-time grant to 2010 LegaciesNow for training and research activities. To date, however, results from this are not available. The Synovate research, meanwhile, suggested that the Games did not change perceptions of access to public spaces (Yuen & Winram, 2010).

2010 LegaciesNow

As noted earlier, the 2010 Games were also the first to include an organization that had as its mandate the responsibility for ensuring legacy. 2010 LegaciesNow was created in 2000 to spearhead the most comprehensive approach to legacy of any major sporting event to date. It established itself as an innovator in sports development and a leader in building partnerships and sport initiatives in recreation, community, the arts, literacy and volunteerism. In 2002 the 2010 LegaciesNow program was transferred from the Vancouver 2010 Bid Corporation to a not for profit society to the 2010 LegaciesNow Society, with a mandate to ensure a strong and lasting sport system for the region. To achieve this it developed several specialist programs in partnership with other agencies and these now focus on sport and recreation, arts, volunteers and literacy (Taylor & Edmondson, 2007).

2010 LegaciesNow was given the mandate to pursue legacies of capacity and opportunity – in addition to the more traditional legacies seen in host cities such as facilities and programming (Boeck, 2007). One specific example related to the Paralympic Games was Bridging the Gap, a recruitment and development initiative of BC Wheelchair Sports. 2010 LegaciesNow is the main funding agency for this program designed to introduce and support continued involvement of individuals with physical disabilities in wheelchair sports.

Within the organization presently are six areas of priority. They include physical activity and healthy living, sport and recreation, arts, volunteerism, literacy and accessibility (2010 LegaciesNow, 2010). Within each of these are five priority groups including youth, youth at risk, aboriginal peoples, inner city residents and people living with a disability. Specific to the Paralympic Games then, 2010 LegaciesNow was hoping to ensure an increase in opportunities for persons with a disability in the areas of physical activity, healthy living and sport, to assist VANOC in making the 2010 Games a model of access and inclusion for future Olympic and Paralympic Games, to identify and address systemic issues related to inclusion of persons with disabilities in the BC Sport system and to leverage the Games to build and enhance partnerships for sport. So far, several programs have already been initiated to assist towards achieving these goals. They include BC Sport Participation focusing on sport participation in community and school based sport, Game Plan BC focusing on high performance athletes, SportFit which addresses computer platform interactive Games to encourage children to discover sport, programs related to accessible Sport Tourism, Measuring Up – a program to help communities become more accessible and inclusive, and accessible playgrounds.

The Canadian Federal Government's also had a 2010 Games Legacy Plan, with a Disability Focus. Primarily, the legacy here was through funding programs including the Canadian Paralympic Committee and other disability sport organization, directly to elite athletes and funding to create Physical Education manuals for teachers assisting them to adapt fundamental motor skill learning for children with disabilities.

VANOC, meanwhile, had as its vision a stronger Canada whose spirit was raised by its passion for sport, culture and sustainability, which is a dedicated legacy specific to the Games. As it related to sustainability for both Olympic and Paralympic Games one of the six goals was accessibility and social inclusion. Within accessibility VANOC targeted venues, transportation, operations, special events, accommodations and communications and wrote guidelines to lead the organization to meet these goals. And through awareness, facilities, recognition, profile and engagement with others VANOC hoped to be the catalyst for change for these legacies to be sustained long term. To ensure a physical legacy from the Games VANOC facilitated a partnership between the Whistler Adaptive Sports Program (WASP) and Whistler 2010 Sports Legacies (WSL2010), and on January 29th 2009 these two groups signed a Memorandum of Understanding outlining the commitment to partner in the creation of a 2010 Paralympic Games legacy for athletes with a disability. This partnership will result in a world-class training centre in Whistler at which individuals with disabilities can engage in recreational and athletic pursuits following the Games. At the centre of the partnership is the Whistler Athletes' Centre, part of the Whistler Athletes' Village, located in Whistler's new Cheakamus Crossing neighbourhood. The fully accessible complex includes: a High Performance Centre featuring: a strength and conditioning gym and a gymnastics hall, along with office space for the headquarters of Whistler 2010 Sport Legacies, the Whistler Adaptive Sports Program (WASP) and other partner groups as well as an Athletes' Lodge featuring up to 76 accessible rooms (of 100 total rooms) restaurant space; and 20 town homes. The Whistler Adaptive Sports Program will be able to significantly expand its range of programs through the use of the centre and accommodations to athletes with a disability and teams who will train, compete, and live in the 'Sea to Sky' region after the Games (Coward & Molloy, 2009).

The Canadian Paralympic Committee is also planning for a legacy from the Games even though their primarily role was to prepare the Canadian team competing at the Games. The CPC Board and staff recognized that there were tremendous potential and opportunity for the national Paralympic Committee to benefit from the Games being held on home soil. More specifically beyond the team goals for the Games, the CPC hoped to leverage the Games to build awareness of Paralympic sport and passion. This was specific to media, corporate Canada and public attitudes.

Henry Storgaard, the CPC's CEO noted that prior to the Games the CPC's goals were "recognition, recruitment and investment, and we achieved all of those," He further noted that "Thanks to the incredible performances of our athletes, and the extraordinary media and television coverage, public response to these Games has shown there is an interest in Paralympic sport. Our goal now is to work with our members, athletes, government and sponsors to keep the interest alive—for the benefit of our Paralympic athletes, as well as all Canadians with a disability" (Canadian Paralympic Committee, 2010).

Lastly legacies were also to be felt from the Games themselves for future hosts. The 2010 Games were the first Games for many initiatives. In addition to those already listed these Games were, the first to have a trademark Act approved for Paralympic marks, the first to establish a legacy fund that included support for Paralympic athletes and coaches and the first to negotiate a share of Games operating surplus. As we have seen in prior Games once these types of initiatives have started they often continue. These alone are significant legacies for the Paralympic Games and movement as a whole.

Interestingly, in SportBusiness.com's annual ranking of the world's greatest sport cities in 2008, Vancouver placed 5th. The Vancouver 2010 advantage was attributed to Vancouver winning the right to host the $1.4 million budget Wheelchair Rugby World Championships in September 2010 at the Richmond Olympic Oval, which was converted to a multi use facilities after it hosted the speed skating events at the 2010 Olympic Games (ABC News, 2008). There was no mention of a disability related event in any other write up of the other top ten cities and to the author's recollection this was the first time a disability sport event was ever even noted in the rankings.

Some might argue that the greatest instrument of the Paralympic movement is the Games themselves. By delivering an extraordinary Games, the hosts in turn leave a positive legacy, showcasing the above mentioned initiatives and raising the bar for the Paralympic Movement as a whole. International Paralympic Committee president Sir Philip Craven even went so far as to declare Vancouver 2010 the "the best ever Winter Paralympic Games" (Canadian Paralympic Committee, 2010). The local community also apparently agreed with 229,626 tickets being sold representing 84% of tickets available which was the highest number of tickets ever sold at a Winter Paralympic Games (Canadian Paralympic Committee, 2010c). Finally, the pre and post survey conducted by Synovate on behalf of the OGI noted that throughout Canada perceptions of the impact of the Games improved dramatically. Hopefully the Games' legacy can continue to build upon these compliments and continue to provide benefits for years to come.

References

2010 LegaciesNow (2010) *Our Programs*, Available at: (http://www.2010legaciesnow.com/)(accessed June 24, 2010)

ABC News (2008) *Melbourne retains ultimate sports city title*, Available at: (http://www.abc.net.au/news/stories/-2008/04/01/ 2204562.htm?section=sport)(accessed 10th November 2008)

Boeck, D. (2007) *Leveraging the Games: How do we create tomorrow's opportunities today?* International Inklusiv Interdisziplinar. Hofmann- Verlag, Schorndork, Berlin.

Cashman, R. & Darcy, S. (2006) *Benchmark Games: The Sydney 2000 Paralympic Games*, Sydney: Walla Walla Press.

Canadian Paralympic Committee (2010) *Paralympic Winter Games Launch New Era fo the Canadian Paralympic Committee*, Available at: (http://www.paralympic.ca/Media/Vancouver- 2010-Paralympic-Winter-Games-launch-new-era-for-the- Canadian-Paralympic-Committee.html)(accessed June 24, 2010)

Canadian Paralympic Committee (2010b) *CPC Gauges Public Support of Paralympic Athletes in a Snapshot Survey*, Available at: (http://www.paralympic.ca/Media/CPC-gauges-public- support-of-Paralympic-athletes-in-a-snapshot-survey.html)(accessed June 24, 2010)

Canadian Paralympic Committee (2010c) *Canada's Olympic Broadcast Media Consortium Delivers Record Hours of Coverage of Vancouver 2010 Paralympic Winter Games,* Available at: (http://www.paralympic.ca/page?a=237&lang=en-CA)(accessed June 24, 2010)

Coward, D. & Molloy, K. (2009) *Vancouver 2010 Paralympic Winter Games – A Catalyst for Change,* Presentation to the Canadian Paralympic Congress, June 12, 2009, Vancouver.

Environics Research Group Limited (2004) *Canadian Attitudes Towards Disability Issues; 2004 Benchmark Survey,* Office for Disability Issues Social Development Canada, Ottawa, ON.

Goodwin, D., Gustafson, P. & Hamilton, P. (2006) *The Experience of Disability in Physical Education in Stones in the Sneakers* (eds.) G. Dickinson, S. Rae & G. Millburn, The Althouse Press, London, ON.

LeClair, B. (2009) *2010 Legacies Now*, Presentation at the CPC Annual Congress, June 11, 2009, Vancouver

Legg, D. (2000) *Strategy Formation in the Canadian Wheelchair Sports Association (1967-1997)*. Doctoral Dissertation, Edmonton, AB: University of Alberta.

Legg, D. (2009) *Measuring the Legacy of the 2010 Paralympic Games*, Insert to the Olympic Games Impact Study, Ed. R. Vanwynsberghe, University of British Columbia. Vancouver, BC.

Levitz, S. (2010) *2010 Paralympics about changing minds, not capturing hearts*, Available at: (http://www.cp24.com/servlet/an/local/CTVNews/20100312/100312_paralympics_start?hub=CP24Sports)(accessed June 17, 2010)

Taylor, M. & Edmondson, I. (2007) Major Sporting Events – planning for legacy, *Municipal Engineer, 160*(4): 171-176.

Qualtrough, C. (2009) *2010 Games Plan*, presentation at the Canadian Paralympic Congress, June 12, 2009, Vancouver.

UBC (2010) *Social, environmental and economic pre-Games impacts were reported in December 2009*, Available at: (http://www.publicaffairs.ubc.ca/2009/12/04/pre-Games-impact-study-for-2010-olympic-winter-Games-finds-modest-benefits/)(accessed June 17, 2010)

VANOC (2009) *VANOC Transfer of Knowledge Report to the IOC / IPC,* PPL Games Knowledge Report. Vancouver, BC.

Yuen, S. & Winram, J. (2010) *2010 Post – Paralympic Games Impact*, Synovate Research Reinvented, Vancouver, BC.

Chapter 12
London 2012

The Right Choice for the Paralympic Games?

Tony Sainsbury

Introduction

On a memorable July day in Singapore 2005, Sebastian Coe, Chairman of the London 2012 Organising Committee for the Olympic & Paralympic Games, promised the IOC and global sport that the occasion of a London Games would be used to regenerate youth's love of sport.

Since winning the right to be the 2012 Host City on that auspicious day this mantra has driven all who work on this project.

For the first time ever in a Bid presentation there was a genuine inclusive guarantee that 2012 would became 'everyone's 2012' - able and disabled persons alike.

This chapter while focussing on London 2012 is inevitably influenced by this author's previous experiences at Paralympic Games since 1980 (see chapter 5 for Sainsbury's reflections on the 1988 Seoul Paralympic Games).

The reader will also find that this chapter is much more opinionated and discursive in style than others of a more academic nature. However, as I understand it the nature of the overall approach was to include both practical and theoretical approaches.

My aim has been to examine the association of the Paralympic Movement and Games with the Olympic Games because the London context and world-changing scale of any Paralympic Games legacy is a consequence of that link.

I intend to propose a set of criteria, which in my opinion underpin any 'Paralympic legacy debate'. That is - 'What conditions prevail in a 'Host country' where the Paralympics are to be held? How are disabled people viewed – as assets or liabilities?'

I have some difficulty with the association of the words 'regeneration and Paralympics' in the same phrase except in the broadest sense where it is applied on an individual basis to those who become disabled.

In that sense one might argue that the genesis of sport for those with a disability, moreover for those who become disabled and are not born with a disability, is about a regeneration of the human spirit – to paraphrase that great Atlanta 1996 strap-line the 'The Triumph of the Human Spirit'.

Those people with spinal cord injuries on the grounds of Stoke Mandeville in 1948 had no idea of what they were starting not just for themselves but for others.

Yet within themselves they rediscovered a different fire that confirmed for each a new **'me'**. Even 'Poppa Guttmann' in his wildest dreams, and in spite of his words about an Olympics for the Disabled, could never have imagined the event on the world scale we saw so wondrously displayed in Beijing in 2008.

Notwithstanding the above comments, people with disabilities and the Paralympic Games have a unique opportunity to exploit (in the best possible way) all the regeneration, physical and social that will occur as a consequence of the 2012 Games.

To best understand this opportunity I will examine the process of Bidding for, and Winning the Games and thereafter managing that win – all in the context of London 2012.

And finally I shall try to summarize the key ingredients necessary to deliver successful Paralympic, and by association Olympic Games.

The underlying principle of that delivery is the consequence of the challenges and benefits of the very complex relationship between the IOC and IPC.

Should this relationship not exist in the way it does then the context and outcomes would be very different and many would argue significantly diminished.

Students need only examine the history of the 'Deaflympics' as they are now called to understand why the IOC-IPC relationship is so critical.

The genesis of those Games dates from the early part of the twentieth century and therefore deaf sport is the oldest sport organisation of any group that can be classed as 'disabled'. And regrettably in my opinion these Games have a limited impact not only on their own world but the world around them.

This is not to denigrate the athletic success of the event or the participants themselves, which is extraordinary as I know from personal experience having attended their Games in Sofia, Bulgaria in the early 1990s.

However, when they leave town what remains? What is there to show for their time there? That is the essence of this discussion.

IOC – IPC historical relationship

What then was the Paralympic Game's initial legacy? Probably like the deaf, outside their own isolated sports world, not much. I remember throughout the 1980s in so called 'developed' countries including the UK having to carry athletes up sets of stairs onto transport or into accommodation – the external impact of the Games was therefore small.

However, the athletes were phenomenal role models not only to those who aspired to be athletes with disabilities themselves but to other people with disabilities who discovered other pursuits whether business, the arts, or politics, because of the evolving higher profile of sportsmen and women with disabilities.

Collectively, people with disabilities in the UK, Canada, Australia and other countries who were the founders of sport for the disabled became a vociferous voice that was not prepared to take a backward step.

And it is perhaps a perception of a non-challenging profile that enabled the Paralympic movement to 'sneak up' on the Olympic one and with the help of some enlightened insiders become embedded in the Games element of Olympic activity.

By this I mean that the motivation to include elite athletes with a disability in any major sports event has always been an initial paternalism. There is no criticism intended by this remark because if I am totally honest it was the basis of my initiation to my own Paralympic journey in the mid 1970s.

Why do I say sneak up?

Well until the creation of the IPC in 1989 there had been a benevolent relationship with the IOC. The disability sport movement had been awarded a special status within the IOC and even had an IOC member specially assigned to that relationship in Walter Troeger.

Before the marketing gurus descended, the word 'Olympics' had been conjoined with the word 'Special' to provide that unique status on some of the most disadvantaged in our society, those with intellectual disability: unthinkable in today's environment of ambush marketing.

It was only the intervention of IOC President Samaranch upon his election which started to bring about significant change: he personally encouraged Los Angeles 1984 to include wheelchair track events within their programme.

When the Games were awarded to his home town of Barcelona the organising committee declared fairly publically that they did not want to organise the Paralympic Games.

But 'pressure' from ONCE * and Samaranch saw the delivery of outstanding Barcelona Games both Olympic and Paralympic and witnessed the beginnings of a positive relationship between the two. The eventual catalyst of which was Paralympics 'Korea 88' use of the Olympic venues.

I use the word 'beginning' because the relationship was pretty volatile at this stage and neither partner I suspect had any idea where it might lead.

As I prepared to write Chapter 9 of the London 2012 Candidate File at the end of 2003 I believed that understanding the reality of the IOC-IPC relationship was key to the part the Paralympic element might play in any London 2012 success.

I cannot claim sole credit because it was suggested to me by many that in such a delicate undertaking there was a real danger of over-emphasising this aspect and suggesting that somehow there would be a joint decision making process as to the host.

It has been suggested by some that the most comparable endorsement of any Bid to that of the IPC is the International Federations' acknowledgement of the technical robustness of a Candidate City's plans. International Federations pay less attention to the overall Games strategy, the transport plans, athletes and spectators generally, ticketing, villages and the myriad of other aspects of either Games.

Failures in the Paralympic sports technical area can indeed now signal an overall failure for the Bid as some recent past attempts have shown. Lack of attention in this area is seen as an insult to the whole process. As one former IPC Ex-Board member once remarked "Theme 9 of the Candidate File on the Paralympic Games will not win the right to host both Games but it could lose that right now"

Another key for London was to recognise that the way of creating a successful Paralympic balance with the other elements was important. The emphasis in the 'Bid documentation' was to acknowledge that the whole process was essentially an IOC activity. And that we, London and the IPC were being invited to be 'guests' at the party and to temper our ambition, limit our aspirations at least verbally either in documents or in presentations to those aspects that would enjoy general universal support within the Olympic Movement.

Those aspects included such issues as legacy, social conscience and the demonstrable ease of delivery of a conjoined event of two Games. In effect not to proselytise!

I realise that some might interpret this as being false to those who entrusted us with this Paralympic task. But this was not the case. To bring about change we first had to win. To deliver lasting legacy we had to be the next Host City even though bidding itself brought many benefits.

Colleagues in both Olympic & Paralympic movements with whom I have worked for over thirty years advocated this balance.

Why so cautious?

To be frank yet non-critical, not everyone within the Olympic or Paralympic Movements see the importance of the Paralympic Games as a compulsory element within the process of offering oneself as a candidate city or putting on the Olympic Games.

They argue from a variety of different positions. Some suggest that the Paralympic Games is too dependent on the Olympic Games when it could (might) enjoy a status of its own similar to that of the Commonwealth Games.

There are some who come from cultures and backgrounds where people with disabilities have few or any rights or place in those societies. And therefore do not see the rational of such inclusion.

There are others who just don't see the Paralympic Games as Olympic business.

Some see the Paralympic Games as a distraction from the 'main event' both to the public and to the Organising Committee.

Each perspective, while perhaps contentious, is an understandable point of view. So for the moment the relationship remains fragile and it is perhaps London's task as part of its legacy to strengthen that relationship not by any ethical debate but by holding a Paralympic Games which demonstrates in every way the potential of the relationship to enhance both Movements.

Criteria: Paralympic legacy pre-Games analysis

London's approach (and one relevant to any city aspiring to be a Games city) was to examine the following criteria to understand in a quite detailed way where the State and the Society of the London and the UK as aspirant host sat –

- What laws exist to support and protect disabled people, i.e. the individual rights of disabled people?
- What regulations exist concerning accessibility and the physical infrastructure of the world we live in – architecture, transport, public realm, etc?
- How are disabled people treated in the media – on television, in the press on the radio?
- Are there high profile public figures with disabilities – politicians, actors, TV presenters, etc?
- How is Paralympic and disabled sport perceived?
- Is the national Paralympic team high profile? Does it have a recognisable following?
- Is there a vociferous and active disabled persons' lobby?
- Does paternalism towards disabled people still exist and what form does it take?
- Do corporations and employers of large numbers of staff have active diversity and inclusion policies towards engaging disabled people?

Indeed, many might risk suggesting that in 'developed' countries all the boxes created by the above into some sort of matrix might get a positive tick. I prefer to see such a matrix with a scale of 1 to 10 against each element.

By doing so in 2003 at the time of the Bid it was clear that London, along with many others, vis-à-vis disabled people could not claim a clean sweep of 10s.

In some areas, over the past fifty years we have made phenomenal progress. And it is not by accident that this period has coincided with the evolution of disability sport in an organised way: making as it has a significant contribution to the inclusion agenda for disabled people.

Therefore at the drafting stage instead of providing an agenda of potential London 2012 Paralympic legacy/outcomes, the act of analysis itself made me pause and ask the question - Would the Games (by association this meant both Games, Olympic and Paralympic) be better invested in a Host City whose matrix scores were predominantly 2s and 3s? As the impact of holding the Games would be so much more significant.

Chapter 5 on the Seoul Paralympic Games in 1988 in which I reflect on my experiences as a volunteer Chef de Mission there, reveals the fantastic impact and legacy of hosting the Paralympic Games.

However notwithstanding that as a possible dramatic outcome elsewhere the enthusiasm and energy that could be created even about the possibility of holding the Paralympic Games in the land of its genesis, and my own country never deserted me.

The UK had, in 1948 during the time of those 14th Olympic Games, started a process that extended beyond sport and would touch society generally. It was a world leader in this regard. It was an exemplar of the possible. The approaching 14th Paralympic Games in 2012 should be the catalyst of a new set of outcomes not just Games related but for society too. If such legacies are not apparent in 2013 then an opportunity will surely have been missed.

Although the criteria in the matrix referred to might only move one or two points with a UK based event, the significance of those moves could be incalculable. Our approach here has been to align as closely as possible the outcomes presented in Singapore for both Games. Inspiring the youth of the world to engage and embrace sport has resonance for all.

And as stated previously, we can point to the impact in past years of those individuals in the disability world who adopted sport as part of their life-style. London will demonstrate to anyone who might doubt the efficacy of holding both Games together that it is possible to do so with a very positive outcome on the balance sheet and minimal additional activity on the operational delivery side.

The key is that the model has to be 'appropriate' to the host country and for us here in the context of London and not one imposed externally. To reinforce these words, London's approach might not be the approach of Rio (2016) or Sochi (2014) or future Bid Cities.

At the 'Bid stage' it was very important to get the messages right. London was less specific in some areas about outcomes rather choosing to set general objectives which could become more detailed later. The following statement about the Athletes Village is a good example.

"Any London residential development is subject to a number of imperatives -

- a significant proportion is made available as affordable housing (basically for essential workers)
- a minimum of 10% is available as fully accessible or adaptable housing for disabled people (increasingly in the UK to a standard known as ' Life Time Homes') "

Now while in a development of a 100 houses or apartments such standards might seem insignificant, in the Athletes' Village which originally was in excess of 3000 dwellings the accessible element is important not only numerically but in ensuring that the future community is both inclusive and integrated: because of design & build considerations, the latter is much more of a challenge than might at first be realised.

The physical consequences for the general infrastructure of such planning directives extend beyond the design of the accommodation alone. All those elements which support the new community are also impacted – the roads, transport systems, schools, hospitals, etc. This 'instant' post-Games community will be composed of the diversity planned for and therefore is made ready in every way as part of its overall development strategy and not piece by piece over many years with possible dilution with the passage of time.

The above statement simply represents the general London planning perspective.

When one overlays the Paralympic requirement the accessibility component increases many fold as the legacy accessible/adaptable accommodation alone cannot provide for the numbers of Paralympians requiring it. The Games team need to find innovative solutions which change the mind set of design while being mindful of resources and sustainability.

For example, make all door widths standard but of the 1000 ml. variety might be a major principle providing the opportunity for wheelchair resident use anywhere.

Similarly it is important to understand the 'wheelchair user in the Paralympic family' because not all wheelchair users require fully accessibly designed facilities: many can live with minor adaptations. But if they cannot get into the apartment in the first place significant flexibility is lost in the critical Games allocation process.

Wheelchair users are also not the sole beneficiaries of excellent accessible infrastructure. Obviously families with small children benefit as the lifts can take their buggies and prams and they too don't struggle to get into their apartment or house. To reinforce the point the most significant issue is the potential impact on future inclusion in the post-Games community as to the spread of useable accommodation throughout the development. This is a real Games consequence.

The outcome is that people with a disability have greater choice within the development as to where they wish to live rather than being confined to some 'specially constructed' part of a project.

Another good example of legacy choice revolves around spectators. Is it more important to fill seats or generate income for the Paralympic Games?

The answer of course is that both are important. In the past selling Paralympic tickets and generating income has been regarded as a secondary function by many Organising Committees. The viewpoint being that it was more important to fill seats than to realise that by literally giving this spectacle away it was never going to develop a worth, a value of its own.

Sydney 2000 surprised itself when SOCOG/SPOC generated significantly more income than its budget because it had invested in many promotional activities prior to the Games which sensitised the public to the excitement they might expect: a strong Australian Paralympic team was a further factor as previously indicated in the matrix. London intends to try and get both 'very right'. If we achieve an outcome where ticket income contributes to a balanced budget then we will also accomplish other positive outcomes on the way. For example, our aim is to encourage people to buy tickets because they are attending an exciting sports event rather than seeing it as a charitable contribution.

However we do realise that as in the case of Sydney significant education of Paralympic sport and innovative marketing strategies will have to precede the ticketing launch.

This example further reinforces the importance of the initial matrix analysis. A Bidding City/Host City needs to know its own context. The conditions exist in the UK to approach ticketing, spectators and income generation as a low/medium risk (poor attendance) whereas in some situations it might be considered high risk.

As stated previously at the 'Bid stage' such outcomes were less tangible and have only been worked through because of the total commitment and approach to an integrated plan. Anticipated outcomes at every point however need to be defined, regularly monitored and evaluated.

In the Bid document, page 173, the opening page of chapter 9 Paralympic theme states – the "Purpose and Promotion" as:

- Strengthening the Paralympic Movement
- Accessible and inclusive designs for all facilities
- Maximising media coverage

These general statements were enhanced with other undertakings because of the conditions prevailing at the time –

"All spectators will travel to the Paralympic venues by fully accessible public transport......"

Again this statement could not have been made if significant elements of this infrastructure did not already exist. In London 2012's situation this was the case – all public bus services had low-level ramped entry; all local trains would be accessible within 12 months; a significant part of the underground which served the venues was already accessible and London had the best fleet of accessible taxis anywhere in the world - 20,000 of the famous black cabs!

One might suggest that the above undertaking applies equally to the Olympic Games and therefore when one analyses Theme 9 of any Candidate File the majority of statements have this dual application. The question needs to be asked then is whether there is even a need for Theme 9?

Politically the answer is probably yes. Yes from an IOC perspective as it positions the Paralympic Games in their context as an invited partner.

Yes from the IPC perspective as the undertakings and proposed outcomes can be identified specifically as a consequence of holding the Paralympic Games.

There is a strongly held view that that to do otherwise might result in 'two Games, one event' simply coalescing into one event, the Olympic Games and as a consequence eroding the distinctiveness of the Paralympic Games.

Maximising outcomes/legacy

The Games, both Olympic & Paralympic are a massive undertaking for a host city. Every day that passes, leading to the Olympic Games Opening Ceremony there is the real danger of the Paralympic element being subsumed.

This is rarely an intentional act but one created by the circumstances with the immense pressure to get the whole event which starts with the Olympic Games off to the best possible start.

Is there a secret formula to guarantee that this does not happen? Is there a Games organising model which will provide for equal emphasis for both Games? The answer unfortunately is no.

But the matrix analysis previously referred to might help determine the model for each Host with a couple of basic principles applying.

The Organising Committee leadership, as here in London must be totally committed to both Games, philosophically and practically.

From the first moments of the formation of the Bid committee, an unshakeable understanding of the principle of inclusion for all aspects of the Games' event while maintaining the distinctiveness of each is critical.

One error in the past has been to simply see the Paralympic Games as a mini Olympic Games. In the early days of the Games this issue was less important than creating the more physical tangible, practical links to the Olympic Games organisation: Seoul's 1988 Paralympic Games were really the first time this physicality existed.

The opportunity, therefore, to 'exploit' all the Games' potential legacies including those particularly for people with a disability and the way in which society perceives their status has to be vested from the top of the organisation as the starting point.

Without that commitment discussing models is immaterial.

The second element to ensure equal emphasis for both Games is to be certain that all commitments, legislative changes, modifications of regulations, reinforcements of obligations are encapsulated for both Games. And not simply by inference – read Paralympic whenever you see the word Olympic.

The legislation for London 2012 was prepared in advance of the bid in Singapore to ensure that it was enacted within months of a successful decision. The Olympic marks had been protected by legislation for many years in the UK under a previous act.

But the London Olympic Games and Paralympic Games Act 2006 provided the same protection for the Paralympic marks vested with the British Paralympic Association for the first time among all the other Games' time requirements.

The consequence of the discussions which led to this legislation has been that the Minister charged with the responsibility for overseeing Government's involvement within the UK Government Cabinet, (Tessa Jowell at the time of writing) was known as the Minister for the Olympic and Paralympic Games.

These issues are not incidental to positioning the organisation effectively for delivery of all potential outcomes including Paralympic related ones. The caveat for any 'Paralympic organisational model discussion' is that one cannot be prescriptive and therefore no attempt is made here to define what the ideal model might look like. However, two distinct elements seem to emerge as key components supported by leaders specifically working at the highest level of Paralympic integration and coordination.

The two elements are –

- positioning the Paralympics Games - made up of communications strategy; marketing activities involving distinct branding; promotional activity; Paralympic events; association with national activity; Paralympic ambassadors and speakers; lobbying; diversity and inclusion activity (internal to the company and with external partners)
- detailed operational planning as an integral part of every Games dependent function; single function director or head responsible for both Games delivery; planning to be conducted simultaneously as sometimes Paralympic issues will determine Olympic ones; every planning session, strategic or operational to include Paralympic implications agenda item.

Previous Games have worked with good and poor examples of the above. So below are a couple of examples which are working for London. In the first instance the establishment of an 'Inclusion and Diversity' function demonstrates daily internally and externally that LOCOG is committed to its values and is not simply advocating a change applicable to others.

In a letter to The Telegraph newspaper (22.12.09) the following was stated:

"......51% of LOCOG employees are female and almost half the senior management team are women. 13% of LOCOG employees are from an ethnic minority background or heritage. LOCOG is the first organisation – from the public or private sector - in the UK to achieve the Gold Standard from Diversity Works for London and now asks suppliers to take part in it as well, many of them engaging in diversity for the first time. LOCOG is also the fastest organisation in the UK to achieve the Equality Standard for Sport and now encourages all Sports Governing Bodies to follow suit, sharing best practice to help".

The ability to influence others to these sorts of good practice demonstrates the power of a Games Organising Committee and its commitment to legacy.

In terms of the second element each LOCOG Director has specific responsibility for the delivery of each Games, both Olympic and Paralympic.

There is a Director of Paralympic Integration, Chris Holmes a former gold medal winning Paralympian, whose role is to ensure that each function holds true to the inclusion value; promotes the Paralympic Games and contributes to the operational delivery of the Games. Only time will tell but these are positive measures which hopefully will come to fruition at the London 2012 Paralympic Games.

Conclusions

The following represent five important principles to be taken into account in planning for future Paralympic Games in order that legacies can be ensured:

At every stage in the evolution of the Paralympic Movement the quality of the relationship between the IOC and IPC is critical to the delivery of the Paralympic Games.

The legacy and positive outcomes of the Paralympic Games are achieved by 'exploiting' the infrastructure and delivery imperatives of the Olympic Games.

Analysis of key criteria/characteristics of the Host country will help determine both what might be achieved; what the priorities might be and the best model to deliver those outcomes.

A fundamental promotion of the Paralympic Games has to be part of the company philosophy and the make-up of the senior leadership.

The outcomes for the Paralympic Games have to be embraced by every function and in every aspect of the way in which the company does business.

As stated from the outset of this chapter 'there is no clear or simple model which applies in every situation to maximise legacies from the Paralympic Games'.

While the Olympic Games can claim phenomenal physical regeneration and legacy to which the Paralympic Games can contribute, it is the Paralympic Games that can truly bring about fundamental universal social change.

Notes

* The views expressed in this chapter are those of the author alone and not the London Organising Committee for the Olympic and Paralympic Games Ltd.
* ONCE – National Organisation of the Spanish Blind: multi-national company employing 1000s of blind people in Spain with social, economic, recreational, housing projects funded by Spain's national lottery also managed by ONCE.

Chapter 13
The Paralympic Games

Legacy and Regeneration in Brazil

Fernando Telles Ribeiro

Introduction

The world is waiting for Rio de Janeiro 2016 and its Olympic legacies but the world should also want to know whether there will be legacies from the Paralympic Games in Brazil? However, at this point in time there is no developed legacy plan for the 2016 Paralympics Games which have included different groups of athletes with physical and intellectual disabilities. There is a suggestion towards a continuing development of a model of legacy but this is by no means implies 'developed in stone'.

By taking into account the historical developments and the legacy approach that has been applied to the traditional Olympic Games (Poynter, 2006), this chapter aims to provide an historical and analytic overview of the Paralympics Games in the Brazilian context. I will also focus on national Brazilian developments based on their meaningful impacts of legacy, which are founded on the hypothesis that structural and managerial developments which occurred in Brazil, were the result of the progressive changes and patterns which evolved in the international versions of the Games. (Poynter, 2006). The main difficulty in carrying out research for this chapter was related to the fact that there are scarce research data about the legacy of Paralympic Games, not only in Brazil, but on the international academic scene, hence the rationale for this book. Indeed, historically until London, the Paralympic Games are usually only mentioned in a single, generic and conclusive paragraph in the Games' bid documents and excluding Sydney in final reports by the organizing committees of Olympic host cities.

Generally speaking, Paralympic sport in Brazil has been beset with problems over issues such as limited space for displacement of the athletes and the limited number of sport facilities available with adequate equipment. To raise these points now while we are six years out from the Games and establish a new methodology for evaluating the post-games legacy is an important issue for future studies and the construction of models to evaluate the impact of Paralympic Games in Rio and other host cities. This perspective is particularly true for Brazilian concerns either from an academic or managerial perspective. In short thus far, the challenge here in Brazil is to bring about the expected and meaningful legacy and regeneration contributions for the city of Rio de Janeiro as a result of it hosting the 2016 Paralympic Games, following the Summer Olympiad (2012-2016). What follows is an historical perspective of Brazilian Paralympic sport in order to place future goals in context.

Historical background: (CPB - Comitê Paraolimpico Brasileiro, 2009)

In 1975, in Rio de Janeiro, Professor Aldo Miccolis founded the National Association of Sports for the Disabled. The purpose was to aggregate and join all sports performed by athletes with all kinds of physical and mental disabilites. As the years passed, the different modalities were divided into specific categories. For example, in the 1980-1990s most associations were founded: the Brazilian Association for the Amputees – ABDA, the Brazilian Association for Sports for the Blind – ABDC (1984) and the Association for the Mentally Impaired – ABDEM (1989) and finally the Brazilian Confederation of Sports for the Deaf – CBDS (1997), which represents Brazil in the International Sports Committee for Deaf People. Coincidentally, focusing international landmarks of this 1980-1990 period, it is important to mention that the IPC – International Paralympic Committee was founded in 1989, following a global tendency toward the creation of National Paralympic Committees (NPCs). For example in the Barcelona Paralympic Games (1992), the creation of National Paralympic Committees became urgent, since the IPC needed entities at the national level as affiliates were then able to aggregate those modalities for people with disability. In this regard the BPC – Brazilian Paralympic Committee was founded In November of 1995.

Objectives of the BPC

In formal terms, the general objectives of the new entity were defined as follows:

- To enhance the visibiity and empathy of the Paralympic Movement with regards to media and the general public;
- To consolidate the Paralympic Movement in Brazil, aiming at full development and diffusion of high-performance sport activities for disabled people in the country;
- To maintain a nucleus of communication and sport marketing as a mean of integrating press, advisory and public relations, such as the promotion, of visual communication and marketing;
- To establish an operational and promotional structure for the events in condition to respond to the expectations and strategic interests of both partners and their clients;
- To develop and establish the sponsorship of a program of human resources development in the form of seminars, administration workshops and sport marketing in regional and national areas, providing modernity and instrumentalizing associations, affiliates and clubs supportive of paralympic activities;
- To create, develop and establish a national program of licensing for the Paralympic Movement;

The operational objectives were as follows:

- To provide technical and scientific conditions for the development of athletes for the national Paralympic representations;
- To create a national ranking for the Brazilian Paralympic athletes;
- To standardize methods and tools for the evaluation of performances by the athletes;
- To stimulate the organization of national competitions in order to motivate and to identify new talents;
- To stimulate the participation of Brazilian athletes and Paralympic teams in international competitions;
- To improve professional qualification to human resources acting either in supportive functions or in output relations of the production, as referred to the Paralympic process of development.
- To stimulate the professional qualification of Paralympic athletes, aiming at planning and preparing them for post-career activities;
- To identify work conditions for Paralympic athletes for their future social and professional inclusion;
- To develop and strengthen the Brazilian Paralympic sport in general;
- To provide an adequate infrastructure for the development of high performance sports for people with disabilities throughout the country;

- To establish quality guidelines and criteria of management for the Affiliated Associations and Paralympic Clubs, aiming at standardization of managerial tools for the follow-up process, projects and results.

In short, these objectives raise a central question for this chapter: to what degree are such general and technical objectives adopted institutionally by the CPB and how will this be used at the Rio 2016 Paralympic Games? Indeed, will the Games, as part of the Olympiad, help to bring about improvements in the city's quality of life for people with a disability by addressing the important issue of social inclusion? To what extent will there be inclusion in the most competitive event in history? To answer these questions an analysis of the conceptual framework of the Paralympic Movement are addressed, and later associated to the specific political, institutional and cultural conditions of Rio de Janeiro. This will be attempted in order to present some basic considerations and suggestions for future Paralympic developments.

Existing Accessibility Infrastructure

With regards to the existing accessible infrastructure Rio 2016 is committed to providing a fully accessible Games for both the Olympic and Paralympic Games. Actions include:

- Adoption of accessibility legislation, which is considered one of the world's most comprehensible national accessibility laws, and a United Nations reference for limited mobility or special needs requirements – the agreement to adopt this legislation is a bid legacy;
- Establishing a panel of national accessibility experts to work with Rio 2016's Accessibility Manager and appointing independent international experts to review all venues, infrastructure projects, cultural facilities and the general city environment;
- Providing integrated accessible seating for each client according to IPC requirements;
- Installing accessible toilets at a ratio of one for every 15 spectators requiring accessible seating;
- Using press and broadcast camera platforms from the Olympic Games as accessible seating platforms for the Paralympic Games;
- Applying the IPC's accessibility guidelines;
- Minimizing transition work between the two Games.

In addition to these items, further information regarding the design and construction of all Games venues may be found in the United Nations Convention on the Right of Persons with Disabilities and its Optional Protocol, which was signed by the Brazilian Government in 2008. Rio's current built environment is in great need of upgrading. While competition venues for the 2007 ParaPanamerican Games were designed with international standards of accessibility, older venues still require refurbishment. All being well, this work should be completed by the time of the Games. While the transport infrastructure is currently partially accessible, Brazilian law requires all facilities and transport modes to be fully accessible by 2014 and new hotels throughout the city are required to have 5% accessible accommodation.

The city environment is a blend of historical, protected areas and modern, newly developed sectors. Accessibility levels within the city reflect this mix. Several initiatives have been launched by the City to improve the accessibility levels of the built environment, including the installation of accessible public telephones and the construction of over 1,000 ramps. Furthermore, a program of 'Accessibility in the Neighborhood' has begun to transform key neighborhoods.

Accessibility Standards / Integrated Planning and Delivery

The Rio 2016 Paralympic Games like all other major games must comply with national and international accessibility standards, in particular the IPC accessibility guidelines and the United Nations Convention on the Right of Persons with Disabilities and its Optional Protocol. Also, the three levels of Government must be able to guarantee that accessibility will be fully integrated into the planning and construction phases for both Games.

Disability Awareness / Comprehensive Education and Planning

Another issue of great concern in the contemporary view of the Paralympics is that of 'Disability Awareness'. The concept that both Olympic and Paralympic Games will incorporate accessible facilities, operations and training is presupposed to be the cornerstone of Rio 2016's planned training programs. People with disabilities would then participate, relating their experiences and advice on the optimal behaviors of the workforce.

Therefore, the program may include:
- Accessibility and the Paralympic Games – covering the history of the event, the range of Paralympic sport and how it helps barriers to be broken down;
- Workforce accessibility sensitivity – how to adapt to differences and to communicate, assist and guide people with accessibility needs. The program will be delivered to the entire Rio 2016 workforce, including security personnel and other contractors;
- Security screening procedures for people with disabilities – how Games security staff can perform their tasks efficiently yet still respect the dignity of people with disabilities;
- School education – establishment of Paralympic education lectures for primary and secondary levels and special education.

With these proposals in mind, Rio 2016 is being planned to provide incentives via all three levels of Government and sponsors to develop accessibility training programs for those working in the hospitality and tourism industries. Indeed, the Municipality of Rio de Janeiro will create a seal of approval for companies and professionals who participate in specific courses as well as those that retrofit their facilities according to international accessibility standards. Again, such initiatives presuppose to raise awareness among the Games workforce, as well as the general public, ensuring that all communication, assistance and conflict resolution will be treated with professionalism and sensitivity.

Press and communication vision of the Paralympic Games

Depending on the ability of the management group, the Rio 2016 Paralympic Games should be a platform for change. If success is met, the expected changes in the built environment, in perception, in sports participation and in media coverage of Paralympic sport will be achieved. If so, investment in accessibility regulations and infrastructure will change the lives of the inhabitants of Rio, making Rio a friendlier city for those with disabilities. Likewise, the sporting excellence of Paralympic athletes will continue to change society's perception of people with disabilities. In this favourable scenario, the positive transformation of Rio will be accelerated by hosting the Olympic and Paralympic Games.

Some recent historical events that point to this most optimistic outcome include Brazil acquiring significant experience in promoting the Paralympic Movement. Since the 2004 Athens Paralympic Games, the Brazilian Paralympic Committee (BPC) has developed a strong relationship with the media. TV coverage had an important impact on the way Brazilian society now perceives people with disabilities and as Paralympic athletes became effective ambassadors; people with disabilities have begun to have their own role models.

As argued in the local newspapers the BPC has continued to build its relationship with the media, as the 2007 Para-Panamerican Games included: 1084 accredited media from 14 Brazilian TV Networks, 11 foreign television networks and more than 340 written press organizations providing media coverage. Indeed, at the 2008 Beijing Paralympic Games, there were more impressive numbers: more than 130 live hours of live television, 25 hours of news dedicated to the Paralympic Games on national television and more than 1400 press articles (unknown source). With such growth in coverage of Paralympic sport it is anticipated that challenges in communicating the vision will be no different from those for Olympic Games. Rather, the Rio 2016 Paralympic Games will represent a significant opportunity for the consolidation of the Paralympic Movement, not only in Brazil but also through South America and beyond (Official 2016 Bid Document, 2009). However, as we will discuss in the last part of the chapter, it is difficult to divorce the Paralympics from the Games as a whole, and, in the case of the 2007 Para Panamerican Games, not everything went as well as is being announced for the 2016 Olympiad, an important issue for a more careful assessment of the legacy factor in this field in Brazil.

Adapted Sport: a social perspective

Another highly significant aspect of Rio 2016's goals is represented by the social dimension of adapted sport events. Following Doll-Tepper (1994) as an initial approach, mainstream concepts have been adopted at the international level that Rio organizers and promoters will be trying to address in the following areas:

- Each country, region or city should accelerate the introduction of the process of new regulations in favour of the same rights and accessibility to both sport and recreation facilities for people with disabilities;
- Both physical education and sport should be offered in an integrated fashion in schools, sport clubs and also considered in social programs. The principle of "sport for all" should be emphazised;
- The professional formation, both at the academic and non academic levels, should be stressed and understood as an objective contribution to the process of social integration;
- The social agents of people with disabilities: family, friends, teachers, etc. should be aware that they represent an important factor in the social integration process;
- The lack of representativeness in sport participation involving girls and women with disabilities, indicates a need to develop specific emphasis to enable more effective participation;
- The media coverage given to sport or persons with disabilities should be changed by giving more importance to the sport itself and less importance to the incapacities of the persons performing them;
- International sport megaevents, such as European and World championships including the Olympic Games, should be a forum for athletes with a disability. To achieve this it is necessary to develop closer relationships between international sports organizations and and sport organizations supporting sport for the disabled.
- It will be also necessary to indentify investigations in sub-disciplines of sport sciences. Fortunately, sociologists and psychologists have just started to study more deeply issues related to people with a disability and their participation in sports.

All these initiatives can be considered important steps towards full inclusion of people with a disability, specifically in physical education and sports in Brazil. The objective to be achieved is the quality of life for all. To bring all this about is a great challenge for the local organizers, given the immense social dimension of the Games and the intricacies of bringing together so many different athletes from every corner of the world. In particular it is important to stress the fundamental role of research centers at the university level to assist local governments in such entreprises as the current work conducted by the research team at LERI – London East Research Institute. Here they are conducting research that is being used by the Rio municipal government to critically examine the various phases of the implementation process in Brazil, especially with regards to the social and economic impacts on local neighborhoods and low-income communities. Should a further similar action be adopted by the Rio or Brazilian governments, an important process of impartial assessment of legacy gains could be added to these actions for the improvement of quality of life in Rio, especially from the point of view of the population with a disability.

Conclusions

Paralympic sport has experienced a significant development during the last quadrennial in both Brazil and worldwide. The learnings overtime by the Brazilian Olympic Committee may work as a model for resource investments, professional training and organization of megaevents and hopefully this will benefit the adapted sport image, which will then translate into acceptability, respect and inclusion of persons with disabilities throughout different sectors of the society.

The 3rd Para-panamerican Games (2007 PARAPAN) have been considered by my colleagues as among the best ever organized international sport mega-event. I argue here that the investments for the PA games were high and much of the planning dedicated to transportation, accessible sport facilities, opening and closing ceremonies, volunteers and other relevant aspects may be viewed as a strong potential to assure a successful Paralympic Games in 2016.

By hosting the Games of 2016, the city of Rio de Janeiro has an unique opportunity to turn into reality the most legitimate aspirations, not only of Paralympic athletes, but the expectations of a whole community of people with a disability, whatever their disability – in line with promotional and technical objectives of the CPB - Brazilian Paralympic Committee.

Gains of *hard* or tangible legacy such as accessibility of the existing and future Olympic infrastructures, were a firm commitment assumed when winning bid of Rio 2016: "...While competition venues for the 2007 ParaPanamerican Games were designed with international standards of accessibility, older venues require refurbishment. This work will be completed for the Games..." (COB, Rio 2016, 2009). It is then hoped that the role of the Paralympic Games is to be a catalyst for urban regeneration: "...while transport infrastructure is currently partially accessible, Brazilian Law requires all facilities and transport modes to be fully accessible by 2014. New hotels throughout the city will have 5% accessible accommodation" (COB, Rio 2016, 2009).

No less relevant, but of great importance as well, are the gains of *soft* or intangible legacy. The ample public visibility impact of the event will enhance respect and admiration for the para-athletes resulting in changed attitudes toward disability, contributing to break conscious or unconscious prejudice and barriers.

Finally, legacy and regeneration are not a status to reach or an ultimate objective to be achieved. On the contrary, they are an expression of progressive accomplishments and multidisciplinary approaches: a continuous vision and a paradigm of positive legacies and regeneration for the city of Rio de Janiero, for the country Brazil and the rest of the world.

References

Comite Olympico Brasileiro, Rio 2016 Bid Document, Chapter 10, Accessibility. Available at: (http://www.cob.org.br/-home/home/asp)

Canadian Olympic Committee (2009) History of the Paralympics, Paralympic Schools Program. Available at: (http://www.paralympic-education.ca/content/history)

Comite Paraolimpico Brasileiro. Availableat: (http://www.cpb.org.br/institutional/conheca)

Doll-Tepper, G. (1994) Deporte Adaptado – Perspectiva Social. *Apunts. Education Fisicia Deportes* (38), 21-25

Mataruna, L. (2008) *Avaliação das estruturas, organização e operacionalização dos Jogos parapan-americanos Rio 2007*. In L. DaCosta, D. Correa, E. Rizzuti, B. Villano, & A. Miragaya (Eds), *Legados de megaeventos esportivos* (pp. 519, 537), Brasília-DF: Ministério do Esporte & CON- FEF: Rio de Janeiro-RJ

Poynter, G. (2006) Working Paper in Urban Studies, *From Beijing to Bow Bells: Measuring the Olympic Effects*. London: London East Research Institute

Chapter 14
Winter Paralympic Games

Founding Legacies 1976 - 1980

Ted Fay

Introduction

This chapter will focus almost exclusively on the events, key issues and athletes, coaches, sport officials and others involved in the founding, evolution and initial growth of the Paralympic Winter Games from 1976 - 1988. Unlike its summer counterpart, which has enjoyed increasing interest from both scholars and the media over the past five years, the Winter Games have not received equal attention. What follows is a chapter that strives to provide a foundation, both from historical and critical perspectives, upon which future scholarship and more broadly-based media attention regarding the Winter Paralympic Games can ensue with recognition of the legacy these Games provided.

Historical Underpinnings

The segment of the Paralympic Winter Games (PWG) discussed in this chapter will be referred to as the Founding Era: 1976 – 1988 and will be presented through a series of brief summaries of four Games (1976, 1980,

1984 and 1988). Although there is a desire to delve deeply into the stories of each, unfortunately there is not space to adequately address the biographies of key athletes and other key difference makers.

The information used in this chapter (1976 – 1980) has been drawn from both primary and secondary sources including the author's own first hand experience that spans nine consecutive Paralympic Winter Games as a cross-country race guide (1980), head coach of U.S. national cross-country team (1984 – 1988), Technical Delegate overseeing all Paralympic cross country skiing and biathlon competition at three Paralympic Winter Games (1992 – 1998), Chair of the ISOD (1988 – 1992) and then IPC Nordic Sport Section (1990 – 1996) and finally as technical classifier for Paralympic cross country skiing and biathlon competition (2002 – 2010).

In many respects, the rich history, as well as more critical perspectives, of the Paralympic Winter Games has yet to be written. To its credit, the International Paralympic Committee commissioned a book that provides some of the broad historical textual elements of the Paralympic Winter Games (IPC, 2006), as well as attempting to aggregate race results and some pertinent data associated with each of the ten Winter Paralympics dating back to the initial Winter Games in Ornskoldsvik, Sweden in 1976 by providing this information on its website (www.paralympic.org). What this website lacks, however, is a deeper context of each of these Games that can only be gleaned from a behind the scenes knowledge and perspective. As one of those voices, this author will attempt to provide some additional observational perspective and context to the data presented.

The Beginnings

By most accounts, the inception of the Paralympic Winter Games came about more as a serendipitous rather than strategic act. Hans Lindstrom of Sweden, who has been appropriately recognized as one of the founders and key difference makers of the Paralympic Winter Games, describes a very ad hoc process that took place during a bathroom break at the 1974 General Assembly of the International Sports Organization for Disabled (ISOD). There was concern among some ISOD delegates that the nascent 1974 World Ski Championship for the Disabled held in Grand Bornand, France would not be continued due to an absence of commitment from any of the competing European nations to organize the 1976 World Championships (IPC, 2006).

Faced with this uncertainty, Dr. Bengt Nirje, founder of the Swedish Sports Organization for Disabled (SHIF) and an ISOD Vice President, suggested to his fellow Swedish delegates, Hans Lindstrom and Bengt Holden, SHIF President, that there was a potential opportunity to create the first Paralympic Winter Games and host them in Sweden. This vision and quick action by Nirje to the ISOD General Assembly led to the selection of the city of Ornskoldsvik to host the first Games, which also would be the first

Paralympic event that was open to athletes with other disabilities than spinal cord injuries such as athletes with an amputation or visual impairments (IPC, 2006).

Retrospectively, the advent of the Paralympic Winter Games in 1976 served as a laboratory for new thinking and innovation for the Paralympic Movement given that the history and practice of winter sports for athletes with a disability such as alpine and cross-country skiing was focused more on 'the sport and functional abilities and not so fixated on disability'. Because winter sports are strongly influenced by the environment and nature where they are practiced (e.g., terrain, weather, temperature) and are gravity-influenced activities in which equipment can help mitigate the disparities between disability types, alpine and cross-country skiing would became the innovators for change within the Paralympic Movement with benefits ranging from sport governance to classification of athletes.

Leading up to the 1976 Ornskoldsvik Games, it was not surprising that certain countries were well positioned to take leading roles in their respective traditional sports of alpine or cross- country skiing. Sweden, Norway and Finland led the way with respect to organizing and dominating Nordic skiing, while the traditional central European powers of Switzerland, Austria, Germany and France were dominant when it came to alpine skiing. It should be noted that some of these respective countries also had a long tradition of using winter sports as a means of rehabilitation of war veterans and victims of war (e.g., World War II) back into society. It is at this nexus of where rehabilitation goals and objectives intersect or meet sport goals that the Paralympic Winter Games began. It was also during this time period that active sport centers for individuals with disabilities were being created throughout Scandinavia, Europe, and in North America (Fay, 1994a and b).

It is also not by coincidence that the first two Paralympic Winter Games would take place in Sweden and Norway respectively. The leadership of the sports centers for people with disabilities in Bollnas in Sweden and at Beitstolen in Norway was a very strong influence as these institutions were recognized as innovators and pathfinders in promoting winter sport activities for people with a wide variety of disabilities The 1970s were also a time of turmoil and transition for a new generation of war veterans from the United States seeking ways to reclaim their active lives in the aftermath of the Vietnam 'war (Briggs; 2009, Batcheller, 2002). From this generation of veterans would come athletes who would emerge as some of the newest and strongest voices and leaders within the development and emerging governance of alpine and cross country ski skiing for individuals with disabilities.

Voices

It was from this group along with select group of strategic allies, that new battlegrounds were engaged over whether or not alpine and Nordic skiing would be organized and governed as cultural/identity events or as truly competitive and elite sporting events. Ian Brittain in his book, *The Paralympic Games Explained*, does an excellent job in outlining the discourse surrounding whether or not the Paralympics are a cultural/identity Games or an elite sporting event (Brittain, 2010). He effectively articulates the shift from the early period of the Paralympic Movement as led by Sir Ludwig Guttman, founder of the international disability sport movement, when sport was defined as a tool for rehabilitation and social integration to more recently when the International Paralympic Committee amended its mission statement to reflect a more elite, high performance set of goals and objectives (www.paralympic.org). This mission statement had the overall goal for each Paralympic sport to become an integral part of the international sport governance system for "able- bodied" athletes or as an independent sport organization overseeing a unique disability sport such as goalball or wheelchair basketball (Brittain, 2010).This is akin of the International Olympic Committee's amending the Olympic Charter in 1985 to purge any reference to the word "amateur" and create eligibility criteria that has allowed professional athletes to compete in the Olympic Games (Pound, 2004). It is within this context that the next sections will briefly outline the legacies of the four Paralympic Winter Games being reviewed.

The Cultural/Identity Games era: 1976 - 1988

This period includes the four Paralympic Games beginning with Ornskoldsvik, Sweden as the host city in 1976 and ending in Innsbruck, Austria in 1988 which holds the distinction of the only city to host two Olympic (1964 & 1976) and two Paralympic (1984 & 1988) Winter Games. This era is being defined by the author as the Cultural/Identity Games Period for a variety of reasons. The first and foremost was that it was managed through a multi-disability sport organizational governance system that focused on participation and not elite sport performance. Alpine and cross-country events were not standardized from one disability grouping to another, but there was an evolving classification system from same type of disability (1976 – 1984) to a more functional classification system beginning in 1988 based on similar ability or performance potential (Deville, et al, 1985).

Most alpine and cross-country ski athletes were not specifically trained at a high level. Most athletes were still multi-sport athletes who did not specifically focus on a winter sport. Events had a wide variance of numbers of participants ranging from 1 to 30 per racing class by 1988. Classification was not standardized using uniform acceptable testing methods (1976 -1984). Race courses varied widely and were not often challenging to the most talented athletes. Teams were housed in hotels and the Games often served as social as well as sporting events as evidenced by the following quote from Reinhild Moeller, German Alpine Paralympic Champion, 1980 -1998, describing her first experience in Geilo, Norway in 1980.

"It was very exciting to see so many ski racers with a disability from so many different countries. We all had two things in common, we had a disability and we wanted to face equal competition with worldwide standards. The ten days of competition had a taste of a festival, a meeting with old friends." (IPC, 2006, p. 16)

As described by Brittain "cultural games have as their aim and ethos of fostering self-respect and belief amongst their participants as well as helping to solidify their social identity as a group", (Brittain, 2010, p. 92). Ironically, as these Games helped bring athletes, coaches and games officials together in a international community of solidarity supporting broad participation of athletes with a disability in a winter sport, it also demonstrated the nasty and often discriminatory behavior of disability politics and hegemony based on the pecking order of disability type.

For example, the United States sent two separate teams to Geilo in 1980, which were organized by disability and sport type. The alpine team was comprised of men and women with locomotor disabilities, while the cross country team was made up of men and women who were blind or visually impaired. As a cross country race guide within that team, it felt as if these were two distinct teams from different countries. This was reinforced two years later in Switzerland at the 1982 World Ski Championships for the Disabled when the U.S. alpine and cross country teams arrived on different international flights, stayed in different hotels, were outfitted in different uniforms and marched in separately at the opening ceremonies. By 1984 in Innsbruck, this type of segregationist policies by sport and disability type was challenged by the U.S. cross country coaching staff and succeeded in integrating its own team by staying together as a united cross country team. Even though the model of separateness was most blatantly practiced by the United States team in 1980 and again in 1982, most national teams were very segregated by virtue of disability grouping (i.e., cultural/identity grouping). This was reinforced by the fact that a number of countries had separate sport governing bodies overseeing sport for individuals with disabilities based on the disability/identity grouping and not based on sport (DePauw & Gavron, 2005, Fay 1994a).

It was during this founding period that the international sport governance overseeing the Winter Games management was also somewhat Balkanized between the International Sport Organization for Disabled (ISOD) that managed the officials and rules governing athletes with a physical disability and the newly formed International Blind Sports Association (IBSA) who took control of those events involving athletes with visual impairments. The International Stoke Mandeville Wheelchair Sports Federation (ISMWSF) was responsible for athletes with spinal injured athletes while the Cerebral Palsy – International Sports and Recreation Association (CP-ISRA) was responsible for athletes who had cerebral palsy as well as neurological disabilities. This de-centralized governance structure made games management nearly impossible at times because of different rules for different disability groups witin the same sport that did not necessarily square with the common practice within that sport. It also required multiple chief event officials, such as the alpine and cross-country skiing Technical Delegates, to manage different races within a given sport that often was highly political and redundant. During this time the classification system for athletes was also evolving and was managed by doctors with some help from physiotherapists that relied almost exclusively on a medical, rather than a functional model of classification. This was consistent with a rehabilitation approach to maximizing participation and not a high performance sport model that emphasized intensive training and sport specialization (DePauw & Gavron, 2005).

Ornoskoldsvik – February 21st – 28th, 1976

As noted earlier, the inaugural Paralympic Winter Games was created upon the success of the first World Ski Championship in alpine and cross –country skiing held in 1974 in Grand Bornand, France for athletes who were visually impaired (cross-country) or had amputations (alpine and cross – country). The Ornskoldsvik Paralympic Organizing Committee (OPOC) had less than 18 months in which to organize these inaugural Winter Games, which included nearly 250 athletes from 16 nations from 4 continents (Europe, North America, Asia and Africa). International governance of the 1st Paralympic Winter Games was under the direction of the International Sports Organization for Disabled (ISOD) in cooperation with the International Stoke Mandeville Games Federation (ISMGF), which was the founding governing body of the first Paralympic Summer Games in Rome in 1960 (IPC, 2006).

Many of the racing classes had very few athletes within each grouping and the rule that there must be at least 5 athletes from 3 nations and two continents to have a valid race had not yet been introduced by ISOD or ISMGF. Thus, a number of athletes were declared the winner by virtue of just finishing. It is therefore difficult to assess the athletic ability and performance level of many of these medalists due to a lack of a reasonable critical mass of athletes in their racing class. For example, Canadian Lorna Manzer became the first athlete in Paralympic Winter Games history to medal in both alpine (2 bronze) and cross-country skiing (1 gold) in the same Games, however, her gold in the cross-country 5 kilometer race had no other competitor in her particular class (www.paralympic.org).

It is worth noting that the Ornskoldsvik Paralympic Winter Games were held after the conclusion of the Olympic Winter Games which were held in Innsbruck, Austria from February 4th - 15th. This became the first time that the Paralympics were not held within the same country as the Olympics, thus breaking a tradition started in Rome in 1960 by Sir Ludwig Guttman (Brittain, 2010). The most profound founding legacy of the 1976 Paralympic Winter Games was that it established the viability of staging a Winter Games in the same year as the Paralympic Summer Games that would be hosted for the 5th time in Toronto, but in the following summer. In essence, the 1976 Games in Ornskoldsvik were skiing Games and there were only two sports on the official program (alpine and cross country skiing) with the addition of the other Paralympic Winter Games sports of ice sledge speed racing (1980), biathlon (1988), ice sledge hockey (1994) and curling (2006) to be added at later Games. The pomp and circumstance of these inaugural Games was very modest with no significant media presence, no spectacular opening or closing ceremonies, and no centralized Paralympic village to allow for easy mixing of athletes and/or team officials with teams loosely organized with minimal technical support and coaching staffs (IPC, 2006).

Geilo, Norway – February 1st – 7th 1980

Unlike its predecessor, the Geilo Organizing Committee had more time in which to organize the 2nd Paralympic Winter Games that included 299 athletes (229 men, 70 women) from 18 nations from 4 continents (Europe, North America, Asia and Africa). This represented over a 40% increase in the number of competitors taking part as well as the addition of two new nations (Italy and New Zealand). The Games, which preceded the Olympic Winter Games in Lake Placid (February 13th – 24th), remained under the international governance of the Games remained under the direction of the International Sports Organization for Disabled (ISOD) in cooperation with the International Stoke Mandeville Games Federation (ISMGF). This was the second consecutive time that the Paralympic Winter Games were not held in the same country as the corresponding Olympic Winter Games in the same year (www.paralympic.org).

Even though the difficulty in assessing top performances based on the strength of a given racing class remained as it was in 1976, the quality and level of the performances in both alpine and cross country skiing seemed to improve and become more competitive in a number of racing classes. Ice sledge racing was introduced as a medal sport for the first time, thus expanding the Paralympic Winter Games The ice sledge racing track was an outdoor, natural track laid over a high school cinder track which was common in Norway and other countries near the Arctic Circle at the time.

Downhill (ski) sledge racing also made its debut as a demonstration sport and acted as a precursor to alpine sit-skiing. With a ski course traversing an alpine slope with high bank turns, the downhill sledge races resembled more of a toboggan or luge racing than skiing. It is interesting to reflect and wonder why there was not more interest in developing a modified luge event for athletes with a disability given the interest created by this event? Other legacies of Geilo included the patronage of the Games by the Norwegian Royal Family along with the presence of the first United States Alpine and Nordic teams. Geilo would be Games that launched the Paralympic careers of a number of athletes, race guides and national team coaches who would later become leaders of Paralympic skiing in the late 1980s and into the new millennium. As with the 1976 Games in Ornskoldsvik the pomp and circumstance at Geilo was also modest with no significant media presence, no spectacular opening or closing ceremonies, and no centralized Paralympic village. The major difference was that the teams were better prepared and organized with increased technical support and coaching staff.

References

Batcheller, L. J. (2002) *Alpine Achievement: A chronicle of the United States Disabled Ski Team.* Fairfield, CA: 1st Book Library Publishers.

Briggs, C. (2009) *Disabled Skiing: Disabled Veteran Discusses The U.S. Disabled Ski Team's Beginnings* http://www.disaboom.com/athletes-with-disabilities/disabled-veteran-discusses-the-us-disabled-ski-teams-beginnings

Brittain, I. (2010) *The Paralympic Games Explained.* London: Routledge.

DePauw, K. P. & Gavron, S. J. (2005) *Disability Sport* (2nd Ed.). Champaign, IL: Human Kinetics Publishers.

Deville, A., Blomquist, B., Kipfer, M. & Altenberger, R. (1985) *Functional Classification System for Disabled Skiing.* International Sports Organization for the Disabled (ISOD). Monograph.

Fay, T. G. (1994a) *Top level winter sports for the disabled.* Proceedings from the 2nd Paralympic Congress. Olso, NOR: Norwegian Ministry of Culture.

Fay, T. G. (1994b) *Technical developments for winter sports athletes: An interrelationship of research and practice.* In R. D. Steadward, E. R. Nelson, & G. D. Wheeler (Eds.) *VISTA '93 – The outlook.* Edmonton: ALB: Rick Hansen Centre.

International Paralympic Committee (2006) *Paralympic Winter Games: 1976 – 2006. Ornsdkoldsvik – Torino.* Bonn, Germany: International Paralympic Committee.

Chapter 15
Winter Paralympic Games

Founding Legacies 1984 – 1988

Ted Fay

Innsbruck, Austria, January 14th – 20th 1984

The Winter Olympic city of Innsbruck was selected to organize the 3rd Paralympic Winter Games, which included 419 athletes (325 men, 94 women) from 21 nations from 4 continents (Europe, North America, Asia, Oceania and Africa) who vied for 315 medals in three sport disciplines (alpine skiing, cross country skiing, and ice sledge speed racing). The Games preceded the 1984 Olympic Winter Games in Sarajevo (February 8 – 19) and were the first Winter Games governed under the direction of the International Coordinating Committee (ICC) that had been formed in 1982 after the 2nd World Ski Championships for the Disabled in Leysin, Switzerland with the purpose of providing a means to incorporate newly formed international sports organizations for the disabled (e.g., International Blind Sports Association, CP - ISRA) and that focused on new categories of athletes competing in the Games such as athletes with cerebral palsy (IPC 2006).

With many more medals at stake and on home turf, Austria emerged as the most dominant nation of the 1984 Paralympic Winter Games by taking 70 total medals including 34 gold. The number of racing categories was increased in alpine skiing from 6 to 9 with the addition of blind and visually impaired skiers taking part for the first time and more subclasses being created for physically disabled athletes. There was also an increase of racing classes in cross-country as well with the introduction of two sit-ski classes for the first time. The number of medals expanded dramatically almost twofold from 168 total medals awarded in Geilo in 1980 to 315 in 1984.

By adding new racing categories representing different disability groupings and therefore different ability and skill levels, the race organizers were faced with serious challenges in their selection of the race venues to accommodate the top level athletes while retaining a reasonable margin of safety. An additional problem of a severe lack of snow also forced the race organizers to call upon the Austrian army to help bring snow down from the nearby high glaciers and prepare the race tracks by hand. Indeed, there was no snowmaking equipment available in Austria and/or the central European alpine nations to assist the Innsbruck Organizing Committee as was done in Lake Placid for the 1980 Olympic Winter Games.

The 1984 Games were unusual in that multiple relay teams from the same nation were allowed to compete, thus giving host nation Austria and Finland the opportunity to win gold and silver in their respective relay events. This practice would be changed for succeeding Paralympic Winter Games.

Sarajevo, Yugoslavia, February 8th – 19th

This was the first-ever Winter Olympic exhibition event for Paralympic athletes. It included 30 male alpine, giant slalom athletes in four different racing classes that included both leg and arm amputees. Reports from Sarajevo do not describe a well organized and well integrated set of events, but rather a hastily held set of competitions. The athletes were also housed and accredited apart from the Olympic Village and were not seen as a part of their respective national Olympic teams. The athletes were not allowed to wear the national uniforms of their respective Olympic teams or take part in the Opening and Closing ceremonies of the Olympic Games. The most positive legacy of this experience for the athletes and coaches was that it was perceived as a breakthrough event that laid the foundation for the next set of exhibition events staged in Calgary at the 1988 Winter Olympic Games (Briggs, 2009).

Innsbruck, Austria, January 17th – 24th 1988

Due to organizational issues associated with the 1988 Calgary Olympic Organizing Committee, Innsbruck was once again called upon on relatively short notice to organize the 4th Paralympic Winter Games. Ironically, the Calgary Olympic Organizing Committee, who would turn down the opportunity to organize these Games, would agree instead, to host the second alpine and the first – ever cross country ski exhibition events for Paralympic athletes during the course of the Olympic Winter Games (February 13th – 28th) one month later. Because the 1988 Paralympic Winter Games occurred one month earlier than the Olympic Winter Games, the Innsbruck Paralympic Winter Games served as de facto qualifying events for their respective Olympic exhibition events for the three –track alpine races (LW 2) for men and women and the B – 1 cross country races for totally blind men and women. The importance of these exhibition events will be addressed later in the next section.

Participation data from the 1988 Games reveals a very interesting trend for the Paralympic Winter Games in that there was a significant decrease in the number of athletes from 419 in 1984 to 377 athletes in 1988, while at the same time, there was an increase of one new nation (the Soviet Union) bringing the total to 22. There was also a corresponding drop in the number of medals awarded from 1984 to 1988 even though new sports and events were added to the Games program. Biathlon, a new discipline of alpine mono-ski, and a new category for blind athletes that split the B – 2 class for visually impaired athletes into two groups (B - 2 and B - 3) to better differentiate athletes with wide ranges of visual acuity for both alpine and cross country skiing provided new medal opportunities for athletes. The biathlon race for three physically disabled racing classes added nine new medal options for cross country athletes and thus really did not have an effect of bringing new specialists to the Paralympic Winter Games. A similar effect occurred in splitting the B 2 group into B – 2 and B - 3 categories in that it simply reassigned existing athletes by reducing the 1984 start fields in each respective alpine or cross country race roughly in half. Correspondingly, the mono-ski alpine races for men and women added 10 new medals while also attracting a whole new group of eligible athletes (Fay, 1989).

This seemingly contradictory data actually has a relatively straight forward answer. With respect to a decline in athlete participation, there was an 8 % decrease in the number of men competing in all sports (325 to 300 athletes), coupled with an 18% decrease in the number of women (from 94 to 77 athletes). One explanation for this drop in participation numbers even despite the evidence of new sports and racing classes being added was that the athletes were beginning to be subjected to higher national qualifying standards in concert with an overall increase in the skill and competitiveness within racing groups. This new trend or shift was led by several nations such as the United States, Germany and Norway taking the lead to hold their athletes to higher performance standards.

There are several potential explanations for the decrease in the total number of medals awarded from 315 to 279 that might be related to the cancellation and/or combining of race classes in either alpine, cross country and/or ice sledge racing. Some of these cancellations were based on new governance criteria from the ICC that stated there needed to be a certain number of athletes from a specific number of nations and from at least two continents in order to hold a competition otherwise an event in a given racing class would be cancelled.

A cursory look at each sport respectively, however, reveals a different and far simpler explanation for the reduction of medals awarded. Alpine as an example was a case of addition and subtraction with the net effect being fewer medals awarded and by adding men and women sit-ski races, alpine skiing increased its medal total by 10 medals and by an additional 6 medals for two new B – 3 races for men. This was offset by the men's slalom race in the LW 3 class not being run, thus eliminating 3 medals along with only 2 medals awarded for the LW 1 racing class providing a loss of 5 medals. Despite these changes, this still left a positive net of 11 medals gained. The women saw an increase of 4 medals with the addition of the LW 10 racing class for mono-skiers, but also experienced a reduction of 9 medals by the elimination of the two races for LW 5/7 racing class that were run in 1984, but not in 1988 as based on the new eligibility criteria regarding too few nations rule for an actual net loss of 4 medals from 1984. The biggest change and surprise, however, came as the result of the complete elimination of the men's and women's alpine combination race, thus wiping out 43 total medals in one fell swoop. Thus, alpine skiing accounted for a gain of 11 new medals counterbalanced by a loss of 47 medals awarded in 1984 for an overall net loss of 36 total medals not awarded.

One of the legacies of the 1988 Paralympic Winter Games was the introduction of a new sport of biathlon race for three standing physically disabled racing classes. The competitors shot twice from the prone position using air rifles on a 10 meter range while completing the 7.5 km event. The equipment including the air rifles and targets used by the competitors was crude by modern biathlon standards. Although an acoustic system had been developed in Sweden that allowed blind and visually impaired athletes to be able to sight and shoot at a target that interacted through sound with a special scope, it was felt that the results were too inconsistent to be able to hold a fair competition. This event, however, was the launch point for biathlon becoming one of the most spectator-friendly and dynamic of all the sports conducted at Paralympic Winter Games (Fay, 1989, IPC, 2006).

These were also the first Paralympic Games, Summer or Winter, to welcome the Soviet Union which only sent a small cross country team made up of blind and visually impaired athletes. This would be the first and last time that the USSR would compete in the Paralympic Winter Games under the aegis of the Hammer and Sickle with the impending fall of the Berlin Wall in 1989.

The Games were also the second Winter Games governed under the direction of the International Coordinating Committee (ICC). There was, however, already a movement starting in 1987 to create a new and more integrated international governing body, the International Paralympic Committee (Brittain, 2010, DePauw & Gavron, 2005). The IPC would officially take over managing the Paralympic Winter Games from the ICC beginning with the Lillehammer in 1994. 1988 also witnessed a significant changing of the guard with respect to overall sport leadership within the International Sports Organization for the Disabled with control being shifted in alpine skiing from the central European powers of Austria, Switzerland, and Germany to North Americans such as, Jack Benedick and Ted Fay and Canadian, Jerry Johnston (Fay, 1994a & b).

Other legacies of the 1988 Games related specifically to new challenges to games management. By adding new racing categories representing different disability groupings and therefore different ability and skill levels, the Innsbruck race organizers were faced with serious challenges in their selection of the race venues to try and accommodate the top level athletes while retaining a reasonable margin of safety. Initial selection of alpine and Nordic venues erred towards very easy race courses that did not fully challenge the best skiers. The cross country ski and biathlon ultimately were moved to Seefeld, the site of Olympic and World Championship events, however these courses were modified to the point where they were quite flat without any significant uphill or downhill challenges (Fay, 1993).

Calgary, Alberta, Canada -, February 13th - 28th 1988

Slightly over two weeks after the conclusion of the 1988 Paralympic Winter Games a select group of male and female Paralympic athletes would re-assemble in Calgary, Alberta as part of two exhibition events hosted by the Calgary Olympic Organizing Committee. The format of these exhibition events had been significantly modified from the first-ever exhibition races held as part of the Sarajevo Olympic Winter Games in 1984. The 1984 events were contested in giant slalom in four different categories for standing disability classes for men only. The 1988 events included a giant slalom event for men and women respectively who had above-the-knee amputations and used a single ski with two outriggers as poles. These exhibition events included cross-country events for the first time with a 5 km race for totally blind men and women. Each start field included the top eight competitors in their respective racing classes as based on the results from the 4th Paralympic Winter Games conducted a month earlier in Innsbruck, Austria (Fay, 1993).

Contrary to the Paralympic Winter Games, these Olympic exhibition events received far more press and broadcast coverage in both North America and Europe and proved to be a critical lasting legacy of the Founding Era of the Paralympic Winter Games. There were a number of convergent factors that led to the profile of these exhibitions being raised beyond an afterthought. First, the law of unintended consequences was in play as both the American and Norwegian Olympic ski teams had less than stellar results. The United States was completely shut out of all ski-related medals in alpine, cross country, ski jumping, Nordic combined and biathlon, while the usually reliable Norwegians were left with but three silver and two bronze medals in the Nordic events and no gold in events they traditionally dominated. The Norwegian press and television was in an uproar, while ABC television was left searching for a few good stories regarding U.S. athletes to fill its many broadcast hours back to the viewers back in the United States (Fay, 1989 and 1993).

For the Norwegians, Hans Anton Aalien, a totally blind cross country skier, would emerge as an overnight front page story in his native land as he captured the only gold medal in any Winter Olympic event for Norway at the 1988 Games as he led a Norwegian-Swedish sweep of the 5 km cross country medals. Multiple Paralympic gold medalists, Ake Petterson from Sweden won the silver, while Asmund Tveit won the bronze. Tveit's bronze also received a lot of attention from the Norwegian press because he was guided by Kjtell Ulvang, who was the younger brother of Vegard Ulvang, who had just won an Olympic bronze medal in the 30 km classic event several days before.

Despite finishing out of the medals, John Novotny from the U.S. and his race guide Craig Ward also garnered nearly 5 minutes of prime time ABC Olympic television coverage through a special segment hosted by ABC announcer Bill Koch, 1976 Olympic silver medalist in Innsbruck. The segment featured the two former U.S. Olympic athletes, Ward (captain of the 1980 U.S. cross country team in Lake Placid) and Koch (1976 Olympic silver medalist in Innsbruck and 1980, 1984 and 1992 Olympian), trading positions as they demonstrated the challenges in guiding a blind skier through the turns, uphill and downhill sections of the demanding Canmore Olympic course at 'normal' race speeds. This segment proved to be longer than all other segments featuring the U.S. Olympians on the U.S. Ski Team at the 1988 Games (Fay, 1989, Fay, Wolff and Hums, 2007).

Also featured on ABC's prime time coverage was the spectacular sweep of the women's giant slalom exhibition medals by U.S. athletes Diana Golden, Cathy Gentile, and Martha Hill. Coupled with Greg Mannino's silver medal, the United States led the medal table for the 4 Olympic ski exhibition events with a total of 4 including one gold, two silvers and a bronze. This nearly equaled the total of six medals won at the 1988 Olympic Winter Games by all U.S. Olympic athletes none of which was accomplished by a ski athlete (Golden, 2010 a & b, Briggs, 2009).

Golden, a multiple gold medalist in downhill and giant slalom at the 1988 Paralympic Winter Games and gold medalist in the Olympic giant slalom exhibition event in Calgary, was ahead of her time in that she became a fully sponsored ski racer supported by an array of sponsors including Visa, Subaru of America, and Chap-Stick. At the time in 1988, it was estimated that she was the third highest supported women on the U.S. Ski Team including all able-bodied athletes. Golden also forced the adoption of the 'Golden Rule' which allow ski athletes with a disability to start in the early seed groupings of U.S. Ski & Snowboard Association sanctioned races and race against 'able-bodied' competition. Also worth noting was the position taken by the United States Olympic Committee and other participating nations in accepting the alpine and Nordic Paralympic athletes into their respective delegations as full members of their 1988 Olympic Team. This meant the athletes, guides and coaches were able to march in Opening and

Closing Ceremonies, be given a complete kit of U.S. Olympic clothing, be credentialed as Olympians to have full access to all Olympic venues and be granted full privileges as a member of their respective Olympic Team. This valuing of Paralympians was unprecedented at the time and would become a matter of hot debate at future Olympic Summer Games with respect to the treatment of Paralympic exhibition athletes in track and field. Ironically, the athletes involved in the Olympic exhibition skiing events in 1988 were given the most equity with respect to their Olympic counterparts than at any Olympic Games from 1984 – 2004 (Legg, Fay, Hums & Wolff, 2009; Fay, Wolff & Hums, 2007, Fay, 1989 and 1999).

References

Briggs, C. (2009) *Disabled Skiing: Disabled Veteran Discusses the U.S. Disabled Ski Team's Beginning.* Available at: (http://www.disaboom.com?athletes-with-disabilities/disabled-veteran-discusses-the-us-disabled-ski-teams-beginnings)

Brittain, I. (2010) *The Paralympic Games Explained.* London: Routledge.

DePauw, K. P. & Gavron, S. J. (2005) *Disability Sport (2nd Ed.).* Champaign, IL: Human Kinetics Publishers.

Diana Golden Biography (2010) Available at: (http://sports.jrank.org/pages/1665/Golden-Diana.html) (accessed 26th November 2010)

Diana Golden – Awards and Accomplishments (2010b) Available at: (http://www.sports.jrank.org/pages/1665/Golden-Diana-Awards-Accomplishments.html) (accessed 26th November 2010).

Fay, T. G. (1989) Beyond the medals and fanfare: Nordic skisport – health and excitement for all. *Palaestra,* **6**, 37 – 45.

Fay, T. G. (1993) *Integration of athletes with disabilities in international sport: Consensus or Discord? The Paralympians view.* Paper presented at annual meeting of International Paralympic Committee Sport Council. Northampton, ENG: International Paralympic Committee.

Fay, T. G. (1994a) *Top level winter sports for the disabled.* Proceedings from the 2nd Paralympic Congress. Olso, NOR: Norwegian Ministry of Culture.

Fay, T. G. (1994b) *Technical developments for winter sports athletes: An interrelationship of research and practice.* In R. D. Steadward, E. R. Nelson, & G. D. Wheeler (Eds.) *VISTA '93 – The outlook.* Edmonton: ALB: Rick Hansen Centre.

Fay, T. G. (1999) *Race, gender, and disability: A new paradigm towards full participation and equal opportunity in sport.* Doctoral dissertation. University of Massachusetts Amherst.

Fay, T., Wolff, E.A., and M.A. Hums (2003) IPC Sport Cla- ssification Systems and the Public Perception of the Paralympic Games: Implications on Marketing, Media Coverage and the Management of the Games. *Proceedings of the 2003 VISTA Paralympic Congress, Bollnas, Sweden.* CD version.

International Paralympic Committee (2006) *Paralympic Winter Games: 1976 – 2006. Ornsdkoldsvik – Torino.* Bonn, Germany: International Paralympic Committee.

Legg, D., Fay, T. G., Hums, M. A. & Wolff, E.A. (2009 Fall) Examining the inclusion of wheelchair exhibition events within the Olympic Games 1984 - 2004. *European Sport Management Quarterly.* **9**, 3.

Chapter 16
Winter Paralympic Games

Summary of Legacies 1976 - 1988

Ted Fay

Summary of the Founding Legacies 1976 – 1988

The legacies of the four Paralympic Winter Games from 1976 – 1988 provided a rock solid foundation from which a clear transition from cultural to high performance Games could take place. Beginning as a gathering of predominantly recreational athletes participating in a ski festival in 1976 and ending with top level performances by highly competitive athletes in exhibition events for cross country and alpine skiing at the 1988 Olympic Games, this period truly set the stage where the Paralympic Winter Games have now evolved and which feature intense, elite high performance athletes where the difference between winning and losing is a matter of seconds seriously impacting national pride and substantial financial gain (Putin, 2010). The entry of the Soviet Union cross country team in Innsbruck in 1988 would be the precursor for the inclusion of the new countries of Russia, Ukraine, Belarus, Kasakstan, Estonia, Latvia in 1992.

It is during this period that the Paralympic Winter Games added two new sports of ice sledge speed racing (1980) and biathlon (1988) and allowed the addition of free technique cross country skiing races for the standing physically disabled racing categories. Introduction of a biathlon event for men with a visual impairment and the allowance of free technique cross country skiing races would have to wait until the 1992 Paralympic Winter Games in Tignes/Albertville, France.

The host city and region of Innsbruck, Austria provided the opportunity in 1984 and again in 1988 for alpine, biathlon, cross country, and ice sledge speed racing athletes to compete on former Olympic and World Championship competition venues for the very first time. Opening and Closing Ceremonies evolved from an afterthought with the march of nations to more of a theatrical spectacle held in a former Olympic venue used for ice skating and ice hockey events during the 1964 and 1976 Olympics. The logos of the 1984 and 1988 Innsbruck Paralympic Winter Games uniquely utilized the Olympic rings in combination with a stylized version of a Paralympic symbol.

Sport Governance

The 1988 Games were the second Winter Games governed under the direction of the International Coordinating Committee (ICC). There was, however, already a movement starting in 1987 to create a new and more integrated international governing body, the International Paralympic Committee. The IPC would officially take over managing the Paralympic Winter Games from the ICC beginning with the Lillehammer in 1994 (Brittain, 2010; DePauw & Gavron, 2005).

At this time there was a very strong effort to move the governance of alpine and Nordic skiing following the 1988 Innsbruck Paralympic Winter Games under the auspices of the International Ski Federation (FIS). This movement led to a series of meetings with the FIS during and after the Calgary Olympic exhibition events and led to the establishment of a new Committee on Disabled Skiing in 1989, but stopped short of full inclusion of disabled skiing into the FIS (Briggs, 2009, 2010, Fay, 1989).

IBSA did not support this move by the ISOD Chairs to advocate for greater integration and inclusion with the mainstream ski racing community. IBSA, for example, refused to change its cross country rules to correspond with the FIS cross country rules that had evolved in the early 1980s to include free technique and classic style races. IBSA claimed that blind and visually impaired athletes were incapable of learning and performing the skills of free technique or skating style of skiing, although many athletes performed this technique quite well in non-IBSA sanctioned races. It is at this juncture that a major power struggle began to ensue between ISOD and IBSA over whether the Paralympic Winter Games would remain a more open, participatory ski festival or become more like its elite, competitive able-bodied cousins (Fay, 1989 and 1993).

It is worth noting that the United States Disabled Ski Team (USDST) was created in 1986 under the governance and auspices of the U.S. Ski Team making it the first national team in Paralympic history, Summer and

Winter, to be integrated into a national governing body of an Olympic sport. This also included the full integration of national championship races for athletes with a disability into the U.S. Cross Country Ski Championships beginning in 1987 with equal status with able-bodied skiers. Even though, the U.S. Alpine Championships remained two separate events held at different times and a different venue, the status of championship medals was recognized as having equal status by the US Ski Team and US Ski and Snowboard Association (Fay, 1989, Fay, Hums & Wolff, 2007, Fay & Wolff, 2009).

This was an amazing change from the separatist, segregated entry of the United States into the Paralympic Winter Games just eight years before in 1980 in Geilo, Norway and the fight to field alpine and cross country teams that integrated athletes from physically disabled and visually impaired disability racing classes as one united team. This led to a sport specific and not disability specific shift in the technical organization and selection of coaching staffs for the U.S. team (Fay, 1989 and 1999).

Sport Classification Systems

As with the advent of new events (e.g., alpine and cross country ski skiing) and sport disciplines (e.g., ice sledge speed racing and biathlon), better organization by host cities through more professional event management, use of previous Olympic venues (e.g., Innsbruck in 1984 & 1988), the increase in athlete abilities and performance, and the addition of new nations, another lasting legacies from this Games period was the evolution and adoption of sport classification systems that are still utilized in some form over twenty-five years later. A group of visionary physiotherapists from Austria, Germany and Switzerland created a functional classification model for grouping athletes with a physical disability into like-type race groupings (Deville, et al, 1985, Fay, 1993 and 2000).

Pioneers of this effort established an initial three class system for sitting athletes (Group I, II, & III) based on level of neurological impairment and a nine class (LW 2 – 9) system for standing classes. This allowed a testing system which focused on the key bio-mechanical elements of alpine or Nordic skiing, as well as ice sledge speed racing and its relationship to an athlete's trunk strength, balance and mobility. Although improved over time, one of the enduring legacies of this testing early regimen that is still in use as recently as the 2010 Vancouver Games has been the tilt table (Deville, et al, 1985).

Ted Fay from the United States, with support from Ingalill Bartlett from Norway and Rolf Hettich from Germany, began creating a time factor system in 1986 after the conclusion of the 1986 World Ski Championships for the Disabled in Salen, Sweden in which athletes with different disabilities from different racing classes were combined into one racing group using a time formula based on international race results (Fay, 1989; Lannem, et al, 2009). This system was used as early as the 1992 Winter Paralympic Games in Albertville/Tignes to help combine the women's cross country standing classes (LW 2 – LW 9) into a large enough critical mass to be able to stage a valid competition. Otherwise there would have been too few athletes from too few nations to be able to award gold, silver and bronze medals in racing groups of less than 3 which had happened in 1976 and in 1980. This system, although refined through more performance-based scientific study and the application of more complex computer-aided statistical modeling programs, created in the late 1980s is now the basis for having just three sets of medals awarded for all cross country, biathlon and alpine events at the 2006 and 2010 Winter Paralympic Games (Fay, 1989, Lannem et al, 2009, IPC 2006). Alpine adopted a similar system in the early 1990s (IPC, 2006).

Chapters 14, 15 and 16 Final Thoughts

Legacies of Paralympic Winter Games have evolved and emerged over the past thirty years born from a gathering of recreational athletes participating in ski festivals (e.g., early Paralympic Games and World Championships) that provided opportunities to compete with athletes with similar disabilities and build new friendships to events featuring intense, elite high performance athletes where the difference between winning and losing is a matter of national pride and financial gain as expressed by Soviet Prime Minister, Vladamir Putin at the close of the 2010 Vancouver Paralympic Games (e.g., Putin, 2010). From these, a set of overarching legacy issues have emerged existing both at the national and, international level.

One of them relates to the current and future overall governance and management of each sport. The General Assembly of the International Paralympic Committee voted in 2000 to force all Paralympic sport, both Summer and Winter, to be become independent, sport-specific international governing bodies by 2016. Based on current practice, this could mean the creation of a completely new Paralympic sport international federation (e.g., the International Disabled Ski Federation), the absorption into an existing international sport federation that currently oversees non-disabled related competition (e.g., the International Ski Federation), or a third possibility of being assimilated by an international organization for sports for the disabled such as the International Wheelchair and Amputee Sports Federation (IWASF).

Examples of each of these models already exist within the family of IPC Summer sports, however, wheelchair curling is the only winter sport that is part of an outside international sport governing body (World Curling Federation). The remaining four sports of alpine skiing, biathlon, cross country skiing and ice sledge hockey still currently operate as IPC sports that are governed under the auspices of the IPC as multi-disability sports for athletes with a disability and are managed through a respective IPC Sports Committee (Brittain, 2010). Cross country skiing was the first ever IPC Sport Committee established in 1990 under the direction of the author. The IPC alpine committee was established soon after under the leadership of Jack Benedick of USA and Jerry Johnston of Canada. In both instances, the intent was to accelerate the tacit relationship these two sports had with the International Ski Federation beginning in 1989 to having the FIS fully embrace and incorporate these two disciplines within its operating structures including FIS World Ski Championships and World Cups (Fay, 1993).

Despite a growing consensus among competing nations and efforts of key individuals within the alpine and cross country ski racing Paralympic community, this goal has yet to be realized. Recently, another international governing body, the International Biathlon Union (IBU), has become more interested in potentially absorbing at least a portion of the IPC Nordic Sport Committee within its aegis. This represents both an opportunity and a dilemma for a number of athletes and nations from a logistical perspective in that typically Paralympic athletes compete in both disciplines and most national Paralympic teams do not distinguish between their cross country and their biathlon teams as their Olympic counterparts do. This also sets up potential conflicts on a national level between two separate governing bodies. Conversely, it also expands the possibility of increased support and interest in developing and sustaining each sport within a given nation.

One IPC winter sport that did not make its debut in the 1980s (circa 1994) is ice sledge hockey. The legacy from the early development period of the sport in the 1970s and 1980s is again an evolution from a small separate disability sport movement to an apparent move to be absorbed by the International Ice Hockey Federation (IIHF). Increased integration and support by Hockey Canada and USA Hockey of their respective national sledge hockey teams portents well for the future shift from the IPC to the IIHF. The increased media and broadcast exposure, plus growing fan interest as demonstrated by sold out semifinal and gold medal games at the last three Paralympic Winter Games sledge hockey tournaments suggests that the IIHF could realize a clear benefit by developing a new niche to its brand as its displayed through IIHF World Championships, Olympic and Paralympic ice hockey tournaments. If for some reason the IIHF declines the chance to take over the governance and management of ice sledge hockey, then there is the possibility of the nations forming a separate federation (e.g., International Sledge Hockey Federation) or being housed under the umbrella of the International Wheelchair and Amputee Sports Federation. If the IWASF were to assume this responsibility, it would represent a dramatic shift away from the movement toward sport-specific, mainstream governance that has been fought for by athletes and coaches for over 30 years (Brittain, 2010).

With the shift to more acceptance of Paralympic athletes and teams into national and international sport federations, is the future destined to see a new legacy of full inclusion within the Olympic Games and IF World championships or World Cups? What will the 20-year legacy of winter (1984 and 1988) and summer exhibition events (1984 – 2004) eventually have on this debate. It is worth taking note that the treatment of athletes with a disability, coaches and game officials taking part in exhibition events at the 1988 Winter Olympic Games in Calgary, Alberta were the zenith of equity and inclusion in the Games for athletes with a disability (Legg, et al, 2009).

According to the author, who participated as a Nordic coach for the U.S. Olympic Team at the 1988 Olympic Games, athletes with disability participating in alpine and Nordic ski events in Calgary were housed, clothed, and credentialed in the same manner as all other Olympic demonstration sport athletes (e.g., short track speed skating, curling, freestyle skiing) at a level equal to Olympic athletes from their respective nations. It should be noted that all three demonstration sports in Calgary became full medal Olympic sports at subsequent Olympic Games (Legg, et al, 2009, Fay & Wolff, 2009).

References

Briggs, C. (2009) *Disabled Skiing: Disabled Veteran Discusses the U.S. Disabled Ski Team's Beginning.* Available at: (http://www.disaboom.com?athletes-with-disabilities/disabled-veteran-discusses-the-us-disabled-ski-teams-beginnings)

Brittain, I. (2010) *The Paralympic Games Explained.* London: Routledge.

DePauw, K. P. & Gavron, S. J. (2005) *Disability Sport (2nd Ed.).* Champaign, IL: Human Kinetics Publishers.

Deville, A., Blomquist, B., Kipfer, M. & Altenberger, R. (1985) *Functional Classification System for Disabled Skiing.* International Sports Organization for the Disabled (ISOD). Monograph.

Fay, T. G. (1989) Beyond the medals and fanfare: Nordic skisport – health and excitement for all. *Palaestra,* **6**, 37 – 45.

Fay, T. G. (1993) *Integration of athletes with disabilities in international sport: Consensus or Discord? The Paralympians view.* Paper presented at annual meeting of International Paralympic Committee Sport Council. Northampton, ENG: International Paralympic Committee.

Fay, T. G. (2000) Strategic approaches to vertical integration & equity for athletes with disabilities: An examination of a critical change factors model. In G. Doll-Tepper, M. Kroner, & W. Sonnenschein (Eds.). *New horizons in sport for athletes with a disability.* Holt, MI: Partners Book Distributing.

Fay, T.G., Hums, M.A. and E.A. Wolff, (2007) *"Critical change factors model: understanding the integration process of sport opportunities for athletes with disabilities into national governing bodies and the United States Olympic Committee" CSSS Staff Presentations.* Paper 7. Available at: (http://www.hdl.handle.net/2047/d10009607)

Fay, T. G. & Wolff, E. A. (2009 Summer) Disability in Sport in the Twenty-First Century: Creating a New Sport Opportunity Spectrum. *Boston University International Law* Journal. 27, 2.

Fay, T. G., Wolff, E.A., Hums. M.A. (September 12, 2007) IPC Sport Classification Systems and the Public Perception of the Paralympic Games: Implications on Marketing, Media Coverage and the Management of the Games. *Proceedings of the 2003 VISTA Paralympic Congress, Bollnas, Sweden.* CD version.

International Paralympic Committee (2006) *Paralympic Winter Games: 1976 – 2006. Ornsdkoldsvik – Torino.* Bonn, Germany: International Paralympic Committee.

Lannem, et al (2009) Cross-country ski classification system

Legg, D., Fay, T. G., Hums, M. A. & Wolff, E.A. (2009 Fall) Examining the inclusion of wheelchair exhibition events within the Olympic Games 1984 - 2004. *European Sport Management Quarterly.* 9, 3.

Little, L. (2010) Armstrong wins gold for Canada and his late wife. *The Vancouver Sun.* Monday, March 22, 2010. C4.

McKnight, P. (2010) Should there be one Games for all? Some Paralympians would like to compete against the able-bodied. And what about the vice-versa? *The Vancouver Sun.* Sunday, March 13, 2010. A9.

Sinoski, K. (2010b) Russian sit-skier evolves into a star. *The Vancouver Sun.* Monday, March 22, 2010. C3.

Yahe, K. (Ed.). (1998) *Trends and Issues in Winter Paralympic Sport: Proceedings of Winter Paralympic Experts Congress – 4th Paralympic Congress.* Nagano, Japan: Nagano Paralympic Organizing Committee.

Part III
Emerging Issues of Paralympic Legacy

Chapter 17
Legacy

Generating Social Currency through Paralympic Excellence

Phil Lane

Introduction

The British Paralympic team's achievements in Sydney 2000, Athens 2004 and Beijing 2008 Paralympic Games arguably make them, over time, one of Great Britain's most successful sports teams of the modern era. It may seem strange therefore that a question needs to be asked of their place in the celebration of Great Britain's sporting achievements. How do we in a country where 'excellence' is acknowledged in every forum, where 'excellence' is the motivation for business, where 'excellence' is a motivating factor in our public services, and 'excellence' is yearned for in education as well as sport, challenge the notion of a Paralympic legacy? It is necessary to ask this question since the debate on sporting attainment and provision in the United Kingdom with its outward appearance of social equity and inclusion consistently fails to appropriately recognise the achievements of many athletes with a disability.

Attention to disability sporting excellence, whilst growing, is remarkably sparse and yet is the very principle that could drive an agenda of debate around social inclusion and social responsibility both within and outside sport. Few countries fail to promote their sporting heroes to encourage national pride and participation and yet, in the U.K apart from Dame Tanni Grey-Thompson and Ellie Simmonds, perception and celebration of disability sport in Great Britain too often remains a politically expedient response. As such, disability sport has stubbornly remained marginalised as a minority interest in the media and public eye.

Nelson Mandela's oft quoted phrase '*[sport] breaks down barriers. It laughs in the face of all kinds of discrimination*'. is blithely attached to Paralympic success with little sense of irony. How appropriate it would be, therefore, for the UK Government's sporting agenda to truly represent this principle and utilise Britain's Paralympic athletes' successes to move the debate forward in British sport. However, it requires acknowledgement that a debate exist on sporting inclusion and not to collude with those who seek to marginalise it by claiming equality of provision is the same as equality of opportunity. How refreshing it would be to exploit an agenda of social responsibility in respect of disability, ethnicity and gender, rather than the overtly economic, and politically expedient, one of health, education and crime. This chapter suggests that the debate is long overdue and what follows highlights some principle ideas which include the notion of legacy as its main agenda.

Background to the principle

Paralympic sport represents a truly outstanding achievement by the UK, firstly in developing the concept through the pioneering work of Sir Ludwig Guttmann at Stoke Mandeville Hospital in the 1940s, and secondly, through the success of its athletes in subsequent Paralympic Games (see Chapters 2 and 3 for further background on Sir Ludwig Guttmann). Harnessing its capacity to motivate and enthuse Britain's disabled (and non-disabled) population to take part in sport would represent a significant contribution to the sporting agenda as well as the health, inclusion and education legacies currently sought by Government.

As a positive example to society, the feats of Britain's Paralympians rank alongside many of the great sporting achievements. The culture of attaining high standards of performance through determination and self-motivation, and dealing with the discrimination that exist towards disability in everyday life and sport, represents a remarkable panoply of achievement that can and should serve to inspire others. It would be ideal therefore, if, in the discussion on British sport, we could be certain that the references to disability were genuinely inclusive and not generically so, and that Paralympic achievements contributed to a culture of social responsibility and accountability and not simply political correctness. However, this is infrequently so and therefore the case for disability sport and sporting inclusion has to be continually restated on all levels, from grassroots to elite performance.

Certainly, others in administration will refer to the advances made under the Disability Discrimination Act [DDA], but, if we are lulled into an impression of an environment and society governed by social responsibility in sport then readers should refer to the regular Disability Sports Surveys undertaken by Sport England. They provide stark and depressing data that serve to further highlight the paucity of sport and leisure provision for people with disabilities in the U.K. For example the following findings are reported:

- Sports participation rates for adults with a disability are significantly lower than for non-disabled adults.
- Past interventions aimed at increasing participation in sport by people with a disability have failed to make significant in-roads into reducing inequity in participation rates across England.
- Much needs to be done to bring participation in sport by children and young people with a disability to a level that is comparable with the general population of young people.
- Overall participation in sport by children and young people with a disability is low in all settings – five per cent do not do sport either in or out of school lessons.
- The number of sports undertaken both in and out of school lessons is significantly lower than the overall population of young people.
- The picture is even more worrying for children with a disability of primary school age and this concern should be extended to those in the older age group: 53% of primary school aged disabled children and 41% of 11-16 year olds are spending less than an hour a week in PE lessons.

Sport England, *Disability surveys*: 2001

- Sports participation among adults with a limiting disability / illness has decreased by 42,800, from 429,500 (6.7%) to 386,700 (6.1%).

Sport England, *Active People Survey*: 2009

Where in the debate on school sport and PE is the clamour for provision for these disabled youngsters? The PESSCL programme [Physical Education School Sport Club Link] is legally inclusive but struggles to practically provide the opportunities that youngsters with a disability need because of lack of knowledge and understanding amongst teachers as much as facilities and resources. Future Paralympians will not happen by chance, they will need the same development pathways and opportunities as their able-bodied peers. They will need teachers as enthused by the prospect of coaching a future Paralympic champion as they are about an Olympian.

We know that not everyone who aspires to be an elite athlete can achieve that challenging goal but if you have a disability it may be a little more difficult than expected. Accessible facilities remain a problem with less than 1 in 150 of the 10% of the UK population with a recognised disability having a fitness venue near to their home that they can access. Progress, through the

DDA is being made, but the installation of a few ramps, a lift and an accessible toilet will not make much difference to the sport experience for most sportsmen and women with disabilities.

Fundamentally, there remains the colossal challenge of shifting attitudes towards Paralympic sport. Having a warm glow as we watch the latest young star on the medal podium won't make 'an iota' of difference to the average child with a disability in Wolverhampton who just wants to play for fun. At this moment in time it will probably not make a great deal of difference to them whether they aspire to be a star of the future themselves or merely to participate recreationally because the pathways are often not there to guide them and neither is the infrastructure to support them. Perhaps, and more crucially, the often patronising attitude displayed towards disability sport and athletes continues to inhibit the investment, both human and financial, that would truly change the life experiences of those with a disability.

Lasting Social Legacies

In the UK it is therefore within this domain that we need to seek the real answers to the legacy questions that have, in recent Games, been posed of Organising Committees and Governments by the IOC (in particular) and the IPC. Much was made in the bidding for the London Games of the need to regenerate East London and re-establish the community spirit that brought cohesion to the old East End with its diverse social mix. Therefore what greater opportunity exists to demonstrate a socially inclusive agenda working in practice than through a Paralympic Games that embraces diversity and celebrates the achievement of athletes with a disability?

Of course the buildings and transport will be accessible but is there the will to encourage the British public and especially the local, socially and ethnically diverse, community in East London to embrace those whose journey to the sporting 'fields of dreams' mirror their own struggle for acceptance and equality. We can but hope that if, by re-establishing the core values in a diverse, yet often socially cohesive, community, we can, through example, influence the hearts and minds of those who may view Paralympic achievement rather more cynically. Only then can we truly say that social responsibility is at the core of legacy of the Games.

Social responsibility may well be attained and demonstrated but what will make those Paralympic medals won in London in 2012 truly meaningful? It will be good enough to know that not only were they won in the toughest competition on earth but it will be because athletes gained the respect of their sporting peers. The respect of fellow athletes (Olympians and Paralympians); the sport; from the family of sport; and the public, will make the true legacy for Paralympians. They do not need the patronising pat on the head but the shared appreciation of beating the odds; overcoming life's obstacles; defeating the world's finest and the understanding that the blood, the sweat and the tears shed are the same for Olympic or Paralympic athlete.

In 2012, the British fans will support the Team as they have done in Sydney, Athens and Beijing and a thousand other less publicised arenas around the world. The public will watch in person, as they have in the past, and in their millions through TV, in a way which has made the BBC's Paralympic coverage the envy of the world. Schoolchildren will enthuse about the day they had off school, the achievements they witnessed and the inspiration of the occasion. If we *can* inspire them, if we are willing to engage their minds then a real Games legacy might just emerge as they become not just the citizens of tomorrow but also its leaders and opinion formers.

However, the crucial factor in the lead up to the Games will be the attitude engendered amongst those who will plan, market and run them. They are the critical components in ensuring the Games environment is both conceptually and pragmatically aligned. Forget the politically inclusive nonsense about using the terms Olympic *and Paralympic* equitably, of inclusive planning and diversity policies. It is the injection of meaningful and genuine conviction that the efforts of Paralympians are worth the investment and that the event is worthwhile, that the competition is as valid, that the achievements are of equal value that really matters. Without that the people of the UK, London, and especially those of the East End in whose name much of the investment has been predicated, will rightly ask 'why'? 'What was it all for'?

The IOC has, in the past, sought a role for the Olympic Games that has embraced world peace, tackled poverty and environmental change, with limited degrees of response and success. Perhaps the IPC by imaginative promotion of the London Paralympic Games offers the chance to really make a difference through an investment in the social currency of a city that prides itself, at least rhetorically, on its diversity and social inclusion. The IPC has long sought a definitive and plausible justification to aspiring 'host cities' for the additional cost of the Paralympics and in China it seemed in touch of the 'holy grail' as the world proclaimed the perceived change in attitude towards the disability community in Beijing. The success of the Beijing Paralympics appeared to represent a paradigm shift in attitude that might otherwise have taken generations to evolve in such a complex and doctrinal nation. Yet, despite the attitudinal shift required for such a plausible and successful Games, the observations and comments made frequently reverted to a review of the ceremonies, the facilities or transport rather than the response of the 'man' in the street.

There is a danger that London will fall into the same self-congratulatory trap recognising, as it surely does, a simple and expedient way to establish its credentials. That building inaccessible facilities is not an option in post-DDA Britain is self-evident and with a (previously) successful Paralympic team there is ample evidence to suggest to an undiscerning audience that the world for those with a disability is as it should be. However, the veneer can be thin as recognised by the writer and international sportsman, Brian

Moore, in a Daily Telegraph article in October 2009. Responding to the public criticism of a joke about wounded servicemen and the 2012 Paralympic team by the comedian Jimmy Carr he contended,

> 'As Carr's comment did not criticise or ridicule the servicemen, the objectors must believe that the subject cannot be the basis of humour and that logically any similarly sensitive subject must also be off limits.
>
> What should outrage people and what really offends servicemen, is the real scandal of under-equipping and over-committing of our armed forces; and the fact that members of the public have complained about having to share swimming pools with amputees.
>
> Unfortunately, as with their service careers, they will find that the attitude of some of the public and officialdom is patronising and occasionally hostile, on the basis that their disability is an unwelcome reminder of the real and brutal consequences of war.
>
> Even though not deliberately so, too much coverage of disability sport is similarly condescending, with the focus being on the injury, its origins and effects, as opposed to the usual features of sport like form, fitness and technique.'

(B. Moore, *Daily Telegraph*, 29th October 2009)

Such an observation from a respected sportsman, lawyer and journalist in one of the UK's leading broadsheet newspapers cannot easily be dismissed. It invokes a worrying analysis of the response by the British public to Paralympic success, because, at least rhetorically, it has been believed that barriers were coming down. Unfortunately the 'public faces' and 'role models' who shed a light onto other aspects and genres of sport and entertainment are not yet replicated in Paralympic sport, even in the UK, where Dame Tanni Grey-Thompson (athletics) and Ellie Simmonds (swimming) are the only likely contenders for public recognition in a world dominated by football. Indeed, Sebastian Coe the Chairman of the London Organising Committee rightly observed in launching the '1000 Days to Go to the Paralympics' event, that:

> 'This is a golden opportunity to raise awareness of Paralympic sport, challenge stereotypes about disability and secure a legacy which will have every disabled child getting greater access to sport'.

(Sebastian Coe, 3rd December 2009)

However, this remains the conundrum for both organisers and Government alike, the opportunity exists (sport and facilities) but what will provide the catalyst to effect lasting change? An analysis of, and investment in, the promotion and marketing of Paralympic sport coupled with a serious addressing of the inadequacies in educational responses, both in opportunity and perception, to those with a disability has to be central to any legacy planning. Merely applauding the architecture and an ephemeral celebration of the medal winners simply will not do.

Conclusive Statements

There is little doubt that the Paralympics has the capacity to effect change and change attitudes. It has both an inspirational and emotive quality as the broadcaster, Clare Balding, wrote with affecting power in an article in the Observer newspaper after the Athens Games. Her report encapsulated the feeling of many involved in Paralympic sport. She argues that:

> 'It is impossible not to be affected by the Paralympic Games. Nothing crystallises more clearly the power of sport to change lives, to motivate, to bond people together, to bring out their inner strength.
>
> For all my intentions to think of it as any other sporting event, I have come away knowing more strongly than ever before that it is not.
>
> It has a purity of intent, a lack of commercialism, a feeling of 'family' to it that sets it apart. It is not often that a sporting event can aspire to such lofty ideals, but the Paralympics bring with them a message that reaches beyond the score in a football match, or a result of a relay race.
>
> In a world that has become increasingly obsessed with achieving the perfect body shape, with judging and being judged by what you wear and how you look, it represents a massive, in-your-face, fingers-up to all that nonsense. There is not a single Paralympic athlete who has not challenged the perception of those around them and the limitations imposed on them by others'.

(Clare Balding, *The Observer* 15th October 2004)

If London 2012 is serious about leaving a lasting legacy then it is in these words that direction and inspiration should be sought. For a nation like Britain, capable of making the financial investment in sport and facilities, those aspects should be regarded as a given. Therefore it is essential that it looks at investment in the emotional and attitudinal legacy of the Games to truly effect change.

In relation to 2012 legacy, marketing and promotion of the Paralympic Games has to be seen as more than an exercise in selling tickets for the event, it has to be part of a thought through and strategically planned promotion of disability sport. The frequently used tactic of bringing in thousands of schoolchildren on discounted tickets is pointless if its outcome is merely to fill stadia. There is the greatest opportunity if the organisers and the IPC have the courage to genuinely educate and engage the young and old alike through imaginative approaches to presenting the Games and real, not perceived, accessibility to the athletes.

However, in the very concept of the 'parallel' Games lays one of the event's great dichotomies – how far must they mirror the Olympics to retain credibility? The IPC has to develop a model that is far more responsive to the host nation market place than the current 'Olympic' based structure and recognise the differing requirements of the host nations. The long road from Seoul to London has secured the same city and venues but in none of the intervening cities has the context for the Games been identical and yet the template for the event has changed little.

For Britain the legacy challenges are as stark as any of the previous hosts but are not manifested in facility and accessibility alone. 2012 is the greatest opportunity to fundamentally change attitudes towards disability sport in a timeframe that would normally be unachievable. If the stakeholders in British Paralympic sport are truly serious about heeding Sebastian Coe's words then this is the time to make not just an investment but the right one.

The outcome of the right investment could not be put more eloquently than in the following words by Brian Moore:

> 'Our support for and our attitude to the Paralympics in 2012 will go a long way to measuring our humanity and maturity, not just our financial support for disabled athletes'. (B.Moore, *Daily Telegraph*, 29th October 2009)

Chapter 18
Paralympic Legacy in Physical

Activity and Health
A UK Perspective

Paul Smith and Scott Fleming

Introduction

Since the first 'World Wheelchair and Amputee Games' took place at Stoke Mandeville in 1948, the Paralympic Games has continued to grow – in scale, and in the quality of athletic performance, and in significance. During the past four Paralympic Games more than 250 World and Paralympic records have been set. There are more participants in an increased number of classification categories[1] across a greater number of Paralympic events. Many Paralympians are full-time, professional athletes, and the quantity and quality of (scientific) knowledge and support they receive continues to evolve. Since the early 1990s there has also been increasing recognition of Paralympic sport in the media. As a sporting mega-event (Horne, 2007), the

---

[1] For a further consideration of classification categories in Paralympic sport, see Jones and Howe (2005) and also Howe and Jones (2006).

2008 Beijing Paralympic Games received an unprecedented volume of media coverage with a tone that was more transparently a celebration of athletic excellence than had been the case hitherto.

The media portrayal of the Olympic Games and the Paralympic Games has a greater impact than merely documenting and broadcasting the outcome of sports contests. The depiction of athletes can also inspire others. One of the most successful Paralympians of all time, Dame Tanni Grey-Thompson, has explained how she was influenced by seeing the success of a multiple Paralympian in wheelchair racing and swimming:

> 'When I was growing up, sport for disabled people didn't get that much coverage on television. But one of my first memories was watching fellow Welsh athlete Chris Hallam in the London Marathon. I remember saying to my mum that I was going to do the London Marathon one day' (BBC Sport, 2005).

For the majority, however, participation in sport is (by definition) not at the level of medal-winning excellence, but more about becoming (more) physically active. For these persons the Para-/Olympic legacies have the potential to be even more profound. To achieve these outcomes, policy statements and intervention projects designed to promote sport participation and increase physical activity (hereafter PA) and should be marked at the fundamental source level. Indeed, it is at the base of the sports development pyramid (Sports Council for Wales, 2005[2]) where it is possible to meet the utilitarian goal of the greatest good for the greatest number[3].

The developments and preparations for the Olympic Games and Paralympic Games in London in 2012 will inevitably lead to urban regeneration in the East End of London – particularly through the building of state-of-the-art facilities, many of which will be situated at the new Olympic/Paralympic Park in Stratford. Yet there is potential to deliver sustainable social, cultural, economic and environmental legacies not only for the host city, but for the country as a whole (Shipway, 2007)[4]. Owing to the increased prevalence of primary and secondary diseases that are frequently associated with ignorance, indulgence and/or inactivity, the (political) climate for sport and PA has changed in the UK. Getting people to be more physically active is

---

2. Naturally, we resist the over-simplified and rather out-dated account of the sports participation pyramid in which the (il)logical inference is that the larger the base of the pyramid, the higher its apex. The theoretical underpinning of effective sports development is clearly more complex than the mere application of a three-dimensional version of the geometry of 'similar triangles'. Yet we do acknowledge that a wider base of the participation pyramid will provide a better foundation upon which sporting talent can be identified and nurtured.

3. Also called the 'greatest happiness principle', this is a version of utilitarianism advanced by English philosopher Jeremy Bentham (1748-1832).

4. Whether these are experienced uniformly throughout the UK is at least contestable (and has been contested in some of the provincial media outlets). But there have been few serious suggestions that parts of the UK outside the capital will not accrue at least some benefits.

now a major political imperative and it is possible that the most important legacy of the 2012 Games could be the improvement of public health.

There are, of course, many agencies involved in developing, promoting and delivering real health benefits. A major challenge, therefore, exists in harnessing the various regional and national stakeholder interests. For example, local authorities, the (locally and regionally managed) National Health Service (NHS), and various Government Departments including Health (DH), Culture, Media and Sport (DCMS), and the National Institute for Clinical Excellence (NICE)[5] all have a role to play. At the outset, however, it is important to note that there is very little evidence to suggest that hosting any previous Olympic Games, let alone Paralympic Games raised levels of participation, nor indeed had any significant impact upon public health, and we will return to this theme later.

Physical Activity, Health and Disability

The link between PA (or exercise[6]) and the pursuit of a healthier lifestyle is unquestionable. There is unequivocal evidence that PA confers many health benefits (Hardman & Stensel, 2009). In a disability[7] context it is evident that an individual's quality of life can be significantly impaired compared to 'non-disabled' counterparts (Barker *et al.* 2009). It is almost certain that failure of disabled individuals to engage in PA will exacerbate their health situation.

In the UK, individuals with a disability are, in general, considerably less physically active than the population as a whole (Sport England, 2001). The 2008 DCMS survey entitled *Taking Part: the National Survey for Culture, Leis-*

---

5. Interestingly, in the USA a programme has also been forged between sporting agencies and their member organisations. For instance, the Paralympic division of the US Olympic Committee has recently signed a memorandum of understanding with the Department of Veterans Affairs, and resulting initiatives will have wide-ranging 'clinical' and 'excellence-in-performance' objectives. An expansion of rehabilitation services and support available to the wider community will also assist the US Olympic Committee identify and nurture athletes who demonstrate true World Class potential, so objectives at both ends of the spectrum of functional capacity.

6. There is an important conceptual distinction between 'physical activity' and 'exercise' – it is essentially a differentiation by the motive for engagement. To illustrate, the World Health Organization (2010) defines physical activity as "any bodily movement produced by skeletal muscles that requires energy expenditure" [emphasis added], while the NHS (2010) explains that the aim of exercise is "to achieve a beneficial level of fitness and health, both physically and mentally". For our purposes, though, we are concerned with the benefits associated with physical activity per se (whether it is for the purpose of exercise or not). Hence we use the term physical activity and its abbreviation 'PA' throughout.

7. We are conscious of the transient and changing nature of the vocabulary used to comment upon these matters. This is not merely about so-called 'political correctness', for we share the view that language is a carrier of cultural values and political (and Political) discourses. For this chapter we therefore adopt the form of language recommended by the British Sociological Association (2004).

ure and Sport revealed (p. 8) that participation by individuals with a 'limited disability' in 'moderate intensity' sport remained largely unchanged between 2005/06 and 2007/08. However, engagement in recreational, 'active sport' became significantly reduced over the same period. Such findings have catalysed the development and implementation of health-related initiatives such as the *Rebuilding Lives Through Sport* campaign that is currently being championed by the UK Spinal Injuries Association.

Disability (or long-term illness) is often associated with secondary health concerns (Barker *et al.* 2009), and the incidence of obesity, for example, is more common in individuals with a learning disability (Marshall *et al.* 2003; Kerr, 2004). The incidence of secondary medical complications and re-admittance to hospital can be substantially reduced through engagement in PA (Scott, 1986). Supervised classes or home-based programmes of PA can result in improvements in both general capacity and functionality, and can bring about other desired metabolic adaptations such as increased insulin sensitivity and favourable changes to the lipid profile (de Groot *et al.,* 2003).

Over a decade ago a consensus statement was published by a panel of experts (Cooper *et al.*, 1999), which focused upon evidence that related PA to health among people with disabilities. They concluded that exercise, in the context of disability, should be studied primarily from the perspective of disease prevention, whilst ensuring that the risk of injury or some other set-back is managed carefully. Five broad areas for future health-related research were identified: (i) epidemiological studies; (ii) the impact of nutrition on an individual's ability to exercise; (iii) cardiovascular and pulmonary health; (iv) disability in children; and (v) accessibility to, and the safety of exercise programmes.

The potential health benefits associated with PA are not restricted to physical change (for example, weight management) and physiological adaptations (such as improving cardio-respiratory fitness). There are also psychosocial benefits to be considered. As well as enhanced psychological well-being (Biddle *et al.*, 2000), individuals in all walks of life use PA to cope with feelings of anxiety in stressful situations, and it has been demonstrated that aspects of mental health can also be improved (Crone *et al.*, 2005; 2006; Taylor *et al.*, 2004). Social interaction through engagement with sport and/or PA can assist is improving an individual's level of perceived self-competence, self-confidence and self-esteem (Page *et al.*, 2001). Moreover, van de Ven *et al.* (2008) concluded that social interaction amongst individuals with spinal injuries helped to develop basic knowledge and life skills. In turn, this led to a greater degree of self-confidence, a greater sense of autonomy and a reduced reliance on others, making sustained participation in PA a more realistic proposition.

On their own, biomedical accounts of health (even those informed by exercise and health psychology) are not sufficient. The prevailing socioeconomic, cultural and environmental conditions are also significant, so too are the living and working conditions as well as social and community influence (Dahlgren & Whitehead, 1992). These take an understanding of PA and health into the sociological domain for there are clearly broader societal constructs that shape life experiences and life chances (Fleming & Jones, 2007). The intersections of class, gender and ethnicity are as obvious in health studies as they are anywhere else (Ahmad, 1993), and participation in sport and PA is also affected (see, for example, Carrington & McDonald, 2001; Scraton & Flintoff, 2002; Roberts, 2004). Many of the other arguments for the benefits of PA resonate with the rationale for the inclusion of physical education in the National Curriculum (Capel, 2000) and the discourses surrounding the importance of health-related exercise in young people's experience of schooling (Armstrong & Sparkes, 1991; AFPE, 2009). There is also an economic incentive to be explored. That is to say, the estimates for the annual costs to the NHS as a result of physical inactivity are between £1 billion and £1.8 billion (DH, 2009). In the period between 2006 and 2007 the indirect costs associated with inactivity for English Primary Care Trusts amounted to over £700 million across the country as a whole (DH, 2009).

An understanding of the Paralympic legacy on health will, therefore, require an inter-disciplinary, multidimensional approach that embraces exercise physiology, exercise psychology, sports development and sociology – and perhaps history and philosophy too. Many of the initiatives being implemented across the UK are multiple agency-based, and draw upon interdependent, complementary themes. For example, the National Healthy Schools Programme (see http://home.healthyschools.gov.uk/) is a joint venture between the NHS, the DH and the government Department for Children, Schools and Families. This country-wide initiative is being implemented in secondary schools, and utilises compulsory elements of the National Curriculum; themes of personal, social, health and economic (PSHE) education, healthy eating, PA, and emotional health and wellbeing are explored. Under this scheme schools are expected to achieve National Healthy School Status, and a clear statement of responsibility ensures that Local Authorities facilitate this process. However, it is unclear whether there is an explicit policy of inclusion to ensure that young people with disabilities have been considered within this strategy.

Barriers to Participation

As mentioned earlier, there is clear evidence to suggest that having a (limiting) disability (and/or a long-term illness) can lead to inequality in terms of PA participation (Sport England, 2001; DCMS, 2008). In addition to general constraints on life opportunities (for instance, socioeconomic class, gender and ethnicity – see above), individuals with a disability are often confronted with further barriers that prevent them from becoming physically active. For example, prosaic geographical situations and relative immobility in an area impoverished of recreational facilities and amenities might prevent some individuals from participating. There is also the economic reality of not being able to afford to use municipal (or other) facilities. People with a disability are far from being a homogeneous group, however, and in reviewing relevant documents and reports it is rare for information to be presented in a stratified fashion. Some sub-groups within the disability community are particularly vulnerable to discrimination, and these variations in personal circumstances will likely create diversity in terms of real or subjective (perceived) barriers to participation.

The most familiar barriers are physical obstructions, such as an inaccessible building; while others may be subjective perceptions[8]. Such challenges, whether taken separately or together, can severely hamper an individual's attempts to become (more) physically active. While the phased implementation of the Disability Discrimination Act has made it unlawful to discriminate against individuals from several perspectives –including employment (1996); service provision (1996; 1999); and access to buildings and premises (2004) – inappropriate access to public facilities (Kehn & Kroll, 2009) remains an issue in isolated cases. Other obstacles to participation include a lack of specialist sporting equipment (Wu & Williams, 2001) and a general lack of time and placing an over-dependence upon others as a resulting of diminished functional capacity (Sport England, 2002; p. 56). Buffart *et al.* (2009) noted that subjective barriers also included perceptions of a lack of energy, a fear of aggravating an existing injury or of acquiring a new injury, and a lack of general information about recommendations for an appropriate physically active lifestyle.

Anecdotal evidence also indicates that minority events amongst existing Paralympic sports suffer simply from the lack of resources needed to create participation opportunities. For example, Handcycling has been a Paralympic Sport since the Athens Paralympic Games in 2004, and Great Britain won a Gold medal in the women's factored time trial in the 2008 Beijing Paralympic Games. Yet there are very few opportunities to participate in Handcycling. To a large extent this is a consequence of the cost associated with specialist (racing) hand bike, which for many is simply prohibitive. Furthermore, owing to the recent and ongoing successes of Great Britain's Paralympic and Olympic cyclists, British Cycling does not explicitly view the development of Hand cycling – either at grassroots or elite level – as a major priority[9].

Physical Activity, Health and the Paralympic Games

Sports Development strategies in many different countries have been predicated on an emphasis of elite sporting success in the hope of a so-called 'trickle-down' effect. The evidence for the success of this approach is, at

---

8. Of course, whether barriers are real or imagined, they become real in their consequences for engagement in physical activity.

9. This example is not being raised as a criticism of the successful strategy currently being implemented by British Cycling, but is offered as an example of a real challenge associated with the development of an existing Paralympic sport.

best, patchy. A report by EdComs (2007) concluded that there is no clear (causal) link of an increase in participation as a result of hosting a major event[10]. Indeed one attempt by Hogan and Norton (2000) to explore the relationship between PA of the general public and national sporting prowess in Australia revealed that these two emphases might even be incompatible. They examined a twenty-year period and showed that significant investment in elite sport (close to AUS$1 billion) had yielded an impressive return in climbing the Olympic medal table from 32nd position in 1976 to 7th in 1996. During an overlapping period, however, physical inactivity also rose from 29.1% of the population in 1984, to 40% in 1999. Though perhaps as guilty of over-simplification as the implied causal link of the 'trickle down' approach, they concluded that it was irresponsible and unrealistic to accept that huge investment at the highest level of sporting achievement would motivate the wider community to become physically active.

More specifically concerning sports mega-events, only limited evidence exists to suggest that previous Olympic Games and Paralympic Games have directly raised widespread levels of PA and/or have improved standards of public health. But it is also true that no previous Olympic Games or Paralympic Games have set out with these twin objectives (Weed *et al.*, 2009). Looking forward to, and beyond the 2012 Games, it is clear that many challenges will exist in securing these long-term outcomes. As Weed *et al.* (2009) note, a systematic evaluation of PA and health-related legacy benefits is essential; it is only through a robust evaluation of the health legacies of 2012 that a baseline (or benchmark) can be established in order to compare and evaluate the efficacy of future sporting events. In reality, whilst an inordinate amount has been written about the Olympic Games, whether neglect, oversight or lack of inclination, significantly less is available in the public domain about the Paralympics. The same is true of the planning and policy domain, for it is true that relatively few new initiatives have been developed to cater for the specific needs and requirements of people with a disability. One argument is, of course, that modern provision for sport and PA (in the UK at least) is required by law, within reason, to be accessible and therefore of benefit to disabled people too. If properly designed to accommodate the particular needs of a variety of constituencies, a preferred approach is one of inclusion and integration, leading to the creation of new opportunities and the concomitant raising of aspirations for disabled individuals to become increasingly physically active. In June 2009 the European Commission advertised an embedded theme of disability sport within a broader announcement concerned with the first *Preparatory Action in the Field of Sport*. A particular emphasis within the disability sub-theme was placed on ways and means by

---

10. The London East Research Institute had suggested that the Barcelona Olympics had increased levels of physical activity, though the methodological basis for such a conclusion was brought into question by Weed et al. (2009) who challenged the veracity of an analysis based on the findings of two separate reports conducted some 10 years apart.

which disability sport and (competitive and recreational) opportunities for people with disabilities could be developed alongside mainstream sport in an inclusive, integrated fashion.

An inclusive approach in the development of participation opportunities for people with disabilities has been the subject of recent reports. By adopting an inclusive, mainstreaming approach to disability sport it should be possible to change attitudes, and go some way to develop communities that are not only creative and vibrant, but also competent and well informed (Sports Council for Northern Ireland, 2005). Published in 2007, *Inclusive and Active: A Sport and Physical Activity Action Plan for Disabled People in London 2007-2012* included the comment from the then Mayor of London, Ken Livingstone that the strategy "... is a key part of delivering this legacy for Londoners, especially disabled Londoners" (Barker & Watson, 2007, p. *i* – emphasis added). The timing of the remark was neither coincidental nor irrelevant because it had become clear that there were important differences in the PA participation patterns of people with disabilities and members of the general public. Specifically, it was noted (Sport England, 2006a) that 20.9% of 'non-disabled' London-based adults participated in at least 30 minutes of PA three times per week, compared to only 9.5% of people with a limiting disability – the lowest participation rate of any of the priority groups identified. From a national perspective an even lower participation rate of 8.8% of individuals with a limiting disability was reported (Sport England, 2006b). More recently, the DCMS (2009) circulated a press release stating that legacy promises would put disabled individuals at the heart of the London 2012 plans – specific pledges were made to change individuals' life experiences.

From an economic perspective, the case for the multiple benefits accruing from a limited resource base is overwhelming. Emerging initiatives aimed at individuals with disabilities using existing or already planned infrastructure, (human) resources and knowledge represents the most (cost-)effective and immediate mechanism through which new opportunities can be created. It is also likely that this approach will provide the greatest long-term sustainability for them. For existing facilities, as indicated above, this may require some structural modification to enable proper access and/or additional bespoke equipment for particular groups. In addition, however, there is the further need to provide additional education and training for coaches, instructors and the essential volunteer workforce to ensure participation opportunities are delivered optimally – that is to say, in a knowledgeable, safe and effective fashion. In the 2009 DH report entitled *Be Active, Be Healthy: A Plan for Getting the Nation Moving*, the recent collaboration between Sport England and the English Federation of Disability Sport to develop an Inclusive Fitness Initiative (IFI) was used as an illustrative example of how this can work. The specific aim of this initiative is to develop 1,000 new IFI facilities across the UK by the opening ceremony of the London 2012 Paralympic Games.

Concluding Remarks

In this chapter we have argued that the Olympic Games and the Paralympic Games have become sports mega-events with the power to influence recreational participation as well as elite performance. The relatively short-lived visibility accorded to individual and team excellence (especially winning medals and breaking championship and World records) is unmistakable, but the longer term and sustainable impact on the engagement of members of the general public in PA and sport may be much more profound. At present little direct evidence exists to demonstrate that a high profile event, such as an Olympic Games or a Paralympic Games, might result in community-wide, health-related benefits. However, the London 2012 bid was the first of its kind to explicitly outline such challenging objectives. It is therefore imperative that the various key (interdependent) stakeholders deliver on such promises.

The health benefits that can be accrued from PA are well established, and apply as much (if not more) to people with disabilities as anyone else. Evidence demonstrates that people with disabilities are proportionally less likely to be physically active than their 'non-disabled' peers. Furthermore, as well as the logistical challenges experienced by all potential participants in PA and sport, other specific barriers to participation are experienced by disabled individuals. In order for the 2012 Paralympic Games to yield the health benefits that may be possible, there are some important emphases that require attention:

- An integrated approach to the planning and delivery of the health benefits of the Paralympic legacy;
- Joined-up thinking and planning amongst the key organisational stakeholders (especially government agencies and departments);
- A consideration of the nature and severity of disability, and the likely challenges that will be encountered in terms of creating new and sustainable participation opportunities;
- The adoption of an inclusive, preferably integrated strategy that attempts to align the (re-)development of disability participation opportunities with mainstream sport;
- Rigorous multi- and inter-disciplinary evaluation of the impact of the Paralympic Games in 2012; and
- Careful and systematic longitudinal analyses of the health-related legacy of the Paralympic Games in 2012 to demonstrate (as far as possible) both the efficacy of the mega-event itself and to act as a benchmark for other similar sports mega-events.

References

Association for Physical Education (2009) AFPE Health Position Paper, *Physical Education Matters*, *3*, 8-12.

Ahmad, W.I.U. (Ed.) (1993) *'Race' and health in contemporary Britain*, Buckingham: Open University Press.

Armstrong, N., & Sparkes, A. (Eds.) (1991) *Issues in physical education*, London: Cassell.

Barker, Y., & Watson, A. (2007) *Inclusive and active: A sport and physical activity action plan for disabled people in London 2007-2012.* London: Greater London Authority.

Barker, R.N., Kendall, M. D., Amsters, D.I., Pershouse, K.J., Haines, T.P., & Kuipers, P. (2009) The relationship between quality of life and disability across the lifespan for people with spinal cord injury, *Spinal Cord*, *47*, 149-155.

Barry, A-M., & Yuill, C. (2002) *Understanding health: A sociological introduction.* London: Sage.

BBC Sport (2005) Meet Tanni Grey Thompson. Available at: (http://www.news.bbc.co.uk/sport1/low/other_sports/disability_sport/4354422.stm) (accessed 30th December 2009).

Biddle, S.J.H., Fox, K.R., & Boutcher, S.H. (2000) Eds. *Physical activity and psychological well-being.* London: Routledge.

British Sociological Association (2004) *Equality and diversity – Language and the BSA: Disability.* Belmont, Durham: British Sociological Association.

Buffart, L.M., Westendorp, T., van den Berg-Emons, R.J., Stam, H.J., & Roebroeck, M.E. (2009) Perceived barriers to and facilitators of physical activity in young adults with childhood-onset physical disabilities. *Journal of Rehabilitation Medicine*, *41*, 881-5.

Capel, S. (2000) Re-reflecting on priorities for physical education: Now and in the twenty-first century. In S. Capel & S. Piotrowski (Eds.), *Issues in Physical Education* (pp. 209-220). London: Routledge, Falmer.

Coalter, F. (2004) London 2012: a sustainable sporting legacy? In *After the Goldrush: The London Olympic Games.* London: Institute for Public Policy Research/DEMOS. Available at: (http://www.nolondon2012.org/SportingLegacyPaper.pdf), (accessed 10th January 2010).

Crone, D., Smith, A., & Gough, B. (2005) "I feel totally alive, totally happy and totally at one": A psycho-social explanation of the physical activity and mental health relationship from the experiences of participants on exercise referral schemes. *Health Education Research*, *20*, 600-611.

Crone, D., Smith, A., & Gough, B. (2006) The physical activity and mental health relationship — A contemporary perspective from qualitative research. *Gymnica, 36*, 29-36.

Dahlgren, G., & Whitehead, M. (1992) *Policies and strategies to promote equity in health*. Copenhagen: WHO Regional Office for Europe [document number: EUR/ICP/RPD 414 (2)].

De Groot, P.C., Hieltnes, N., Heijboer, A.C., Stal, W., & Birkeland, K. (2003) Effect of training intensity on physical capacity, lipid profile and insulin sensitivity in early rehabilitation of spinal cord injured individuals. *Spinal Cord, 41*, 673-9.

Department for Culture, Media and Sport (2008) *Taking part: The national survey of culture, leisure and sport*. Available at: (http://www.culture.gov.uk/images/research/PSA3_report_12_08.pdf), (accessed 8th January 2010).

Department for Culture, Media and Sport (2009). *New legacy promise puts disabled people at the heart of London 2012*. Press release. Available at: (http://www.dcms.gov.uk/reference_library/media_releases/6502.aspx), (accessed 15th December 2009).

Department of Health (2004) *At least five a week: Evidence on the impact of physical activity and its relationship to health*. Available at: (http://www.dh.gov.uk/prod_consum_dh/groups/dh_digitalassets/@dh/@en/documents/digitalasset/dh_4080981.pdf), (accessed 13th December 2010).

Department of Health (2009) *Be active, be healthy: A plan for getting the nation moving*. Available at: (http://www.dh.gov.uk/prod_consum_dh/groups/dh_digitalassets/documents/digitalasset/dh_094359.pdf), (accessed 14th December 2009)

EdComs (2007) *London 2012 legacy research: Final report*. London: COI/DCMS.

European Commission (2009) *Preparatory action in the field of sport: Call for proposals*. [Document number: EAC/21/2009].

Fleming, S., & Jones, R.L. (2007) Sociology for coaches. In R.L. Jones, M. Hughes & K. Kingston (Eds.) *An introduction to sports coaching* (pp. 43-51). London: Routledge.

Grey-Thompson, T. (2008) British Paralympians' early success an inspiration to others. Available at: (http://www.telegraph.co.uk/sport/othersports/paralympicsport/2700019/British-paralympians-early-success-an-inspiration-to-others.html), (accessed 30th December 2009).

Hardman, A.E., & Stensel, D.J. (2009) *Physical activity and health – The evidence explained* (2nd edn.). Routledge, London.

Hogan, K., & Norton, K. (2000) The 'price' of Olympic Gold. *Journal of science and Medicine in Sport, 3*, 203-18.

Horne, J. (2007) The four 'knowns' of sports mega-events. *Leisure Studies, 26*, 81–96.

Howe, P.D., & Jones, C. (2006) Classification of disabled athletes: (Dis)-Empowering the Paralympic practice community. *Sociology of Sport Journal, 23*, 29-46.

Jones, C., & Howe, P.D. (2005) The conceptual boundaries of sport for the disabled: Classification and athletic performance. *Journal of the Philosophy of Sport, 32*, 127-140.

Kehn, M., & Kroll, T. (2009) Staying physically active after spinal cord injury: a qualitative exploration of barriers and facilitators to exercise participation. *BMC Public Health, 9*,168.

Kerr, M. (2004) Improving the general health of people with learning disabilities. *Advances in Psychiatric Treatment, 10*, 200-206.

Marshall, D., McConkey, R., & Moore, G. (2003) Obesity in people with intellectual disabilities: the impact of nurse-led health screenings and health promotion activities. *Journal of Advanced Nursing, 41*,147-53.

National Health Service (2007) *Your health, your choices.* Available at: (http://www.nhs.uk/Conditions/Exercise/Pages/Definition.aspx), (accessed 1st January 2010).

Nazroo, J.Y. (2001) *Ethnicity, class and health.* London: Policy Studies Institute.

Page, S.J., O'Connor, E., & Petersen, K. (2001) Leaving the ghetto: A qualitative study of factors underlying achievement motivation among athletes with disabilities. *Journal of Sport and Social Issues, 25*, 40-55.

Scott, A. (1986) Management of related spinal cord injury problems. *Spinal Cord Injury Nurses, 3*, 3-5.

Scraton, S., & Flintoff, A. (Eds.) (2002) *Gender and sport: A reader.* London: Routledge.

Soundy, A., Faulkner, G., & Taylor, A. (2007) Exploring variability and perceptions of lifestyle physical activity among individuals with severe and enduring mental health problems: A qualitative study, *Journal of Mental Health, 16*, 493-503.

Sports Council for Northern Ireland (2005) *Disability mainstreaming policy.* Available at: (http://www.vagacms.co.uk/content/showcontent.aspx?contentid=1330), (accessed 12th January 2010).

Sports Council for Wales (2005) *Framework for the development of sport and physical activity.* Cardiff: Sports Council for Wales.

Sport England (2001) *Sport equity index for regular participation.* Available at: (http://www.vagacms.co.uk/content/showcontent.aspx?contentid=116), (accessed 12th January 2010).

Sport England (2002) *Adults with a disability and sport national survey 2000-1.* Available at: (http://www.sportengland.org/research/tracking_trends.aspx?sortBy=alpha&pageNum=1), (accessed 13th December 2009).

Sport England (2006a) *Active people survey: London Region factsheet.* (Available at: (http://www.sportengland.org/research/active_people_survey/active_people_survey_1/regional_results.aspx), (accessed 12th January 2010).

Sport England (2006b) *Active people survey: National factsheet.* Available at: (http://www.sportengland.org/research/active_people_survey/active_people_survey_1.aspx) (accessed 12th January 2010).

Taylor, A.H., Brazier, J., Cable, T., Faulkner, G., Hillsdon, M., Narici, M., & Van Der Bij, A.K. (2004) Physical activity and older adults: A review of health benefits, and effectiveness of interventions. *Journal of Sports Sciences, 22,* 703-725.

van de Ven, L., De Witte, L., & Van Den Heuvel, W. (2008) Strategies for autonomy used by people with cervical spinal cord injury: a qualitative study. *Disability and Rehabilitation, 30,* 249-260.

Weed, M., Coren, E., & Fiore, J. (2009) *A systematic review of the evidence base for developing a physically active and health legacy from the London 2012 Olympic and Paralympic Games.* London: Department of Health.

World Health Organization (2010) *Global strategy on diet, physical activity and health.* Retrieved on 1st January 2010 from: http://www.who.int/dietphysicalactivity/pa/en/index.html

Wu, S., & Williams, T. (2001) Factors influencing sports participation among athletes with spinal cord injury. *Medicine and Science in Sports and Exercise, 33,* 177-18.

Chapter 19
Physical Education and the 2012 Paralympic Legacy

From Playground to Podium?

Natalie Campbell

Introduction

In the United Kingdom education, sport and culture continually provide for endless discourse and debate. Interestingly, the reason as to why people choose to participate in such activities has never been fully understood and will undoubtedly continue to be theorised and postulated about for years to come. Many philosophers and academics have sought to address the moral issues surrounding sport, competition and the pursuit of physical excellence. What has been agreed upon in the latter part of the 20th century is the overwhelming medical evidence for the inclusion of physical education (PE) as a school curriculum subject (Marshall & Hardman, 2000). Indeed, Article 1 of the United Nations Educational, Scientific and Cultural Organisation (UNESCO) Charter for Physical Education and Sport (1978) affords PE the status of a 'fundamental right' that should be guaranteed and provided for within educational systems. In the UK particularly, the pedagogy of PE lays down the foundations for the 'physically educated' person and lifelong engagement in regular physical activity (Hardman, 1998). With the winning of the 2012 Olympic and Paralympic bid the word 'Legacy' became the government's 'leitmotif' for PE throughout the country.

Evidence surrounding the importance of PE within schools is readily available and growing. Indeed, empirical studies have long argued that children who regularly participate in sport and / or physical activity develop personally, physically and socially. The agreed importance of the corporeal and intellectual benefits of exposing children to physical education ensures those responsible for educational institutions will endeavour to provide the necessary provisions. Since winning the Olympic bid in 2005, these provisions have never received such attention – from the UK government, the national media and UK national sporting bodies. Sport and PE have attained a position of unprecedented prominence in the government's 'Olympic Legacy' campaign, despite the continuous movements (and reductions) of budgets, buildings and blame. The Olympic bidding document, and the many publications that have followed, have been plumped with the 'promise' of improving the access to and provisions for this 'fundamental right' of physical education.

But what about the 'fundamental rights' of the children and young adults in the UK schools system with an impairment – be it physical or intellectual? Where is the proposed, and indeed 'promised' Paralympic legacy to ensure children with disabilities reap the same benefits to improvements in provisions of PE to able bodied children? The spectacle of the Olympic Games often over shadows that of the Paralympic Games (as was most recently confirmed by the 2010 Vancouver Olympics[1]), with the consequence often being that the Paralympic Games are simply viewed, by many, as a secondary, 'necessity' event, limping along behind the great show, arriving late with a much smaller accolade, with an agenda to tick as many of the required equality boxes as possible. However, with evidence of this disregard and disinterest in disability sport at the elite level, one must question the 'worth' of the Paralympic Legacy and to what extent this legacy will actually filter down to the sports halls and playing fields of the UK. With the epidemic of child obesity being at the forefront of the media's, and the politician's, minds, it appears the Olympic Legacy has been burdened with the responsibility of being the sole rehabilitator of the situation – and PE will be its puppet. So why has the Paralympic Legacy not been granted the same arduous tasks as the Olympic Legacy in terms of improving the provisions of PE and sport in schools for children with impairments or obesity? This is an important question and the following chapter will explore the proposals

---

1. The BBC showed in excess of 90 hours of live coverage during the Vancouver 2010 Olympic Games. The Vancouver 2010 Paralympic Games, however, received no live coverage from the BBC, which instead showed 1 hour highlight shows via the BBC website. Channel 4 has bought the rights to broadcast the London 2012 Paralympic Games.

and promises of the Paralympic Legacy, critique its realisation and examine what the future of adaptive PE and sport might hold for this seeming forgotten group of children.

Intellectual disability

When the news broke of the cheating of the Spanish team in the 'Intellectual Disability' (ID) categories at the 2000 Sydney Paralympic Games there was widespread controversy and disgust – especially as the category of intellectual disability had, only been introduced at the previous 1996 Atlanta Games. With 10 of the 12 players from the Gold medal winning Spanish Basketball team being declared of 'normal' intellect, the team were stripped of their medals and an investigation began. It was later revealed that Spanish athletes in the ID categories for Table Tennis, Athletics and Swimming had also won their medals fraudulently after it was found that Spain had failed to provide the required documentation stating the intellectual capacity of all of its athletes. The result of this disastrous revelation was for the IPC to suspend all ID events until a more stringent and reliable eligibility criteria and testing procedure could be introduced and enforced. Consequently, ID category sports were not held at the 2004 Athens Paralympic's nor at the 2008 Beijing Paralympics.

In November 2009 the IPC lifted the ban on the inclusion of ID sports in the 2012 Games, much to the delight of many sporting organisations representing athletes with learning difficulties. Nick Parr (Secretariat for International Sports Federation for Persons with Intellectual Disability – INAS-FID) highlighted that since winning the bid for the 2012 Games there has been ongoing dialogue between the domestic Mental Health charities, such as Mencap, LOCOG, the BPA, and the IPC as well as the British government and that all are participating in a joint effort to address the issues of inclusion and setting the eligibility criteria. At present, much of the ongoing dialogue between the groups is to ensure the ID category is not exploited. Meaning the need for a lasting sporting legacy to children with learning difficulties in schools is far further down the list of priorities than some might hope. Parr further argues that:

> '.. the involvement of children with intellectual disabilities in sport is perhaps even more important as it provides an opportunity for people to get involved and excel and enjoy competition which is something that might not necessarily prevail in their everyday lives'.

There is no doubt that the Paralympic Games have received greater attention and focus over the last decade, and that the understanding of the Games and the role that it plays to the impaired communities has become much deeper. The introduction of Paralympic athletes such as Dame Tanni Grey-Thompson and Eleanor Simmons as role models has helped to 'normalize' the Games and promote the idea of 'inspiring' young disabled children to become Paralympians one day. However, can the same be said for children and young adults with learning difficulties? Where are their Paralympic heroes? Who will be responsible for encouraging them to strive for Rio 2016? Parr comments that the:

> '...learning disabilities section does not benefit so much from these role models of disability sport...' and that '...we are a long way behind other impairment groups in terms of the development of coaches, programmes and opportunities. Hopefully 2012 will give us an opportunity to make up for lost ground'.

With many disability sporting initiatives (both from NGBs and from Sport England and UK Sport) targeting wheelchair, and amputee athletes, there is little evidence to suggest that the Paralympic Legacy for intellectually disabled children will be of any impact, or indeed of significance. Parr feels this *'... undermines the disability and fails to develop meaningful sporting opportunities'.* It is hoped that the inclusion of the ID category in 2012 will help to begin to fill the exceptionally large gaps in terms of recognizing athletic achievement; however, it appears the Paralympic Legacy of the 2012 Games has failed to reach one of the most underrepresented groups in sport.

References

Hardman, K. (1998) 'Threats to Physical Education! Threats to Sport for All', paper, I.O.C. VII World Congress 'Sport for All', Barcelona, 19–22 Nov. cited in Oxley, J. (1998) 'Never Mind Literacy and Numeracy: What about Physical Education?', *Bulletin of Physical Education 34(1):* 55–7.

Marshall, J., & Hardman, K. (2000) The state and status of physical education in international context. *European Physical Education Review, 6(30):* 203–299.

Chapter 20
Urban Regeneration and Paralympic Legacy for London 2012

Gavin Poynter

'It is vital that disabled people benefit from the once-in-a-lifetime opportunity presented by the Games. It's the opportunity to make a real and lasting change, to showcase disabled people's talents and not just in the sporting field, but through employment, through positive role models and through the disability arts programme. Such a legacy will live past 2012 and take us toward a vision of disability equality by 2025'.
Jonathan Shaw, British Minister for Disabled People, (3rd December 2009)

Introduction

The above Minister's statement was published with one thousand days to go before the Paralympic Games commence in London in 2012. It was accompanied by a commitment to publish, in spring 2010, a Disability Legacy promise focused upon three themes – increased sports participation, improved business services for disabled people and changing attitudes, particularly toward inclusion. The government's commitment to transforming the lives of persons with a disability sits alongside five other visionary promises, including its commitment to achieve the social transformation of East London – a relatively socially deprived area of the city. In making its commitment to specific benefits to be sought from hosting the Paralympic

Games in 2012, the British government has integrated into the concepts of 'regeneration' and 'legacy' the inclusion of disabled people, perhaps in a more systematic way than any other previous host city.

This chapter is divided into three parts. First, it explains the concepts of 'regeneration' and 'legacy' in the context of the hosting of mega events over recent decades and identifies the specific ways in which London has come to be considered as the 'Legacy Games'. The argument here is that urban regeneration schemes, associated with previous host cities, have often achieved mixed outcomes for a city's existing residents, especially its poorer communities, often reinforcing social inequalities rather than reducing them. Second, London 2012's approach to legacy is discussed with particular reference to the visions of social transformation to be achieved in East London. The chapter concludes with a brief examination of the social legacy goals to which the key stakeholders aspire from hosting the 2012 Paralympic Games.

Urban Regeneration and Olympic Legacies

The potential of festivals, exhibitions and mega events to catalyse programmes of urban regeneration emerged in the USA in the 1970s. In America, federal aid for cities significantly diminished and local governments had to seek new sources of finance for their development plans (Castells, 1980, p. 14). The more entrepreneurial US cities, are often located in regions most affected by de-industrialisation and economic restructuring, adopted a policy of consumption based economic development which focused on the post-industrial service-based industries (Andranovich, Burbank and Heying, 2001, p. 114). By the mid 1980s, in the wake of the economic crises that signalled the end of the post-war boom, hosting the Olympic Games seemingly provided a compelling prize for the entrepreneurial city that sought a little 'fantasy' in the not too distant future. Los Angeles (1984) commenced this trend by hosting a Games that was privately funded with high revenues realised from selling promotion and broadcast rights to television networks and other commercial sponsors (Preuss, 2004, p. 16). The surplus achieved by Los Angeles revealed the potential offered by using a mega event and a globalised media to brand a city on an international scale.

In the post cold war twenty first century, this projection of a city or host nation's identity has become a more complex affair. Performance Events have been utilised by hosts in part to offset domestic disintegrative and fragmentary social tendencies that have accompanied the transition of city and national economies toward more flexible, service-oriented activities operating in a global market economy (Roche, 2000, pp. 220-1) or, as with the case of Beijing (2008), to contain the social disruption arising from rapid urbanisation and economic expansion (Perry and Selden, 2000, Nolan, 2004). Recent host cities have also sought to use mega-events to re-present themselves in various ways to the wider world through 'place marketing' – revealing, for example, their capacities for innovation and the clustering of high value-added service activities and enhancing their competitive advantage over other cities as a result. (Buck, Gordon, Hall, Harloe and Kleinman 2002, pp. 2-5) Each host city and nation has utilised the event to then achieve specific local and national goals. For Barcelona (1992), the Games represented an opportunity to redevelop the city using a mix of public and private sector funding that balanced commercial and social aims. The aggressive commercialism of Los Angeles and the tourist orientation of the Fantasy City model were modified and the Barcelona approach emerged as an alternative to obtaining a post-Games regeneration legacy (LERI: 2007).

Since 1992, 'Legacy' has assumed a growing significance to the IOC – as its evaluation process has incorporated environmental and other social dimensions - and is now firmly focused upon non sport-related outcomes as a source of social and political legitimation for hosting the Games. The Barcelona inspired modification of the 'commercial' approach to hosting the Games was replicated by the London 2012 bid, with 'legacy' becoming an integral theme in the candidature document and pre- and post-event phases of the project. In this sense, legacy as a managerial discourse promoted by IOC 'brand managers', teams of international management consultants and regeneration professionals, assumed a new social dimension with London's successful bid, including its focus upon the long term regeneration of a deprived area of London and its commitment to engaging with young people to inspire them to become involved in sports.

The legacies to be achieved as a result of London hosting the 2012 Olympic and Paralympic Games have been the subject of numerous policy documents produced by central government, the City's mayoral office and the five local authority 'Olympic' boroughs. The promises and their associated policies have provided a framework through which the 2012 stakeholders have committed to achieving a positive legacy for the *existing* or *resident* population of East London, through a programme of urban development that seeks to reduce social inequalities rather than reinforce them as has happened as a result of several regeneration projects initiated in past host cities such as Atlanta (Poynter and Roberts, 2009). An important component of this social policy framework is the 'Disability Legacy promise' through which the needs and interests of people with disability will be incorporated into the wider socio-economic legacy objectives of the Games. In this manner, London 2012, has integrated the Paralympics into the narrative of regeneration that aspires to address infrastructural development and different dimensions of social inequality.

This linking of social policies and programmes to hosting mega-events has several origins. Competitive sport has assumed a significant role in contemporary popular culture, 'a key place in the expressive life of societies' (Rustin: 2009: 6) and the Paralympics have secured an increased role in this process since its organisational integration with the Olympic Games in 1992, the subsequent rise in media coverage of the Paralympics and the emergence of national squads of elite disabled athletes (Gold J. and M. Gold 2007: p. 85). Technological improvements in sport have 'supported the movement of Paralympic athletes in space in a positive and life changing manner' (Edwards, A., O.J. Schantz and K. Gilbert, 2009, p. 248) and, in turn, sport governing bodies and other national and international institutions have been pressed into reviewing their assumptions about the provision of 'separate, segregated opportunities for sport, leisure and cultural activities by persons with a disability' (Fay T. and E. Wolf 2009, p. 231). These developments within the world of sport have interacted with wider social debates to ensure that the Olympic and Paralympic Games' association with 'good city building' has assumed new dimensions. These relate to such policy themes as design, access and social inclusion; elements of which were clearly evident in previous Games in the twenty first century but which have now become an integral part of London's 'legacy games' (Cashman, 2008).

London 2012: the Legacy Games

The focus of Olympics-led regeneration in London is the five East London Olympic boroughs of Newham, Tower Hamlets, Hackney, Waltham Forest and Greenwich. They have rising populations, a high percentage of young people compared to the rest of England and relatively high levels of social deprivation. Since the nineteenth century East London has provided the location for manufacturing industries and the city's docklands. It housed the city's working classes and remained, throughout the twentieth century, relatively poor compared to the rich west of London. When the docks closed in the 1970s and 1980s, the area suffered major job losses in traditional manufacturing and processing industries from which many parts have not recovered. By the beginning of the twenty first century, the extensive regeneration of London's Docklands and improvements in infrastructure had created a sub-region that is socially polarized, containing pockets of relative affluence within an area that has a high concentration of poverty and deprivation.

The hosting of the Olympic and Paralympic Games in 2012 is aimed at accelerating a process of extensive social and economic renewal that addresses these underlying social and economic issues. In linking the games to the social transformation of East London, the government and the key stakeholders in 'London 2012', have embarked upon a new and highly ambitious interpretation of the games' contribution to the social legacy to be achieved by hosting the world's most prestigious sporting event. The policy focus of legacy is a set of five government aspirations/promises:

- Promise 1: Making the UK a world-leading sporting nation.
- Promise 2: Transform the heart of East London.
- Promise 3: Inspire a generation of young people.
- Promise 4: Make the Olympic Park a blueprint for sustainable living.
- Promise 5: Demonstrate that the UK is a creative, inclusive place to live, visit and do business.

The five promises are at the centre of the Legacy Masterplan Framework (LMF). Whilst the promises have UK-wide dimensions, two directly relate to East London – transforming its social and economic position and ensuring that the Olympic Park development exemplifies forms of city building that enshrines sustainability. The East London dimension incorporates at sub-regional level a more detailed policy and investment strategy, developed over 2009, called the Strategic Regeneration Framework (SRF). In early 2010, the SRF was the subject of debate amongst the 'London 2012' stakeholder network (primarily central government, the London Mayor's Office and London Assembly and the five local Olympic local authority boroughs) with discussions focused upon the ways in which the 'convergence' of East London with the rest of London may be achieved through the identification of specific policy objectives and the setting of performance targets for improving the socio-economic position of resident communities. In developing the SRF, local policy makers are seeking, for example, to improve education and housing provision and generate employment and reduce 'worklessness' within their existing communities, achieving levels of performance in these areas that are equivalent to the average for the city of London as a whole. It is recognised that such goals can only be achieved over time and that the transformation catalysed by hosting the Olympic and Paralympic Games is but one component of this complex process.

The political leaders of the five Olympic boroughs summarized the concentration of deprivation and the need for social transformation in a publication in April 2009. They focused on the incidence of high levels of child poverty and its multiple causes and called for a 'plan' to improve their area:

> 'This is the area of the most concentrated deprivation in the country and has the biggest intra-regional gap between the most prosperous and most deprived parts of the region. The current employment rate in the five boroughs is only 60% (2007) and we would need to see another 100,000 residents in work if we were to even approach the national average, and that is without modelling for the current levels of population churn; one in three households across the 5 boroughs with dependent children contain no adult in work; a child in one of the 5 boroughs is twice as likely to grow up in a workless household as the rest of England; there are major challenges in the overcrowding and quality of our housing and the gap between housing affordability and earnings; our boroughs look run down in many places and that reduces the level of civic pride, resulting in high levels of littering and graffiti, low levels of resident satisfaction and well-being, and reducing levels of property and business desirability.
>
> These five boroughs are the place which will need transformational change if Government is to achieve its national aspirations to eliminate child poverty; an 80% employment rate; 79% of working age adults qualified to level 2 or above and 56% to level 3 and above; 3 million new homes in London; 70,000 new affordable homes per year; and to halve the number of households in temporary accommodation. These social and economic conditions raise a wider question of social equity given the opportunities already seen in growth points of such significance as Canary Wharf and the expectation of the impact of the Olympics.

> The persistence of the deprivation also shows that the realisation of regeneration in this part of London as an Olympic Legacy will not bring benefits to the communities living in the area unless there is an explicit and focused plan to ensure that socio/economic conditions improve in line with the physical development of the area'.
>
> Source: Five Olympic Boroughs (2009) Draft Multi Area Agreement, p. 5.

The Legacy Masterplan Framework (LMP) is, in turn, supported by Area Plans which focus upon proposals for the development of high quality and sustainable communities in six locations within the vicinity of the Olympic Park, Stratford. The Area Plans aspire to provide a significant increase in housing (10,000-12,000 new homes) and contribute to the development of a 'new town' within East London bringing with it new employment opportunities for the resident population. An important component of this regeneration narrative is enhancing employment opportunities for local disabled people. 18.6 percent of the UK's population of working age were registered as disabled in 2006, with approximately 2.6 million in employment and three million without work. Of that three million, at least one million wished to work. The employment rate within the UK for disabled people of working age was 50 percent in 2006, well below the 80 percent level of non-disabled people. In the five host Olympic boroughs only 33.7 percent of the disabled community were in employment in 2006, well below the national average of 50 percent (ODA 2007). A glance at one important area of social policy, employment, clearly indicates that disabled people, living within the vicinity of the London 2012, experience significant disadvantage in the local and city-wide labour market with this position worsening as a result of the 2008-9 economic recession.

The LRF, and linked policies, aim to address this employment 'gap' and other major issues such as housing and the provision of education and training opportunities. The government's Disability Legacy promise is focused upon employment, showcasing disabled people's talents and the wider promotion of a positive understanding of disability. The framework for the development of this policy in the course of 2010, is provided by the Olympic Delivery Authority's (ODA) Inclusive Design Strategy, published in June 2008 which pledges to host 'the most accessible games ever' (ODA: 2008: p. 2), and incorporates the Commission for Architecture and the Built Environment's (CABE) five principles of inclusive design:

- Place people at the heart of the design process
- Acknowledge diversity and difference
- Offer choice where a single design solution cannot accommodate all users
- Provide for flexibility in use
- Provide buildings and environments that are convenient and enjoyable for everyone to use;

> Source: ODA (2008) 'Inclusive Design', Inclusive Design Strategy, London: ODA, June 2008 p. 6.

The strategy is complemented by the ODAs 'Inclusive Design Standards' document written for all planners, designers and developers associated with the London 2012 project. Improving accessibility through infrastructure development and improvements to transport networks is a further feature of preparations for 2012, through developments to, for example, the Jubilee Line underground service and the Docklands Light Rail along with the provision of the world's largest fully accessible bus fleet and 20,000 accessible taxis for use in 2012 (LOCOG 2007).

The over arching national, city-wide and sub-regional government strategies to promote inclusion and accessibility are supported in London 2012's pre-event phase by a number of other initiatives, many led by UK Sport and the British Paralympic Association (BPA). UK Sport, for example, in collaboration with local councils and authorities within the UK launched, in November 2009, a talent search for potential athletes for the 2012 Paralympic Games Other elite and wider participation initiatives include Deloitte's sponsorship of Disability Sport – a £1.7 million programme aimed at enhancing the performance and achievements of British athletes at the 2012 Paralympic Games and 'Inclusive and Active' - a 'Sport and Physical Activity Action Plan for Disabled People in London' (2007 - 2012) led by the Mayor of London, National Health Service (NHS) London and the London Sports Forum for Disabled People.

Evaluating London's Paralympic Legacy

Whilst it is perhaps too early to establish the evidence-base to evaluate the range of Paralympic legacy programmes and policies associated with London 2012, some initial conclusions may be drawn. First, the national and sub-regional policy frameworks and programmes link the process of urban regeneration to achieving a social legacy that addresses the needs of existing residents and communities. The multi-ethnic composition of these communities places social inclusion and the necessity to tackle social inequalities at the centre of these policies. Given this social context, the commitment to addressing the inequalities experienced by disabled people has become an important part of the 2012 narrative, extending beyond elite and community sport participation into the discourse of urban regeneration itself.

Second, despite initial expectations that the 2012 Olympic and Paralympic Games would, at least in part, be financed through public/private partnerships, investment in the preparations for the Games – its direct and indirect costs – have been wholly publicly funded. While the 'leverage' model of public/private sector partnership has tended in some past host cities to generate legacies that are favourable to private sector or commercial interests but which reinforce existing patterns of social disadvantage through displacement/replacement and the process of 'gentrification', such an approach has not been adopted by London. The unfolding of the global recession in 2008-9 has tended to strengthen the UK Government's commitment to demonstrate the benefits of public investment in infrastructure and the social programmes associated with the Olympics; though such a perspective and the resulting longer term social benefits may not come to fruition if the requirement to reduce the UK's public debt leads to a future government seeking to recoup some its investment via the (fire) sale of Olympic 'assets' in the period immediately following the completion of the Games.

Finally, the detailed policies and proposals for inclusive design and access and the wider social programme aimed at achieving equality for disabled people (even by 2025) has some distance to go. The government published its five promises concerning social legacy in 2008, the promise to disabled people will not be published until 2010 thus leaving a shorter timeframe for an inclusive legacy to be put in place. An indication of the distance of travel is provided, for example, by statistics relating to the employment of disabled people in the Olympic Park development itself. The government's target of providing employment for three percent registered disabled workers out of the total contractor workforce was not achieved by July 2009 – just one percent voluntarily declaring themselves as disabled, a total of 34 out of a contractor workforce of a little over 800 (LOCOG: 2009). Conversely, by October 2009, the London Development Agency was able to report that its skills development and training support programmes for disabled people had achieved higher levels of engagement than the targets set, with skills programmes in 2007-8 and 2008-9 being provided for 372 against a target of 225 and employment support for 291 against a target of 238 (LDA, 2009).

It appears that the 'legacy Games' is successfully extending the boundaries of the urban regeneration debate to include people with disability in a discourse driven by concepts such as design, access and social inclusion. These ambitious objectives may only be effectively evaluated over time, a period during which the transformative dimension of the social legacy must be sustained in the face of growing pressures to curb public investment in government-led programmes of urban regeneration. If the London Paralympics are to achieve a transformative legacy, the social programmes and infrastructure investment currently attached to this flagship mega event must be sustained well beyond 2012.

References

Andranovich G, M.Burban and C.Heying (2001) 'Olympic Cities: Lessons Learned from Mega-Event Politics'. *Journal of Urban Affairs*, 23 (2), 113-131.

Buck N, I. Gordon, P. Hall, M. Harloe and M. Kleinmann (2002) Working Capital – Life and Labour in Contemporary, London. London: Routledge.

Cashman R. (2008) The Benchmark Games, The Sydney 2000 Paralympic Games, Sydney: Walla Walla Press.

Castells M. (1980) The Economic Crisis and American Society, Oxford: Blackwell.

Edwards A, O.Schantz and K.Gilbert (2009) Technology, Space and the Paralympic Athlete. In *Olympic Cities and the Remaking of London* G. Poynter & I. Macrury (Eds). London: Ashgate Publications. (pp: 243-258).

Fay, T. and E.Wolff (2009) Disability in Sport in the Twenty-first Century: Creating a New Sport Opportunity Spectrum. *Boston University International Law Journal*, 27 (2) 231-248.

Five Olympic Host Boroughs (2009) Olympics Legacy Draft Multi-Area Agreement, April 2009. Availableat: (http://www1.waltham-forest.gov.uk/ModernGov/Published/C00000287/M00002016/AI00011763/$12AppA090422OlympicsLegacyAprilMAA-DraftSubmission.docA.ps.pdf), (accessed 3rd January 2010).

Gilbert K. and O.J. Schantz (2009) The Paralympics: Empowerment or Sideshow, Meyer –Meyer-Verlag, Aachen, Germany.

Gold J. and M. Gold (2007) The Paralympic Games. In Gold J. and M. Gold *Olympic Cities* pp 84-102. London: Routledge.

Jonathan Shaw, Minister for Disabled People, 3rd December 2009 'New legacy promise put disabled people at the heart of London 2012', http://www.culture.gov.uk/reference_library/media_releases/-6502aspx

London Development Agency (2009) Local Employment and Training Framework –Evaluation, October 2009. Available at: (http://www.lda.gov.uk/upload/pdf/Public_Item_03_3_1_Appendix_1-Evaluation_Summary.pdf), (accessed 12th January 2010).

London East Research Institute (LERI) (2007) A Lasting Legacy for London?, May 2007, London: London Assembly.

London Organising Committee of the Olympic Games (LOCOG) (2007) London 2012 Guide to the Paralympic Games, London: LOCOG.

London Organising Committee of the Olympic Games (LOCOG) (2009) Employment and Skills Update. London: LOCOG.

Nolan P. (2004) Transforming China, London: Anthem Press.

Olympic Delivery Authority (2007) Disability Equality Scheme, November 2007, London: ODA.

Olympic Delivery Authority (2008) Inclusive Design Strategy, June 2008, London: ODA.

Perry J. and M. Selden (Eds) (2000) Chinese Society, 2nd Edition change, conflict and resistance, London: Routledge.

Poynter, G and E. Roberts (2009) 'Atlanta 1996: The Centennial Games' in *Olympic Cities and the Remaking of London* G. Poynter & I. Macrury (Eds). London: Ashgate Publications. (pp: 121-132).

Poynter, G and I. MacRury (eds.) (2009) Olympic Cities and the Remaking of London, London: Ashgate Publications.

Preuss H (2004) The Economics of Staging the Olympics – A Comparison of the Games 1972-2008. Cheltenham: Edward Elgar.

Roche M. (2000) Mega-events and Modernity, London: Routledge.

Rustin M. (2009) Sport, Spectacle and Society: Understanding the Olympics. In Poynter G. and I.MacRury (Eds) *Olympic Cities and the Remaking of London*, pp: 3-22. London: Ashgate Publications.

Part IV
Reconceptualising Paralympic Legacies

Chapter 21
A Metasynthesis of Paralympic Legacy
Keith Gilbert and David Legg

Introduction

This chapter aims to analyze the previous chapters in order to contribute to the theoretical development of the processes, outcomes and experiences of the notion of differing Paralympic legacies. The metasynthesis conducted in this chapter aims to build on the previous comments regarding legacy and the successes and failures outlined and noted in the various chapters.

Before embarking on this process it is necessary for us to share our thoughts on metasynthesis? We accept that this term is used to describe the compilation of numerous research studies or pieces of academic work into a single theoretical perspective. Typically this process involves working with quantitative data and its definition revolves around the quantitative analysis of research. A plausible definition is 'meta-analysis provides a quantitative method of increasing sample size to enable a reliable estimate of the most likely effect of an intervention, particularly for studies involving randomized, clinically controlled trials' (Scholfield, 2004, p. 204). However, as the world shifts more towards the qualitative paradigm researchers have moved towards the concept of the term 'metasynthesis'. As Thorne and colleagues (2004, p. 1346) note:

> 'The goal is clearly defined, not mere aggregation to achieve unity; it is not a summary portraying the lowest common denominator. Metasynthesis is not a method designed to produce oversimplification; rather, it is one in which difference is retained and complexity enlightened. The goal is to achieve more, not less. The outcome will be something like a common understanding of the nature of a phenomenon, not a consensual worldview'.

Schreiber (1997, p. 315) suggests three types of metasynthesis exist including theory building, theory explication and theory development approaches. Theory building metasynthesis move the analysis to higher levels of abstraction than is possible when using data from just one sample, the end result of which is a formal theory (Schreiber et al 1997). Theory explication metasyntheses are used to flesh out an abstract concept through deconstruction, reconstruction and synthesis (Fingeld, 2003). Finally, theoretical development metasynthesis focus more broadly on a topic in order to provide a comprehensive analysis of the phenomenon.

The aim in this chapter is to synthesize the findings of the various individual chapters into a comprehensive account of the phenomenon under investigation – the legacy of the Paralympic Games. In this manner this chapter does not seek to deconstruct and repackage the findings from the preceding chapters. In addition, the topics broached by the authors are too broad to allow a thorough exploration of legacy for theory building or explicating approach. As such, a theory development metasynthesis will be undertaken which will involve reanalysis of the original material and the use of an imposed structure to organise findings into processes, outcomes and experiences of legacy. Where appropriate, establishing theories will be used to reflect on the findings and position them within the body of the new literature in legacy research to date. This theoretical critique is vital for development of a literature base in the area of legacy research. According to Morse (2000, p. 715) who insists that:

> '......refusing to place the theory within the context of work that has already been published, is a serious problem. It results in a plethora of small competing contributions to the literature. These contributions are not additive, they do not build on what has been published before; thus qualitative inquiry as a discipline makes only a minor impact and has trouble demonstrating its contribution to science'.

The Characteristics of Paralympic Legacies

The characteristics of the issues related to Paralympic legacies found within this text include historical but more importantly reflective perspectives. These included:
1. disability tolerance, attitudinal change, benchmarking, economics, cultural change,
2. civic pride, reflected glow, cultural considerations, social debate, sporting legacy, political legacy and value of Paralaympic education, improved tourism, developed,

3. infrastructure such as telecommunications, transportation and housing, emotional connection, health, changing perceptions, competition between nations, increased work front ending new facilities,
4. handicapitalism, increased spending power, taking up of exercise, infrastructure, disability friendly infrastructure, social integration,
5. athlete integration, media world exposure, removing perceptions, better organized disability sport, nation building, founding of sports organizations, increasing number of outlets for disability sport, professionalize management,
6. observer programmes, improved technical delivery, improved classification procedures, entertainment, regeneration, renewal, accessibility, increased athletic achievements, increased disability rights, social visibility,
7. Blazesports, creation of employment, increased sport science knowledge, volunteerism, healthy living, sport and recreation, arts, literacy and accessibility, social inclusion, social change, disability awareness training, workforce sensibility,
8. attention to excellence, increased developmental pathways, marketing, improvement of public health, physical activity for all, health related legacy,
9. physical education for disabled students, urban regeneration, design and social integration, inspire a generation of young people, and finally addressing inequality.

If we carefully review and address the list of issues above we will understand that all need to be researched further in the Paralympic contexts and many if not all of the Paralympic legacies are 'soft' and designed to influence the opinions of school children and individuals in the community where the Games are held. The question remains as to which of the above legacies have been planned either by the OCOG, International Paralympic Committee or bidding committee? And how many of them are still in practice? The answer to both questions remains in the negative. These legacies then have likely either already occurred by chance or are on the organiser's wish list for future Paralympic Games. Ideally in the future the Paralympic movement will evolve beyond the scope of providing legacies which are purely serendipidous towards a planned execution of events to support the chance legacies which have gone before. What follows is a metasynthesis of the previous chapters.

History

Clearly one of the most important functions of legacy is its historical significance and Legg and Steadward when describing the start of the Paralympic movement argue that the Stoke Mandeville Games was the first legacy left by people to the Games. This is interesting as nowhere in the legacy literature has anyone commented that 'legacy can only be left by people for people' or 'older generations for younger generations'. Legacy from our perspective then is thus not an act of nature but is instead a purely human characteristic and intergenerational in that older generations bequeath legacy to younger ones. In this way it is doubtful that the people who were involved in those original Games ever realized the immense impact that their initial energetic efforts would have on the legacy for those who followed. This was reflected upon by Pope John XXII himself who commented about the following Games in Rome 'You have given a great example which we would like to emphasize: you have shown what an energetic soul can achieve, in spite of apparently insurmountable obstacles imposed by the body' (Guttmann, 1986). This quote of course has other connotations as we realize that for any legacy to be left behind after any Games there must be large amounts of energy and effort put into the legacy process. It is clear that we owe Sir Ludwig Guttmann a great deal as his legacy to the world has transformed lives and reshaped the world of international sport. Perhaps the best description of the relationship to history and the Paralympics occured with Tony Sainsbury's description of the historical relationship between the IOC and the IPC. He argued that 'holding a Paralympic Games included those aspects that would enjoy general universal support within the Olympic Movement'. And that by 'holding a Paralympic Games it demonstrates in every way the potential of the relationship for both the IPC and the IOC'. Telles Ribeiro agreed with this point and discussed the effect of history on Paralympic legacy by remarking strongly that 'historically, until London, the Paralympic Games are usually only mentioned in a single, generic and conclusive paragraph in the games bid documents and excluding Sydney in final reports by the organizing committees of Olympic host cities'. In short, when developing strategy and plans for future Paralympic legacies there needs to be a careful examination of past legacies.

Beacon Economic Multi-Sport-Events

It is obvious from the chapters presented in this text that there are several 'beacon legacy events' which have left their mark on the Paralympic world. The so called 'beacon Paralympic Games' include Seoul, Barcelona, Sydney and Vancouver. These Games were innovative and stand out organizationally both because they were financially viable and economically sound and left their mark on the legacy of the Paralympic movement as a whole. The four Games noted above highlighted many of the economic benefits from other major multi-sport events which have already been well documented in the Olympic literature which can easily be passed onto the Paralympic arena (see Preuss, 2002, 2004, 2005, and 2006). Also, Patrick Jarvis provides a good account of the economics of the Paralympic Games in chapter 6 where he mentions in his section on the 'context of games legacies' that: 'skeptics see wasted resources' which we argue could be utilized for other important societal issues such as health or education. However, the work of Shuhan and LeClaire specifically has a section on the economics of the Paralympic

Games in China where they highlighted the amendments which were made to the 1991 Chinese Disability Act allowing the promotion of employment for people with a disability. Although the research as stated is good we feel that there still needs to be further research on the economic benefits of staging a Paralympic Games.

Educating Society

Tokyo's games in 1964, as Guttmann remarked, 'left a profound educational value' but the legacy of its educational value since, as previously mentioned, is mostly osmotic in nature. Thus, in our opinion, there needs to be concerted efforts by future OCOG's and Bid Committees to impart the development of a culture of education to the ongoing OCOG impact and the application process. This, of course, was tackled by Vancouver 2010 and as Legg and Steadward argued in chapter 4 when referring to Vancouver's legacy ideas '..these initiatives and vision will have a dramatic impact on Paralympic sport both nationally but also internationally'. Brittain similarly argues from the Canadian context that 'The lessons learned by both the media and the public in Canada following the 'Torontolympiad' appeared to have been quite marked' and that the 'message learnt appeared to have been the importance of removing perceptual, attitudinal and architectural barriers present within Canadian society'. The issues of education and societal change further appears to run throughout the book as other authors such as Jeon and Legg have written a complete section on the societal changes in Korea after the Seoul Paralympic Games. Indeed, Darcy and Appleby also argue that a major part of the legacy of the Sydney Games was the community awareness and 'positive and possible life changing experiences for many Australians'.

There are of course many benefits to the hosting of the Paralympic Games and now that the Games have at long last been eagerly placed on the sporting calendar then we will likely see more legacy outcomes. However, unless there is a concerted effort by administrators and academics alike this will not be forthcoming. There is a need to be sure that educational perspectives are to the forefront of thinking in future bid documents. If the writing and language around Paralympic legacy is placed in the countries bid document, then arguably the OCOG are duty and legally bound to provide the outcomes stated therein. Lobbying for legacy change seems like an easy method to improve the social impacts of the Paralympics by highlighting education and consequently the public's perception of disability sport. Coward and Legg argue further that the four specific questions related to the Paralympic Games which are on the Olympic Games Impact Study (2007) will make a difference as to how people with disabilites are viewed in society. They discuss the second of the four indicators which is 'perceptions of people with disabilities in society' as a method to capture the specific dimensions of social inclusion, attitudinal change and social perceptions. Tony Sainsbury also raised the issue of social capital and Paralympic athletes by asking the question how people with disability were viewed in a 'Host Country' where the Paralympics were held. His final comments were particularly relevant to the development of social context of the Paralympic Games where he argued that 'While the Olympic Games can claim phenomenal physical regeneration and legacy to which the Paralympics can contribute, it is the Paralympic Games that can truly bring about fundamental universal social change' a point which must we feel be one of the most important in this book. Almost all contributors to this text viewed education and social change as important perspectives in the development of legacy. With this point in mind Ribeiro stated that 'Rio 2016 is being planned to provide incentives via all three levels of government and sponsors to develop accessibility training programmes for those working in hospitality and tourism industries'. Finally the chapter by Phil Lane which was almost exclusively on education and the creation of societal change through legacy production. He argued quite rightly in our opinion, 'How refreshing it would be to exploit an agenda of social responsibility in respect of disability, ethnicity, and gender'. He explained this sentiment further in his chapter by highlighting the importance of the Paralympic movement creating a form of social responsibility and that it is 'essential that it looks at investment in the emotional and attitudinal legacy of the Games to truly effect change'.

Media coverage

In our opinion, one area where Legacy can be significantly impacted is via media converage and based on past Games we feel that the International Paralympic Committee can play a significant leadership role. As far back as 1976, we suggest that one of the important legacy events at each Paralympics could be increased media time. Indeed, Brittain in his chapter on the 'Torontolympiad' argued the importance of the media in the development of legacy for the Paralympic Games. He stated that 'although dogged by organizational and financial difficulties Toronto received widespread and on the whole favorable media coverage and public support'. Brittain has long argued for better media coverage of the Games and later in his chapter found the 'way the media portray people with disabilities and disability sport can have a major impact on how other groups and individuals within society view them' (Brittain, 2009; p. 72). There follows an excellent section by Brittain who took an important view of the Paralympic Games time coverage in Canada and elsewhere. It highlighted the comments by Guttmann who even in early days was thankful for all the media coverage that he could get. Twenty years after Toronto, Mushett and Cody argued the value and importance of media at the 1996 Games noting that that even with all the problems which Atlanta had through the Paralympic Games they 'were considered a marketing triumph' with 'more than 2,000 accredited journalists report(ing) on the proceedings'. However, Gilbert and Schantz (2001) in a landmark study found that the coverage was actually not good enough and disappointing considering the number of journalists at the event. Darcy and Appleby also supported the importance of media support for the Paralympics and stated that the Sydney Games set new benchmarks for media coverage on national and international levels. They quoted Goggin and Newell (2001) that 'The coverage by WeMedia was regarded as first rate from a sport perspective and from the perspective of disability representation'. The media then had a major role to play in the development of the Paralympic Games and thus we would argue that media issues for the Paralympics need to be written into future bid documents. Indeed, Appleby highlights the fact that the General Secretary of the IPC at that time explained to her that television coverage at subsequent games were based on the Sydney model which was incredibly successful so the precedent was already set. Looking forward, in his chapter on the upcoming Rio de Janiero Paralympics in 2016, Ribeiro argued that the media should allow Rio to be a platform for change. As an example he noted that: 'Since the 2004 Paralympic Games, the Brazilian Paralympic Committee has developed a strong relationship with the media'. He further stated that 'the Rio 2016 Paralympic Games will represent a significant opportunity for the consolidation of the Paralympic Movement, not only in Brazil but also throughout South America and beyond' and this can only be achieved with the strong support of the media. The importance of media coverage is also highlighted by Campbell who found that in the United Kingdom 'The Vancouver 2010 Paralympic Games' received no live coverage from the BBC, which instead opted to screen 1 hour highlights via the BBC website'. The general consensus of opinion throughout the book, by most authors, is that there needs to be a centrally coordinated media package which delivers the Games on a global scale which is built into the Games bid and also negotiated and supported by the relevant OCOG. What we would argue is that for this to take place and be effective it will require leadership and oversight from the International Paralympic Committee itself. For further information re the relationship between the Paralympic legacy and the media (see Schantz and Gilbert, *The Paralympics and the Media* 2011 forthcoming).

Sport for all

A major legacy for the London 2012 Olympic Games and in many other Olympic Games held prior is getting children and other individuals to exercise and improve their health. It would appear that in this particular area the Games have not lived up to perhaps unfairly high expectations. Therefore if a city or nation state cannot do this for the Olympics how then can we expect to improve the physical activity patterns for youth with disabilities via the Paralympics and should they be seen in isolation at all? That being said we do know that this has been achieved to a certain extent by the communist party in China prior to and following the Beijing Games. As Shuha and LeClair discussed, along with the cultural renaissance in China there were important 'National Health Regulations passed on October 1st

2009 and there has been a National Fitness day negotiated for youth and the elderly and that also the opening of many provincial disabled sports centers and training sites'. Generally however, there appears little difference in the physical; activity patterns of disabled youth after a Paralympic games has taken place in their city. As Phil Lane argues in the context of the United Kingdom '53% of primary school aged disabled children and 41% of 11-16 year olds are spending less than an hour a week in P.E. lessons'. Ribeiro also notes that across Brazil 'both physical education and sport should be offered at integrated places in schools, sports clubs and also considered in social programs. The principal of 'sport for all' should be emphasized'. We recognize, however, that this soft legacy costs money and time to set into practice. It is doubtful that this will occur in some locales such as Brazil because of the lack of funds in the education system and soft legacies like the 'sport for all' concept are difficult to maintain and deliver on a long term basis. And of course these soft legacies are typically the first to get shelved if the Federal or state budgets get slashed in an economic downturn. We are so pleased then that we have the chapter from Smith and Fleming who tackle the important issues of Physical Activity, Health and disability. They argue that 'the link between PA and the purity of a healthier lifestyle is unquestionable'. They go further pointing out that 'The most familiar barriers are physical obstructions, such as an inaccessible building; while others may be subjective perceptions. Such challenges, taken separately or together, can severely hamper an individual's attempts to become (more) physically active'. Natalie Campbell further supported the case of Smith and Fleming and put forward strong arguments for increased physical activity legacy for individuals with an intellectual disability. She advocated more time in Physical Education classes and drove home the point that 'the 2012 Games have so far failed to reach one of the most underrepresented groups in sport' and the general community. Poynter in a final comment also presented a suggestion that 'if legacy has a focus on the long term regeneration of a deprived area of London and its commitment to engaging with young people to inspire them to become involved in sport' then it might fail. These examples thus set a strong case for the soft legacy of Physical Activity for people with disabilities and in our opinion their ideas and ideals should be at the forefront of International Paralympic Committee and OCOG's future thinking.

Final statements

The above five issues of history, beacon economic multi-sport-events, educating society, media coverage and sport for all appear to be the major issues emerging from a meta-synthesis of the chapters in this book. They are all issues, which are geared specifically to the development of legacy in the Paralympic context, and if employed carefully by the IPC, OCOG's and bidding city, could make an outstanding contribution to Paralympic and disability sport across the globe. The recognition of the value from understanding and planning for legacy from major Games is gaining in popularity and Paralympic sport should take advantage of this trend. For example the following words by former British Prime Minister Tony Blair, to a recent conference in Brazil, highlight our legacy thinking. He commented that 'they (Rio de Janiero) need to focus on a legacy that goes beyond sport when the Brazilian city hosts the Games in 2016. It cannot be just about the three weeks of the Games'. Indeed, he provides a great message to the rest of us, 'There is no point doing the Games if there isn't a sense that something is being built for the long term' and 'Part of the legacy is about what sport can do to society. Sport today is far more important that just sport itself' (Blair, 2010). We couldn't agree more.

In this book we negotiated a multiplicity of subject matter on legacy and the Paralympics Games. All the while taking note of arguments, questions and anxieties connected with researching legacy and the Paralympic Games and movement - many of which have been articulated in the final statements in the metasynthesis above. We began with a pastiche of ideas which have developed or been developed over time by other authors in order to provide us with a book about legacy, disability and the Paralympics on a global sense in global societies. We feel that one role for the academic remains to produce research, which tests ideas and also challenges individuals and movements. We also believe that practitioners should be utilizing the research highlighted in this text and utilizing the ideas postulated to support their own work practices, professional development and the profession. All this, we hope, can be achieved through the publication of this book thus leading to practitioners and academics prizing open the fissures in legacy research so that *all* can benefit from the shared ideas.

References

Brittain, I. (2009) The Paralympic Games Explained, Routledge: London.
Fingeld, D.L. (2003) Metasynthesis: The state of the art – so far. *Qualitative Health Research*, Vol. 13 No. 7, pp. 893-904.
Goggin, G, and C. Newell (2001) Crippling Paralympics: Media Disability and Olympism, Media International Australia, No. 97 (Nov.) pp. 71-83.
Morse, J.M. (2000) Editorial: Theoretical congestion, *Qualitative Health Research*, Vol. 10. pp. 715-716.
Morse, J.M. and L. Richards (2002) *Readme first for users guide to qualitative methods*. Thousand Oaks, California, Sage.
Preuss, H. (2000) Electing an Olympic City – A Multi dimensional Decision, *In Bridging Three Centuries: Intellectual Crossroads and the Modern Paralympic Movement*, edited by K.B. Wamsley, S.G.Martyn, G.H.MacDonald, H.Gordon and R.K.Barney ON: Centre for Olympic Studies, UWO, 2000 pp. 89-104.
Preuss, H. (2004) *The Economics of Staging the Olympics: A Comparison of the Games1972- 2008*, Cheltenham, Edward Elgar Pubs.

Preuss, H (2005) The Economic Impact of Visitors at major Multi-Sport-Events, *European Sport Management Quarterly*, Vol. 5 No. 3 pp. 283-304.

Preuss, H (2006) Winners and Losers of the Olympic Games, In *Sport and Society,* (Eds). B.Houlihan, London, Sage Publications.

Schrieber, R. Crooks, D. and P. Noerager Stern (1997) Qualitative Metanalysis. In J.M.Morse (Eds.) *Completing a Qualitative Project*. Thousand Oaks. California, Sage.

Scholfield, M (2004) Sampling in Quantitative Research. In V. Minichiello, G. Sullivan, K. Greenwood A. Axford (Eds.) *Research Methods for Nursing and Health Sciences* (2nd Ed.) Frenchs Forest, New South Wales, Prentice Hall.

Sports City (2010) '2016 legacy must go beyond sport', quoted from Tony Blair, Business Seminar in Rio De Janiero. Available at: (http://www.sports-city-.org/news_details,php?news_id=13477&idCategory=10), (accessed 29th October 2010).

Thorne, S. Jensen, L. Kearney, M.H. Noblit, G and M. Sandelowski (2004) Qualitative Metasynthesis: Reflections on Methodological Orientation and Ideological Agenda. *Qualitative Research Handbook*, Vol. 14, No. 10. pp. 1342-1365.

Chapter 22
Epilogue

The Plot Thins

Keith Gilbert and David Legg

Introduction

Legacy and indeed Paralympic legacy is an important concern which has not been fully explored and there is sparce information in the academic world regarding the effects of sports or civil legacy on a nation state. This was perhaps the main reason for the development of this text. What we have concluded is that while much has been accomplished there is still a great deal that could be achieved in future Games to maximize the legacy impact. We believe that this will require concerted effort from many stakeholders but perhaps most importantly focused leadership from the International Paralympic Committee itself.

If we argue that legacy is the process of developing a new culture in a city by regeneration and providing opportunities for cultural renewal then we need to ask to what extent the Paralympic movement through the auspices of the IPC has control and what role does it play in developing it? The short answer is that based on prior Games it appears to have little control or role. This is conceivably because the IPC appears to have limited direct power with respect to the host cities and without this it cannot effectively play a role in societal or cultural renewal. Basically, in terms of hard legacy, it could be argued that the IPC has been 'riding on the coat-tails' of the IOC, the respective OCOG and nation states in terms of legacy from the Paralympic Games. Indeed, it appears as though most Paralympic legacies occur through a form of Olympic to Paralympic osmosis, locally driven initiatives or serendipity. This is not to say that the contributions of local leaders (who might be argued form the foundation of the Paralympic 'movement') are not valued or important but instead we recognize that perhaps much more can be achieved via Games' legacy through a coordinated and concerted focus from the IPC itself.

In order to clarify this statement we have to reflect on the work in this book, as various authors have argued that the concept of a sporting legacy is in itself problematic when it is used to categorise what is left behind after a Paralympic Games. There have been authors who have referred to the concepts of the two dimensions of Paralympic legacy - principally that of soft and hard legacies. However, it appears as though there are few specific hard legacies which are influenced by the IPC and left behind after a Paralympic Games. We are, of course, aware of specialist transport, (which is almost always in the city already) and the development of the athlete's village to make it disability friendly (mostly wheelchair) by the OCOG. Where we see this being extended for instance is through the IPC influencing the development of accessible sports venues, long term and far reaching commitments to education, and the enabling of the broadest and deepest media coverage possible (as but a few examples). The IPC who arguably are the guardians of Paralympic legacy for people with a disability appear not to have a 'legacy voice' and there is a need to understand who exactly is at the centre of legacy development.

Central figures

When exploring social processes within a nation state there is clearly justification and promotion for a Games Bid and along with the bid comes pressure from interested parties. For example, pressure from individuals who promote legacy form a loose conglomeration of often self interested individuals from business, government, sports executives, and sport stars, who are supported by their media support teams. These diverse groups subsume the needs of the city inhabitants and are allowed either through social status, privilege or new money to become the holders of the 'legacy voice' for the rest of the population.

We also argue that issues of legacy from sporting events go to the very heart of society, and as such we ask the important question as to what sort of society we live in when we need outside sporting bodies such as the IOC and their OCOG's to change and deliver basic services which should be delivered in the context of normal societal structures. It is agreed that the IOC have created a sporting revolution in the delivery of major sporting events by using the legacy term and by making promises and influencing the host's government and business to develop that which probably should have happened anyway - regardless of able bodied or disability focus. Furthermore, governments support the bidding process and persuade their citizenry that they need the sporting event and that there will be tangible legacy rewards for going along with their grandiose plans. Indeed, legacy plans are driven deep into the minds of ordinary people as they imagine and are promised a new utopia with fancy buildings, sports parks, waterways, shops and the promise of a better lifestyle. People are influenced into believing that along with the major sporting event comes a new lifestyle and proof of this is in the fact that there has been billions of tax payers' dollars spent in the name of legacy or what is left behind from recent major sporting festivals. However, we must never forget that many people earn little money or live below the poverty line and if we take the case of east London people are quite poor and only the individuals who have money will likely be fully able to access the Games, and the trappings that are promised through legacy projects. This of course has implications from a disability and Paralympic perspective in that people with disabilities are often under employed and earn less than their able bodied peers and thus perhaps are even further hindered by this challenge.

Beyond the general attention towards cultural renewal is typically a focus on young people and especially relevant for this book are youngsters with disability who become a part of the cultural renewal process. However, what we are manifestly unable to discuss is how this cultural shift and cultural renewal is influenced by legacy promises. Indeed, perhaps in the bidding process and during the games period, legacy functions as a smokescreen behind which important social shifts take place. In actuality legacy is thrust upon people and it is not necessarily democratically structured. In the case of sporting legacy there is perhaps a mindset that promotes the wealthy and administrators who decided upon whether the populous will have the stadia, pools, and trappings of legacy whether they want them or not. Indeed, after the Games have left the city there is nothing left but legacy.

A proposition for the IOC

A final conclusion from our book is that there needs to be further examination regarding the relationship between Olympic and Paralympic legacy particularly if the Games continue with the practice of hosting one after the other? Clearly, Olympic legacy is all about bequeathing amazing sporting facilities (for which the IOC have no fiscal responsibility prior to or after the Games) to a city which can be utilised long after the Olympic and Paralympic Games have moved onto the next host city. As promoted in this book, Paralympic legacy is about developing an understanding in society for the marginalised and changing cultural beliefs and this can only be achieved through soft legacy development. In this manner there needs to be more focus on the benefits and abilities to further develop the soft legacy associated with the Paralympic Games.

The IOC have realised the benefits of legacy and are perhaps using the term as another contemporary pillar along with others such as 'sustainability' to court new cities into bidding for future Olympic Games. In contrast the IPC has little control or presently published focus on legacy. The IOC, meanwhile has successfully set themselves as an organisation concerned with the manufacturer of social change as well as an elite sports organisation – they are continually reinventing themselves and can perhaps be classed as a proxy United Nations who take on social and world issues which are valuable to them such as the previously mentioned sustainability, environment and legacy. In our opinion the IOC could add further financial and political support to the IPC as there can be no better legacy for the International Olympic Committee than to support legacy for the Paralympic Movement.

What we have seen and learned through the development of this book is that tremendous legacies have been left in many if not all the cities examined that have hosted Paralympic Games. We are concerned, however, that the extent or reach of these has perhaps not been fully realized yet we are not naïve to the challenges in doing so from any number of perspectives – be they financial, human resource, or political. What we do hope for, however, is a commitment from the highest levels of leadership in sport, both Paralympic and Olympic, to recognizing and capatilizing on the benefits of hosting Paralympic Games. We look forward to contributing to this process, and watching how future Paralympic Games continue to build upon the traditions and innovations begun by Sir Ludwig Guttmann. Perhaps in twenty years time we will have the privilege of producing a second edition of this text noting the many significant and important legacy contributions from Games to come.